Computer-Assisted Learning for Engaging Varying Aptitudes:

From Theory to Practice

R. Dhaya
King Khalid University, Saudi Arabia

R. Kanthavel
King Khalid University, Saudi Arabia

A volume in the Advances in Educational Technologies and Instructional Design (AETID) Book Series

IGI Global
PUBLISHER of TIMELY KNOWLEDGE

Published in the United States of America by
IGI Global
Information Science Reference (an imprint of IGI Global)
701 E. Chocolate Avenue
Hershey PA, USA 17033
Tel: 717-533-8845
Fax: 717-533-8661
E-mail: cust@igi-global.com
Web site: http://www.igi-global.com

Library of Congress Cataloging-in-Publication Data

Names: Dhaya, R., 1983- editor. | Kanthavel, R., 1974- editor.
Title: Computer-assisted learning for engaging varying aptitudes : from theory to practice / R. Dhaya, and R. Kanthavel, editors.
Description: Hershey, PA : Information Science Reference, [2023] | Includes bibliographical references and index. | Summary: "This book will provide an insight into the practical applications of technology-based learning measures with results, so that the readers will get an explanation and the applicability of the methods"-- Provided by publisher.
Identifiers: LCCN 2022018290 (print) | LCCN 2022018291 (ebook) | ISBN 9781668450581 (Hardcover) | ISBN 9781668450628 (Paperback) | ISBN 9781668450598 (eBook)
Subjects: LCSH: Educational technology. | Computer-assisted instruction. | Learning. | Educational change.
Classification: LCC LB1028.3 .C6388 2023 (print) | LCC LB1028.3 (ebook) | DDC 371.33--dc23/eng/20220718
LC record available at https://lccn.loc.gov/2022018290
LC ebook record available at https://lccn.loc.gov/2022018291

This book is published in the IGI Global book series Advances in Educational Technologies and Instructional Design (AETID) (ISSN: 2326-8905; eISSN: 2326-8913)

British Cataloguing in Publication Data
A Cataloguing in Publication record for this book is available from the British Library.

All work contributed to this book is new, previously-unpublished material.
The views expressed in this book are those of the authors, but not necessarily of the publisher.

For electronic access to this publication, please contact: eresources@igi-global.com.

Advances in Educational Technologies and Instructional Design (AETID) Book Series

ISSN:2326-8905
EISSN:2326-8913

Editor-in-Chief: Lawrence A. Tomei, Robert Morris University, USA

MISSION

Education has undergone, and continues to undergo, immense changes in the way it is enacted and distributed to both child and adult learners. In modern education, the traditional classroom learning experience has evolved to include technological resources and to provide online classroom opportunities to students of all ages regardless of their geographical locations. From distance education, Massive-Open-Online-Courses (MOOCs), and electronic tablets in the classroom, technology is now an integral part of learning and is also affecting the way educators communicate information to students.

The **Advances in Educational Technologies & Instructional Design (AETID) Book Series** explores new research and theories for facilitating learning and improving educational performance utilizing technological processes and resources. The series examines technologies that can be integrated into K-12 classrooms to improve skills and learning abilities in all subjects including STEM education and language learning. Additionally, it studies the emergence of fully online classrooms for young and adult learners alike, and the communication and accountability challenges that can arise. Trending topics that are covered include adaptive learning, game-based learning, virtual school environments, and social media effects. School administrators, educators, academicians, researchers, and students will find this series to be an excellent resource for the effective design and implementation of learning technologies in their classes.

COVERAGE

- Classroom Response Systems
- Adaptive Learning
- Digital Divide in Education
- K-12 Educational Technologies
- Instructional Design Models
- E-Learning
- Virtual School Environments
- Game-Based Learning
- Higher Education Technologies
- Social Media Effects on Education

IGI Global is currently accepting manuscripts for publication within this series. To submit a proposal for a volume in this series, please contact our Acquisition Editors at Acquisitions@igi-global.com or visit: http://www.igi-global.com/publish/.

The Advances in Educational Technologies and Instructional Design (AETID) Book Series (ISSN 2326-8905) is published by IGI Global, 701 E. Chocolate Avenue, Hershey, PA 17033-1240, USA, www.igi-global.com. This series is composed of titles available for purchase individually; each title is edited to be contextually exclusive from any other title within the series. For pricing and ordering information please visit http://www.igi-global.com/book-series/advances-educational-technologies-instructional-design/73678. Postmaster: Send all address changes to above address.

Titles in this Series

For a list of additional titles in this series, please visit:
http://www.igi-global.com/book-series/advances-educational-technologies-instructional-design/73678

Mobile and Sensor-Based Technologies in Higher Education
Oytun Sözüdoğru (University of City Island, Cyprus) and Bülent Akkaya (Manisa Celal Bayar University, Turkey)
Information Science Reference • © 2023 • 335pp • H/C (ISBN: 9781668454008) • US $195.00

Handbook of Research on Fostering Social Justice Through Intercultural and Multilingual Communication
Eleni Meletiadou (London Metropolitan University, UK)
Information Science Reference • © 2023 • 450pp • H/C (ISBN: 9781668450833) • US $270.00

Exploring Comics and Graphic Novels in the Classroom
Jason D. DeHart (Appalachian State University, USA)
Information Science Reference • © 2023 • 331pp • H/C (ISBN: 9781668443132) • US $215.00

Enhancing Education Through Multidisciplinary Film Teaching Methodologies
Jason D. DeHart (Appalachian State University, USA)
Information Science Reference • © 2022 • 310pp • H/C (ISBN: 9781668453940) • US $215.00

Guide to Integrating Problem-Based Learning Programs in Higher Education Classrooms Design, Implementation, and Evaluation
Pam Epler (Youngstown State University, USA) and Jodee Jacobs (Youngstown State University, USA)
Information Science Reference • © 2022 • 246pp • H/C (ISBN: 9781799881773) • US $205.00

IGI Global
PUBLISHER of TIMELY KNOWLEDGE

701 East Chocolate Avenue, Hershey, PA 17033, USA
Tel: 717-533-8845 x100 • Fax: 717-533-8661
E-Mail: cust@igi-global.com • www.igi-global.com

Table of Contents

Preface xiii

Chapter 1
Technology-Based Computer-Assisted Learning: An IoTCAL Overview 1
Sinthuja U., Ramakrishna College of Arts and Science, Coimbatore, India & Hindustan College of Arts and Science, Coimbatore, India
Thavamani S., Sri Ramakrishna College of Arts and Science, India

Chapter 2
Use of CAL-AI in Future Wireless Communication Systems 9
Mahalakshmi M., CMR College of Engineering and Technology, India

Chapter 3
The Influence of AI-Assisted Learning on CAL: A Blueprint 23
Karthik Ganesh R., SCAD College of Engineering and Technology, India

Chapter 4
Instruction Process and Learning Issues in Computer-Assisted Learning: A Detailed Review 36
Banumathi J., Anna University, India & University College of Engineering, Nagercoil, India

Chapter 5
Computing the Cloud Storage for Computer-Aided Learning Access.................55
K. Juliana Gnanaselvi, Rathinam College of Arts and Science, India

Chapter 6
An Overview of the Big Data Technology for Computer-Assisted Learning......66
Sivaranjani R., Hindusthan College of Arts and Science, India

Chapter 7
Analyzing the Novel Approaches for Intelligent Computer-Aided Learning (ICAL)....75
Shaheen H., MVJ College of Engineering, India

Chapter 8
Recent Trends in Nanomaterials: Challenges and Opportunities....88
Kannadhasan S., Study World College of Engineering, Coimbatore, India
Nagarajan R., Gnanamani College of Technology, India
Kanagaraj Venusamy, Rajalakshmi Engineering College, Chennai, India

Chapter 9
Recent Trends in Microstrip Patch Antenna Using Textile Applications....103
Kannadhasan S., Study World College of Engineering, Coimbatore, India
Nagarajan R., Gnanamani College of Technology, India
Kanagaraj Venusamy, Rajalakshmi Engineering College, Chennai, India

Chapter 10
Cloud-Based Detection of Forged Passport and Extraction of True Identity: Surf Match Algorithm for Fraudulence Reduction....120
Kanthavel R., King Khalid University, India

Chapter 11
IoT-Based Solar Charged Wireless Vehicle Parking Network....158
Dhaya R., King Khalid University, Saudi Arabia

Compilation of References....183

Related References....201

About the Contributors....225

Index....228

Detailed Table of Contents

Preface..xiii

Chapter 1
Technology-Based Computer-Assisted Learning: An IoTCAL Overview 1
Sinthuja U., Ramakrishna College of Arts and Science, Coimbatore, India & Hindustan College of Arts and Science, Coimbatore, India
Thavamani S., Sri Ramakrishna College of Arts and Science, India

In today's world, technology is taking over many parts of human existence, and computer aided learning (CAL) is an educational instrument that facilitates learning. Computer aided learning (CAL) is an integrated technology that specific role of IoT in education in a learning environment where a computerized tool is utilized to help a user study a specific topic. Incorporating technologies like artificial intelligence (AI), internet of things (IoT), virtual reality (VR) and augmented reality (AR) in CAL will be driving the present as well as future. The impact of pandemic conditions has resulted in an increase in CAL users, which is expected to make the CAL programme more successful. The proposed IoTCAL ideas are intended to provide a worthwhile learning experience by delivering efficient, engaging, and preemptive context-aware training smart services.

Chapter 2
Use of CAL-AI in Future Wireless Communication Systems..............................9
Mahalakshmi M., CMR College of Engineering and Technology, India

Communication systems have changed dramatically during the last few decades. Wireless communication is one of the few industries that has been able to maintain exponential growth and visionary characteristics for many years. Computer assisted learning- artificial intelligence [CAL-AI] can process vast amounts of data produced by communication systems on a regular basis to give optimal QoS based on insight. CAL-AI is a method for creating "intelligent machines." It is a promising method that has the potential to make significant advancements in the technological area. The authors present a general summary of this groundbreaking method in the realm

of wireless communication systems in this chapter, as well as its future implications. The progress of the information and communication technology industry will be largely attributed to CAL-AI.

Chapter 3

The Influence of AI-Assisted Learning on CAL: A Blueprint 23

Karthik Ganesh R., SCAD College of Engineering and Technology, India

Reading, creating, hearing, witnessing, analyzing, testing, and other activities are all part of a diverse, multilayered, and dynamic learning experience. These layers combine to make learning a unique and personal experience for each individual. Understanding the factors that influence how people learn has a lot of power. When that expertise is combined with artificial intelligence (AI), the authors can develop learning experiences that are beneficial to all students. AI-assisted learning is a learning experience that is adaptive and enhances our natural learning style with machine intelligence (AIAL). AI can recognize trends and make decisions that are beneficial to users. There are numerous different tendencies in memory as it relates to humans in this study. This chapter explains how AI-assisted learning takes into account aspects including a student's background, the subject, modalities, and environment to produce an integrating teachable moment.

Chapter 4

Instruction Process and Learning Issues in Computer-Assisted Learning: A Detailed Review 36

Banumathi J., Anna University, India & University College of Engineering, Nagercoil, India

Computer assisted learning (CAL) has grown in popularity over the past and is also known as computer based instruction (CBI), computer aided learning (CAL), or computer aided instruction (CAI) . For the purpose of this study, we might tell exactly CAL as computer-assisted learning techniques and settings. However, collaboration is the key to comprehending CAL. On numerous levels, computers can help with engagement during the learning process. This chapter looks at CAI in general because CALL and CAI share many aspects. It also goes over broad learning topics like learning styles and tactics, personalized knowledge, as well as the elements that determine the consequences of gaining knowledge. Where necessary, the education learning setting is mentioned, as well as how contemporary CAI knowledge can be applied to the education learning circumstance.

Chapter 5
Computing the Cloud Storage for Computer-Aided Learning Access.................55
K. Juliana Gnanaselvi, Rathinam College of Arts and Science, India

Computer-assisted learning is a type of educational practice that involves the use of computer systems and other technology. It can take many different forms, and it involves a variety of tools and devices, including smartphones, tablets, personal computers, and others, despite its reputation. Different types of software and procedures are used in CAL. It can be used in a variety of subjects, including language acquisition and math. It is also used at all stages of education by then and now booming sectors in the coronavirus pandemic situation, particularly K to 12 programs, distance programs, skills and vocational training institutes, corporate training programs sometimes by individual broadcast trainers. Computer-assisted learning improves the teaching and learning process, resulting in higher levels of engagement and results. However, there are certain disadvantages to CAL. The authors look into the storage purpose of the CAL sessions as well as conversations. This is the time, the authors have to focus on the storage aspect of the CAL sessions, as much as the chats.

Chapter 6
An Overview of the Big Data Technology for Computer-Assisted Learning......66
Sivaranjani R., Hindusthan College of Arts and Science, India

Education has gradually gotten rid of old teaching methods and their limits as society has progressed under the impact of high technology such as big data, cloud computing, network technology, and mobile Internet. This study uses data mining technology to implement educational reforms, creates a computer-aided learning system (CAL) based on data mining, and creates teaching system functions based on real-world data with big data techniques. Many strategies for data analysis are available through data mining. Without the use of automated analytic techniques, the big data now in student databases exceeds the human ability to examine and extract the most important information. Data analytics for CAL will be helpful in evaluating teaching and learning processes, and measures will be taken based on the findings to improve the process.

Chapter 7
Analyzing the Novel Approaches for Intelligent Computer-Aided Learning (ICAL)...75
Shaheen H., MVJ College of Engineering, India

Beyond the spread of the disease and efforts to treat, the coronavirus pandemic has far-reaching implications. It is crystal clear that the pandemic wreaked havoc on critical fields such as healthcare, business, and academic. In terms of academics, one direct outcome of the pandemic's spread was the decision to suspend traditional in-person classroom courses in favor of remote learning and home-based schooling through the use of computer assisted learning technologies, but these technologies confront numerous hurdles. The majority of these issues revolve around the effectiveness of these delivery modalities, as well as engagement and knowledge testing. These difficulties highlight the need for an advanced smart educational system that aids all types of learners, gives teachers a variety of smart new tools, and enables a more flexible learning environment. The internet of things, artificial intelligence and virtual reality is a blooming sector, and IoT-based devices have ushered in a revolution in electronics and information technology.

Chapter 8
Recent Trends in Nanomaterials: Challenges and Opportunities 88
Kannadhasan S., Study World College of Engineering, Coimbatore, India
Nagarajan R., Gnanamani College of Technology, India
Kanagaraj Venusamy, Rajalakshmi Engineering College, Chennai, India

Nanoscience is the analysis of phenomena and material modification at the chemical, cellular, and macromolecular scales, where properties vary greatly from those at larger scales. Nanotechnologies are the regulation of form and size at the nanometer scale in the design, characterization, processing, and deployment of materials, components, and systems. The development of efficient methods for the synthesis of nanomaterials in a variety of sizes and chemical compositions is a hot topic in nanotechnology research. There have been many changes and modifications to the methods for producing metal nanoparticles that provide greater control over the scale, form, and other characteristics of the nanoparticles. These advancements have enabled researchers to investigate quantum confinement as well as other properties that are affected by scale, form, and composition.

Chapter 9
Recent Trends in Microstrip Patch Antenna Using Textile Applications..........103
Kannadhasan S., Study World College of Engineering, Coimbatore, India
Nagarajan R., Gnanamani College of Technology, India
Kanagaraj Venusamy, Rajalakshmi Engineering College, Chennai, India

Wireless body area networks (WBANs) have gotten a lot of interest as the need for wearable gadgets like smart watches, eyewear, and clothing grows. WBAN applications need the use of a conformal antenna. A low-profile IR-UWB antenna and an all-textile higher order mode circular patch antenna for omnidirectional radiation were used to meet this need. To achieve maximum power output, researchers need to maintain the antenna's efficiency as high as feasible while designing a lightweight antenna for wireless power transfer. The need for tiny textile antennas with high gain and broadband features has risen in response to the fast growth of wireless power transfer. Microstrip patch antennas provide a number of advantages, including a cheap cost, a low profile, a light weight, and a simple manufacturing method. Increases in substrate thickness, antenna efficiency, use of a low dielectric substrate, and different impedance matching and feeding techniques are all examples of ways to enhance antenna bandwidth.

Chapter 10
Cloud-Based Detection of Forged Passport and Extraction of True Identity: Surf Match Algorithm for Fraudulence Reduction..........120
Kanthavel R., King Khalid University, India

The forgery of primary documents has become a cause of great concern in recent times. Forged passports have been used in significant numbers, and the number continues to rise year after year. As a result, there is a need for a quick, inexpensive technique that can recognize false passports. This is the same cause why researchers adapted our basic tasks to recognize persons effectively even at a stretch using the SURF matching technique for use in counterfeit passport detection applications. The use of the SURF matching algorithm to identify and so discover the targeting individual has been expanded to the detecting of false passports. This has broadened the area of the paper's application in both detection and tracking and the identification of duplicated passports. The outcome and applicability of our technology can be changed depending on the photographs associated with the input. In the case of a phony passport, the authors' article likewise tries to remove the patient's genuine identity.

Vehicle parking and vehicle parking place have become inevitable things for the present situation and it contributes to traffic congestion in an indirect manner. The proposed work aims to solve the problem of effectively utilizing the available parking space through an IoT-based parking network during peak hours as well as to charge the system with solar energy as a renewable to ensure reliability in terms of saving time, space, and energy. Because IoT can convey information via the network without encompassing human contacts in the cloud and also permits a user to use affordable wireless technology. the innovative idea of this proposed vehicle parking network is of using solar as renewable energy to charge the sensors in the network. Hence, it is proposed to use the Infrared sensor to be positioned alongside the parking space ESP module. IR sensors will update the current state of available parking spaces for ESP uses light energy observed by the sensors will be used to charge the network. The outcome will benefit the users to manage the parking space effectively and efficiently.

Preface

The rapid acceptance and present and future scenario of computer-assisted learning have been the cause and basis of inspiration for editors for the selection of theme for this edited book. computer assisted learning (CAL) presents students with two significant provisions: remedial academic support and experience to computers. Studies have revealed that way into computers with educational software cans appreciably progress student performance in disadvantaged schools. Computer-assisted learning can be any mode of learning that is mediated by a computer and which necessitates no direct communication between the user and a human instructor in order to run. Computers have revolutionized the teaching occupation in numerous ways. Teachers use computers to document grades, calculate averages, manage attendance, and access data on student routine in virtual programs and evaluations. Computers have also completed it easier for teachers to differ their instructional deliverance.

On the other hand, the purpose of computer assisted learning is that it strongly supports the operation of ICT in language learning to get better efficiency and effectiveness of learning that can develop the quality of understanding and mastery of the language learned.

Moreover, computers allow students to be taught by doing rather than trying to take up lines of information from a textbook. They are also given the chances to study by trial and error, which permits them to see how things work rather than compelling them to trust what the teacher speaks. Furthermore, the advantages over computer assisted learning testing that includes overcoming administrative and logistic burdens: The first advantage of the use of computers in language testing is that it helps overcome many of the administrative and logistic burdens associated with tradition testing practices.

In addition to that, computer assisted learnings are viewed as the future of teaching and *learning* and also as a powerful technological machine.

This book carries 11 chapters and each one has its uniqueness in elaborating computer assisted leanings in different ways.

We are in no doubt that this book will be constructive and helpful to the researchers, academicians, and enthusiastic managers to bring up to date them with modern development in the area of computer-assisted learning and to approach with the challenges of the dynamic leaning methodologies. We hope that the book will offer appropriate insights of computer-assisted learning to the students and creates a contemporary interest. We are thankful for the efforts put in by the researchers in terms of quality research work done by them. We put across our gratitude to the reviewers of the various articles for being generous their precious contribution in the form of comments and ideas for the improvement of this edited book. We are also gratified to IGI Global for publication of this book.

We look forward to our commitment to the source of endorsing high quality research work in the area of Computer Assisted Learning will contribute to enlighten our readers in the time to come.

CHAPTER 1: TECHNOLOGY-BASED, COMPUTER-ASSISTED LEARNING – AN IoT CAL OVERVIEW

In today's world, technology is taking over many parts of human existence, and computer aided learning (CAL) is an educational instrument that facilitates learning. Computer aided learning (CAL) is an integrated technology that specific role of IoT in education in a learning environment where a computerized tool is utilized to help a user study a specific topic. Incorporating technologies like artificial intelligence (AI), internet of things (IoT), virtual reality (VR) and augmented reality (AR) in CAL will be driving the present as well as future. The impact of pandemic conditions has resulted in an increase in CAL users, which is expected to make the CAL programme more successful. The aim of this chapter is to propose IoT CAL ideas that are intended to provide a worthwhile learning experience by delivering efficient, engaging, and preemptive context-aware training smart services.

CHAPTER 2: USE OF CAL-AI IN FUTURE WIRELESS COMMUNICATION SYSTEMS

The intension of this chapter is to explore the ideas how to use CAL with artificial intelligence in future wireless communication system. Communication systems have changed dramatically during the last few decades. Wireless communication is one of the few industries that have been able to maintain exponential growth and visionary characteristics for many years. Computer assisted learning- artificial intelligence [CAL-AI] can process vast amounts of data produced by communication systems on a regular basis to give optimal QoS based on insight. CAL-AI is a method for creating "intelligent machines." It is a promising method that has the potential to make significant advancements in the technological area. We present a general summary of this groundbreaking method in the realm of wireless communication systems in this chapter, as well as its future implications. The progress of the information and communication technology industry will be largely attributed to CAL-AI.

CHAPTER 3: THE INFLUENCE OF AI-ASSISTED LEARNING ON CAL – A BLUEPRINT

Reading, creating, hearing, witnessing, analyzing, testing, and other activities are all part of a diverse, multilayered, and dynamic learning experience. These layers combine to make learning a unique and personal experience for each individual. Understanding the factors that influence how we learn has a lot of power. When that expertise is combined with artificial intelligence (AI), we can develop learning experiences that are beneficial to all students. AI-assisted learning is a learning experience that is adaptive and enhances our natural learning style with machine intelligence (AIAL). AI can recognize trends and make decisions that are beneficial to users. There are numerous different tendencies in memory as it relates to humans in this study. This chapter explains how AI-assisted learning takes into account aspects including a student's background, the subject, modalities, and environment to produce an integrating teachable moment.

CHAPTER 4: INSTRUCTION PROCESS AND LEARNING ISSUES IN COMPUTER ASSISTED LEARNING – A DETAILED REVIEW

Computer assisted learning (CAL) has grown in popularity over the past and is also known as computer-based instruction (CBI), computer aided learning (CAL), or computer aided instruction (CAI) . For the purpose of this study, we might tell exactly CAL as computer-assisted learning techniques and settings. However, collaboration is the key to comprehending CAL. On numerous levels, computers can help with engagement during the learning process. This chapter looks at CAI in general because CALL and CAI share many aspects. It also goes over broad learning topics like learning styles and tactics, personalized knowledge, as well as the elements that determine the consequences of gaining knowledge. Where necessary, the education learning setting is mentioned, as well as how contemporary CAI knowledge can be applied to the education learning circumstance.

CHAPTER 5: COMPUTING THE CLOUD STORAGE FOR COMPUTER AIDED LEARNING ACCESS

Computer-assisted learning is a type of educational practice that involves the use of computer systems and other technology. It can take many different forms, and it involves a variety of tools and devices, including smart phones, tablets, personal computers, and others, despite its reputation. Different types of software and procedures are used in CAL. It can be used in a variety of subjects, including language acquisition and math. It is also used at all stages of education by then and now booming sectors in the corona virus pandemic situation, particularly K to 12 programs, distance programs, skills and vocational training institutes, corporate training programs sometimes by individual broadcast trainers . Computer-assisted learning improves the teaching and learning process, resulting in higher levels of engagement and results. However, there are certain disadvantages to CAL. This chapter looks into the storage purpose of the CAL sessions as well as conversations.

CHAPTER 6: AN OVERVIEW OF THE BIG DATA TECHNOLOGY FOR COMPUTER ASSISTED LEARNING

Education has gradually gotten rid of old teaching methods and their limits as society has progressed under the impact of high technology such as big data, cloud computing, network technology, and mobile Internet. This study uses data mining technology to implement educational reforms, creates a computer-aided learning system (CAL) based on data mining, and creates teaching system functions based on real-world data with big data techniques. Many strategies for data analysis are available through data mining. Without the use of automated analytic techniques, the big data now in student databases exceeds the human ability to examine and extract the most important information. Data analytics for CAL will be helpful in evaluating teaching and learning processes, and measures will be taken based on the findings to improve the process. The effectiveness of using big data technology for computer assisted learning has been explained in this chapter.

CHAPTER 7: ANALYZING THE NOVEL APPROACHES FOR INTELLIGENT COMPUTER AIDED LEARNING (ICAL)

This chapter analyzes the novel approaches for making the CAL in an intelligent way. Beyond the spread of the disease and efforts to treat, the corona virus pandemic has far-reaching implications. It is crystal clear that the pandemic wreaked havoc on critical fields such as healthcare, business, and academic. In terms of academics, one direct outcome of the pandemic's spread was the decision to suspend traditional in-person classroom courses in favor of remote learning and home-based schooling through the use of computer assisted learning technologies, but these technologies confront numerous hurdles. The majority of these issues revolve around the effectiveness of these delivery modalities, as well as engagement and knowledge testing. These difficulties highlight the need for an advanced smart educational system that aids all types of learners, gives teachers a variety of smart new tools, and enables a more flexible learning environment. The internet of things, artificial intelligence and virtual reality is a blooming sector, and IoT-based devices have ushered in a revolution in electronics and information technology.

CHAPTER 8: RECENT TRENDS IN NANOMATERIALS – CHALLENGES AND OPPORTUNITIES

The aim of this chapter is to identify the recent trends in challenges and opportunities of CAL. Nano-science is the analysis of phenomena and material modification at the chemical, cellular, and macromolecular scales, where properties vary greatly from those at larger scales. Nanotechnologies are the regulation of form and size at the nanometer scale in the design, characterization, processing, and deployment of materials, components, and systems. The development of efficient methods for the synthesis of nano-materials in a variety of sizes and chemical compositions is a hot topic in nanotechnology research. There have been many changes and modifications to the methods for producing metal nano-particles that provide greater control over the scale, form, and other characteristics of the nano-particles. These advancements have enabled researchers to investigate quantum confinement as well as other properties that are affected by scale, form, and composition.

CHAPTER 9: RECENT TRENDS IN MICROSTRIP PATCH ANTENNA USING TEXTILE APPLICATIONS

Wearable gadgets such as smart watches and eyewear devices are WBAN applications that need the use of a conformal antenna. A low-profile IR-UWB antenna and an all-textile higher order mode circular patch antenna for omni-directional radiation were used to meet this need. To achieve maximum power output, we need to maintain the antenna's efficiency as high as feasible while designing a lightweight antenna for wireless power transfer. The need for tiny textile antennas with high gain and broadband features has risen in response to the fast growth of wireless power transfer. Microstrip patch antennas provide a number of advantages, including a cheap cost, a low profile, a light weight, and a simple manufacturing method. Increases in substrate thickness, antenna efficiency, use of a low dielectric substrate, and different impedance matching and feeding techniques are all examples of ways to enhance antenna bandwidth. This chapter explores the recent trends in microstrip patch antenna using textile applications.

CHAPTER 10: DETECTION OF FORGED PASSPORT AND EXTRACTION OF TRUE IDENTITY USING CLOUD BASED SURF MATCHING ALGORITHM FOR FRAUDULENCE REDUCTION

Forgery of primary documents has become a cause of great concern in recent times. Forged passports have been used in significant numbers, and the number continues to rise year after year. As a result, there is a need for a quick, inexpensive technique that can recognize false passports. This is the same cause why we adapted our basic tasks to recognize persons effectively even at a stretch using the SURF matching technique for use in a counterfeit passport detection applications. The use of the SURF matching algorithm to identify and so discover the targeting individual has been expanded to the detecting of false passports. This has broadened the area of the paper's application in both detection and tracking and the identification of duplicated passports. The outcome and applicability of our technology can be change depending on the photographs associated with the input. In the case of a phony passport, our article likewise tries to remove the patient's genuine identity. A national card is utilized since it has been found to be a trustworthy source of information in the case of nationals. We focused on creating a system that performs admirably in the applications where it can be used.

CHAPTER 11: IoT BASED SOLAR-CHARGED WIRELESS VEHICLE PARKING NETWORK

The vehicle parking and vehicle parking place have become the inevitable things for the present situation and it contributes to traffic congestion in an indirect manner. During busy hours. Typically, the user spends time and money looking for a free parking bay in a particular parking garage. The proposed work aims to solve the problem of effectively utilizing the available parking space through an IoT-based parking network during peak hours as well as to charge the system with solar energy as a renewable one to ensure reliability in terms of saving time, space, and energy. Wireless sensor networks are a perfect choice for vehicle parking systems since these provide for precise monitoring of each loading space's condition if required. Furthermore, wireless sensors also have the benefit of being portable as plenty with self-organizing capability. On the other hand, the Internet of things (IoT) can offer a wireless connection to the tool to keep informed of the parking area's accessibility to reduce traffic congestion and limited vehicle parking. Because IoT can convey information via the network without encompassing human contacts into the cloud and also permits a user to use affordable wireless technology. Besides, the innovative idea of this proposed vehicle parking network is of using solar as renewable energy to charge the sensors in the network. Hence, it is proposed to use the Infrared sensor to be positioned alongside the parking space ESP module. IR sensors will update the current state of available parking spaces for ESP users. Also, the light energy observed by the sensors will be used to charge the network. The outcome of this task will benefit the users and administrators to manage the parking space effectively and efficiently.

R. Dhaya
King Khalid University, Saudi Arabia

R. Kanthavel
King Khalid University, Saudi Arabia

Chapter 1
Technology-Based Computer-Assisted Learning:
An IoTCAL Overview

Sinthuja U.
https://orcid.org/0000-0001-5873-3459
Ramakrishna College of Arts and Science, Coimbatore, India & Hindustan College of Arts and Science, Coimbatore, India

Thavamani S.
Sri Ramakrishna College of Arts and Science, India

ABSTRACT

In today's world, technology is taking over many parts of human existence, and computer aided learning (CAL) is an educational instrument that facilitates learning. Computer aided learning (CAL) is an integrated technology that specific role of IoT in education in a learning environment where a computerized tool is utilized to help a user study a specific topic. Incorporating technologies like artificial intelligence (AI), internet of things (IoT), virtual reality (VR) and augmented reality (AR) in CAL will be driving the present as well as future. The impact of pandemic conditions has resulted in an increase in CAL users, which is expected to make the CAL programme more successful. The proposed IoTCAL ideas are intended to provide a worthwhile learning experience by delivering efficient, engaging, and preemptive context-aware training smart services.

DOI: 10.4018/978-1-6684-5058-1.ch001

INTRODUCTION

One of the most valuable blessings of the digital age is computer-assisted learning (CAL). We can have an abundance of knowledge with only one click. It is the process of learning knowledge through the use of technological gadgets and products. No longer does one have to rely just on books and institutions to obtain education and information. Technology is used in every aspect of education, whether it is medical or civil. Electronic equipment can be used to gain any kind of knowledge in any discipline. In the majority of schools and institutes, virtual learning is replacing classroom instruction. Computers enable smart classes, video classes, online-offline movies, web classrooms, and many other services. Computer-assisted education is a simple and effective technique to absorb and comprehend information. We can learn at any time and in numerous ways using Computer-Assisted Learning. We may watch the films and the recorded tutored sessions at any time and from any location. It has brought value to the realm of education platforms. Learning has grown more exciting as a result of Computer-Assisted Learning. Students have become more independent as a result of computer-Assisted Learning, which has lessened their reliance on teachers and physical instruction. Students' interest is maintained by interactive videos and presentations. The pandemic began in China, where the lockdown was first detected. Education should not suffer as a result of the lockdown. The Chinese government employed tencent classrooms to make education available online. This has been dubbed the "biggest online movement" in Wuhan's educational history. Which has resulted in bringing more equipped tools in teaching and learning practice.

IoT in CAL

The components of the Internet of Things can be broken down into three categories: based on things, internet, as well as semantic (Atzori, Iera, and Morabito, 2010). The first layer is referred to as the "Device Layer." This layer includes sensors, actuators, and an embedded communication hardware system. "Service Layer" is the second layer. The third layer is characterized as "App Layer," and it consists of on demand storage and cloud computing tools for data analytics. The layer provides visualization and interpretation capabilities that may be used on a variety of platforms and for a variety of applications (Gubbi et al., 2013). Although the Internet of Things vision has immense promise for future technology, many complicated technical, social, and economic issues remain unsolved. The significance of hardware and software platforms in accelerating the reduction of concepts to working with prototypes is an intriguing thought in the context of IoT technology in education (Hodges et al., 2012).

IoTCAL TECHNOLOGY LANDSCAPE

In Johnson et al's (2012) "Higher Education Edition", a yearly study that examines the impact of current and future technologies on education, first referenced the IoT in the edition of 2012 and forecasts widespread implementation on/ before 2017. Few of the technologies recommended in table 1 for better understanding of the IoTCAL.

Table 1. Implemented technologies for IoTCAL

Sr.No	Literature	Implemented Technologies for IoTCAL
1	(O'Connor, 2010)	Used RFID tags to track class attendance
2	("Texas Tech University Health Sciences Center in El Paso deploys campus-wide RFID asset tracking", 2022)	Implemented RFID tags to track lab resources
3	(Bolton, 2015)	Introduced IoT course
4	(Byrne, O'Sullivan, and Sullivan, 2016)	Hackathon has conducted for Wearable Technology awareness
5	(Dobrilovic and Zeljko, 2016)	University proposed Low-cost open source platform for student's hands-on.
6	(Mhatre and Rai, 2017)	Proposed prototype in Engineering Education
7	(Hendrick, 2015)	Created IoT cum Cloud computing for education

IoTCAL METHODOLOGY

An IoTCAL will be equipped with a learning environment, it should ideally be as diverse as feasible, allowing learners to create a wide range of solutions. In practice, cost constraints can be severe, particularly in poorer nations, therefore equipment should be carefully chosen. As discussed in the introduction section, in the device layer, the major components should be multipurpose, low-cost microcomputers and microcontrollers that can perform a variety of tasks based on user programming.

Although the running logic can be distributed among devices, it is more convenient to centralize it behind a well-defined web service API. Devices that take measurements (such as sensor nodes) can occasionally report to web services, which act as the system's middleware. If the devices are powerful enough, they can obtain their instructions via polling specified services or by running their own web services for input. In a collaborative, educational setting, the web service concept is extremely useful. Students can create and share their own services; more complicated services can be established by combining student-created services with cloud-based and external web APIs. Client apps, whether they're web-based, desktop-based, or mobile-based, only interface with web services.

Sensor reading reporting was identified as a common situation in IoT applications, therefore the students were given a simple API to utilize for this purpose, which allowed them to save, use, and share sensor readings, as well as import or generate external data for use in simulations of certain scenarios. Students were also provided with an SMS sending/receiving service, and more services might be provided depending on the educational institution's existing infrastructure.

Figure 1. IoTCAL Design

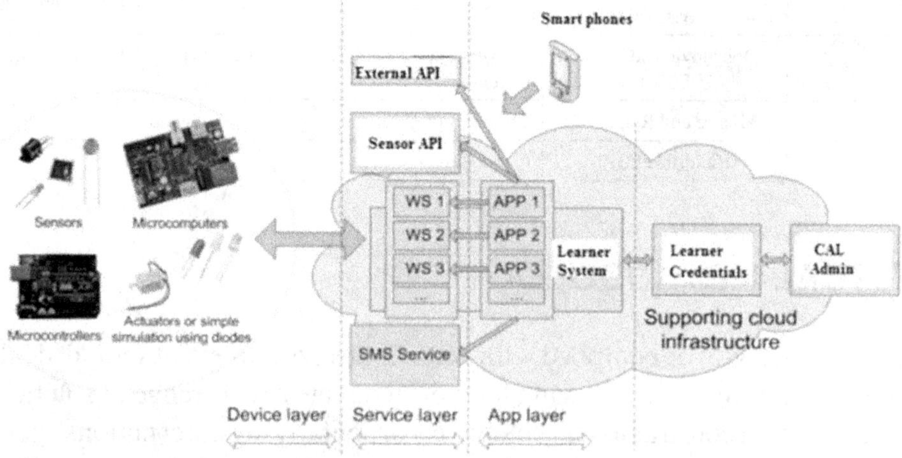

The application of the new model could be quite useful as it involves a huge number of interconnected services, some of which could be combined with current learning systems to make learner activity tracking and grading easier. Although it is not required, using a cloud platform with high scalability and redundancy, as well as greater usage of existing processing resources, is an excellent choice in such circumstances.

TECHNO CAL

This section describes most of the novel technologies which can take the CAL forward, it is always important to notice these technologies here to bring up a better CAL environment. The application of the new model could be quite useful as it involves a huge number of interconnected services, some of which could be combined with current learning systems to make learner activity tracking and grading easier. Although it is not required, using a cloud platform with high scalability and redundancy, as well as greater usage of existing processing resources, is an excellent choice in such circumstances.

The future framework for techno CAL will be constantly revised in light of new technologies like AI, AR, VR and MR which are also incorporated with IoTCAL, experiences and case studies, as well as all global experiences from a more linked perspective. Techno CAL environments, broadly defined, are a new generation of educational systems involving an effective and efficient interplay of pedagogy, technology, and their fusion to improve learning processes. The set of physical and digital venues, situations, and cultures in which students learn can also be classified as modern learning environments. Digital learning environments should always be viewed as the addition of digital technology and related scenarios to a person's current physical environment, altering their whole cognitive representation of their surroundings and, as a result, their behavior and learning processes.

Human learning interfaces are used by digital technologies in a smart learning environment. As a result, a smart learning environment is aware of its surroundings and adapts to the behavior of each learner. AR enhanced by IoT data has a lot of potential for both effective contextual, in-person learning experiences and spontaneous exploration and discovery of the interrelated nature of information in the real world. Not only is the world ready for AR, but it has already begun to embrace it. AR is the real-time integration of digital data with the user's environment. Unlike virtual reality, which produces a completely fictional scene, augmented reality boosted by IoT data works with what is already there and overlays fresh information on top of it. By heightening the contrast between what is genuine and what is computer-generated, this new technology blurs the line between the two (Shoikova, Nikolov, and Kovatcheva, 2018).

Learners can benefit from AI technology by being able to learn outside of the classroom with virtual feedback, which makes learning more engaging and allows material to be tailored to the person. Although different technologies can be adapted by CAL it is also important to notice the security concerns in terms of data storage, information access, and so on. Based on the depicted security concerns we have also carried out few of the works for strengthening purpose.

CONCLUSION

We are concluding the CAL with IoT and some of the blooming technologies, augmented reality will soon overthrow traditional learning methods. VR and MR will completely alter the location and timing of the research process, as well as open up new avenues and approaches. While AR technology has progressed, it can still be challenging for students to utilize; consequently, additional research into the user experience design of IoTCAL applications is required. This idea will be helpful for special learners like deaf and blind.

ACKNOWLEDGMENT

First, our appreciation goes to parents and family for their sacrifice, commitment, and overalls, their support and consistent encouragement. I wish to express my sincere thanks to our Prestigious Institution.

REFERENCES

Atzori, L., Iera, A., & Morabito, G. (2010). The internet of things: A survey. *Computer Networks*, *54*(15), 2787–2805. doi:10.1016/j.comnet.2010.05.010

Bolton, W. (2015). *Programmable logic controllers*. Newnes.

Byrne, J. R., O'Sullivan, K., & Sullivan, K. (2016). An IoT and wearable technology hackathon for promoting careers in computer science. *IEEE Transactions on Education*, *60*(1), 50–58.

Dobrilovic, D., & Zeljko, S. (2016, May). Design of open-source platform for introducing Internet of Things in university curricula. In *IEEE 11th International Symposium on Applied Computational Intelligence and Informatics (SACI),* (pp. 273-276). IEEE.

Gubbi, J., Buyya, R., Marusic, S., & Palaniswami, M. (2013). Internet of Things (IoT): A vision, architectural elements, and future directions. *Future Generation Computer Systems*, *29*(7), 1645–1660. doi:10.1016/j.future.2013.01.010

Hendrick, S. (2015 September 9). Why Gateways and Controllers Are Critical for IoT Architecture. RTInsights. https://www.rtinsights.com/why-gateways-and-controllers-are-critical-for-iot-architecture/

Hodges, S., Taylor, S., Villar, N., Scott, J., Bial, D., & Fischer, P. T. (2012). Prototyping connected devices for the internet of things. *Computer*, *46*(2), 26–34. doi:10.1109/MC.2012.394

Johnson, L., Adams Becker, S., Cummins, M., Estrada, V., Freeman, A., & Hall, C. (2012). The NMC horizon report: 2012 higher education ed. Austin, TX: The New Media Consortium.

Mhatre, L., & Rai, N. (2017, February). Integration between wireless sensor and cloud. In *2017 International Conference on I-SMAC (IoT in Social, Mobile, Analytics and Cloud)(I-SMAC)* (pp. 779-782). IEEE.

O'Connor, M. C. (2010). Northern Arizona University to use existing RFID student cards for attendance tracking. *RFID journal, 24.*

Radiant. (2022). *Texas Tech University Health Sciences Center in El Paso deploys campus-wide RFID asset tracking. Radiant.* https://radiantrfid.com/news/texas-tech -university-healt h-sciences-ce nter-in-e l-pas o-deploys-campus-wide-rfid -asset-tracking/

Shoikova, E., Nikolov, R., & Kovatcheva, E. (2018, March). Smart digital education enhanced by AR and IoT data. In *Proceedings of the 12th International Technology, Education and Development Conference (INTED)*,(pp. 5-7). Valencia, Spain.

KEY TERMS AND DEFINITIONS

AI: Artificial Intelligence
AR: Augmented Reality
API: Application Program Interface
CAL: Computer Assisted Learning
SMS: Short Message Service
VR: Virtual Reality
MR: Mixed Reality

Chapter 2
Use of CAL-AI in Future Wireless Communication Systems

Mahalakshmi M.
CMR College of Engineering and Technology, India

ABSTRACT

Communication systems have changed dramatically during the last few decades. Wireless communication is one of the few industries that has been able to maintain exponential growth and visionary characteristics for many years. Computer assisted learning- artificial intelligence [CAL-AI] can process vast amounts of data produced by communication systems on a regular basis to give optimal QoS based on insight. CAL-AI is a method for creating "intelligent machines." It is a promising method that has the potential to make significant advancements in the technological area. The authors present a general summary of this groundbreaking method in the realm of wireless communication systems in this chapter, as well as its future implications. The progress of the information and communication technology industry will be largely attributed to CAL-AI.

DOI: 10.4018/978-1-6684-5058-1.ch002

INTRODUCTION

Rapid advancements in mobile internet tend to generate massive volumes of network traffic, which necessitates more bandwidth in order to experience it at a higher quality. Wireless networks are evolving towards a diverse paradigm to meet the high demand for data traffic. Artificial Intelligence (AI) can easily process the massive amounts of traffic generated.

CAL-AI is a strategy for creating "intelligent machines," which replicate the functioning of a human mind and learn from their surroundings on a continual basis. Their learning is defined as Machine Learning (ML), and they use it to create a database that categorizes information to assist them in solving problems and providing "intelligent outcomes" similar to human beings depending on the insights gained, increasing the likelihood of success. Intelligent mobile networks are operated more efficiently and autonomously with improved performance thanks to AI. It has the potential to handle unstructured problems by interpreting large volumes of data and compartmentalizing it so that it can be dealt with during the design and optimization phase (Wang et al., 2020).

The Architecture of Artificial Intelligence

Without being expressly programmed, an Artificial Intelligence can assess massive volumes of data generated by several sources such as camera images, various sensors, drones, and surveillance recordings and operate accordingly. These are then combined to build a detailed operating map and database of the network's vast number of devices. It can be used to optimize many functions across wireless networks of varied sizes, such as fault monitoring and usage tracking. By learning the operations of the wireless environment and the network's users in real-time, AI Resource management techniques can run completely autonomously. AI is used to ensure that these management mechanisms grow over time and always function at their best, maintaining network dependability and adaptability by making real-time decisions based on predictions and interpretations of user behavior.

End-to-end optimization is provided by AI, which handles the design complexity of Radio Frequency (RF) communication systems by using robust machine learning techniques to optimize RF characteristics including channel bandwidth, antenna sensitivity, and spectrum monitoring. Physical and signal processing designs (from the OSI model) might be commoditized using this strategy, allowing the RF system's complexity to be addressed.

5G is the networking technology of the future, and with it comes new fast-paced networking possibilities. AI can not only adapt to the new faster network connections, but also take use of them to drastically reduce communication latency, lowering costs and cutting power consumption. It is widely projected to become an increasingly important part of the 5G wireless network and subsequent communication. CogNet 5 will merge AI with wireless communication devices as part of the 5G network. As a result of these advancements, AI can now be employed for physical layer and network management, dramatically improving the performance of wireless networks. 6G will broaden the scope of mobile Internet and be fast enough to allow for real-time off-site processing. As a result, Artificial Intelligence (AI) will play a vital role in the design and optimization of future wireless communication (refer to Figure 1) architectures, protocols, and operational hierarchy.

Figure 1. Wireless Communication

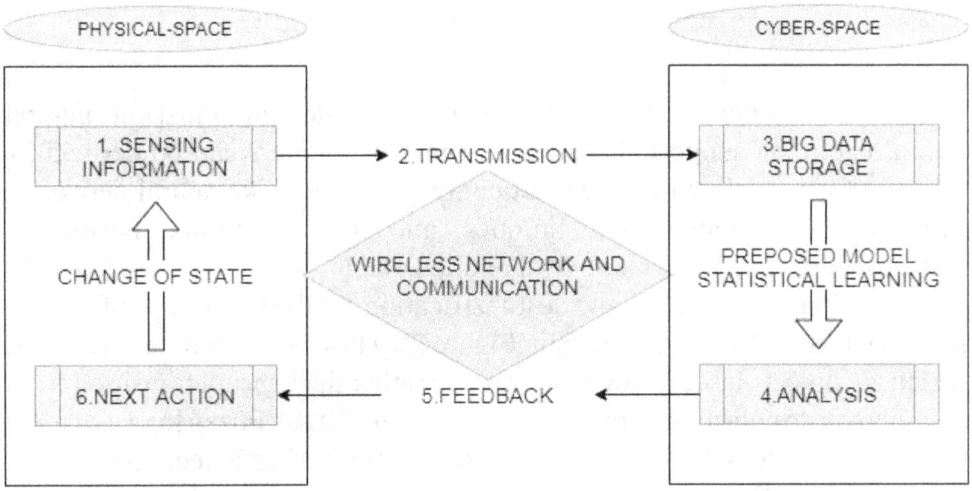

Fuzzy Logic

All variables in this fuzzy logic follow Boolean logic and can be any real value between 0 and 1. (both inclusive). This logic can be totally correct or completely incorrect. Fuzzy logic is used to emulate the human mind's unsure deduction procedure (Banupriva, Pandi, and Prathisha, 2018). This is a system full of unpredictability, ambiguity, imprecision, and vagueness.

Figure 2. Fuzzy Logic Controller

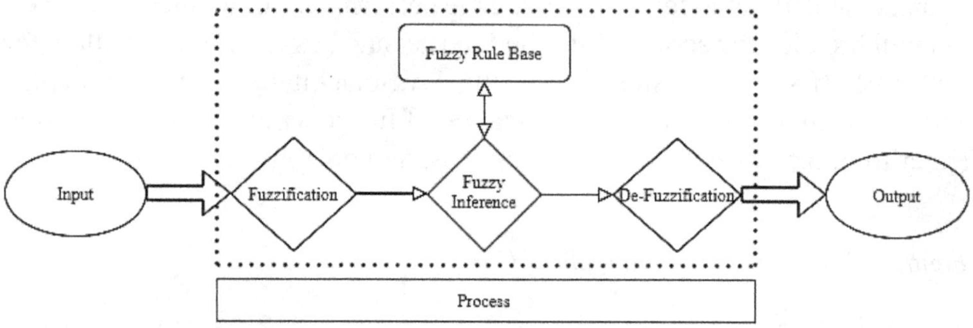

Fuzzy logic, often known as fuzzy control, integrates individual information into a regulation supported structure. These parameters can be derived by merging fuzzy logic with other soft computing fields like neural networks, evolutionary computation techniques, and so on (Cintula, Fermuller, and Noguera, 2021; Erman, Mohammed, and Rakus-Anderson, 2009). Fuzzification, aggregation, and de-fuzzification are the three steps of a fuzzy logic controller (FLC) (as shown in Figure 2). These are based on fuzzy sets, which are object classes with a progressive rather than abrupt transition from membership to non-membership (Silva and Pinto, 2018). Fuzzy logic is widely utilized in wireless communication to solve multi-criteria decision-making problems including network selection, handover control, and so on.

In a wireless communication system, a channel is the medium through which information is conveyed from a transmitter to a receiver using signals. The transmitted data is normally received without any errors under ideal settings. In the case of time-varying channels, adaptive strategies must be applied, and fuzzy techniques and neural networks are very useful in this field. In wireless communication, fuzzy logic is typically used for channel estimation, channel equalization, and decoding.

The channel coefficients in a multi-path fading Code Division Multiple Access (CDMA) (Viterbi, 1995) channel are monitored using a fuzzy tracking approach for channel estimation (Niemi, Joutsensalo, and Ristaniemi, 2000). CDMA is a spread-spectrum technology that allows several transmitters to share the same frequency band. Fuzzy tracking based on Kosko's fuzzy associative memory models and the TSK model, as well as fuzzy logic used in conjunction with adaptive algorithms such as the LMS and RMS algorithms or the inference scheme of a neuro-fuzzy, are among the fuzzy-based methodologies to be used. Channel coding and decoding are critical components of modern wireless communications.

Error-correcting codes for channel coding are employed to achieve consistent communications at Shannon channel capacity rates (Nguyen et al., 2020). The study of Wang and Mendel on fuzzy adaptive filters, both type-1 and type-2, TSK fuzzy logic systems, proved extremely useful in channel equalization. These fuzzy adaptive filters can use human expert feedback as well as training data. Adaptive fuzzy filters were used as the foundation for a Bayesian architecture that incorporates fuzzy base functions (Erman, Mohammed, and Rakus-Anderson, 2009).

A handover system is proposed in (Banupriya, Pandi, and Prathisha, 2018) for Long-Term Evolution (LTE). The proposed method takes into account the field of network coverage as well as the data rate in the proposed handover mechanism. The ping-pong movement is one of the most important handover concerns. The ping-pong consequences of the handover are reduced in fuzzy logic. The algorithm considers the current signal to noise ratio (SNR), observed SNR, serving bandwidth, and intended eNB bandwidth. To detect a ping-pong effect in a low-rate wireless private area network, fuzzy logic is used. Radio access technology (RAT) selection is one of the most difficult aspects of wireless networks.

The network is chosen in two steps: in the first, fuzzy logic is used to determine the out-of-context acceptability of each RAT for delay-sensitive applications and best-effort applications. The findings of the first stage estimation are merged with terminal capacity, user preferences, and operator policies in the second stage to determine each RAT's in-context suitability. The decision is made via a fuzzy multiple attribute decision-making procedure. The signal strength acquired, mobile speed, mobile battery level, user classification, and service kind are five characteristics that determine network selection as input to the fuzzy logic controller (Banupriya, Pandi, and Prathisha, 2018). Acceptable, not acceptable, probably acceptable, and probably not acceptable are the four options for linguistic variables (Banupriya, Pandi, and Prathisha,

2018). As a result, the Fuzzy Logic technique improves comprehensibility while reducing complexity. Its goal is to keep the input to a minimum so that the rule base isn't overly complicated.

1. MACHINE LEARNING IN WIRELESS COMMUNICATION

Machine learning (ML) is a branch of pattern recognition that is based on the idea that machines should be given artificial intelligence (AI) that allows them to learn from past computations and adapt to their surroundings via experience (Chen et al., 2017; Dhaya and Kanthavel, 2021; Andrieu et al., 2003; Freeman, Pasztor, and Carmichael, 2000; Sebastiani, 2002; Collobert and Weston, 2008; Pang, Lee, and Vaithyanathan, 2002; Bishop and Nasrabadi, 2006; Stone and Velsoso, 2000). In machine learning, training refers to the process of teaching the machine learning framework how to achieve a certain goal, such as speech recognition. The training allows the framework to discover potential links between the framework's input and output data. It can be divided into two categories: 1) Supervised Learning and 2) Unsupervised Learning. 2) Learning Without Supervision As shown in Figure 3, there are four types of learning: 1) semi-supervised learning, 2) reinforcement learning, and 3) reinforcement learning. In the construction and dynamic functioning of such a hyper-communication system, ML can play an important role.

Unidentified channel information may mostly be sourced via machine learning approaches based on contact data and previous experiences. ML can be utilized for channel feature prediction, channel impulse response (CIR) modeling, multipath component (MPC) clustering, channel parameter estimation, and scenario categorization based on channel measurement data and environmental information (Wang et al., 2020). A 2D nonlinear complex support vector regression (SVR) centered on an RBF kernel multipath channel was developed to accomplish exact channel estimation in a time-varying rapid fading (Varela and Bourgine, 1992). To lower the computational complexity, machine learning is utilized, which allows the task to be completed with fewer resources (Hyder, Tennakoon, and Jayakody, 2019).

The massive volumes of data produced by big antenna arrays, very high Multiple-Input Multiple-Output (MIMO) arrays, are particularly well-suited to machine learning techniques.

Because parametric models are either inaccessible or inaccurate, traditional prediction algorithms are incompatible. For large MIMO systems using mmWavebeamspace, an approach for deep-learning-based channel estimation was suggested in (He et al., 2018). It can deduce the channel's structure and approximate the channel using a large amount of training data. The scatterer pathways' angles and gains can be defined using sparse spatial structure in mmWave channels (Wang et al., 2020). To assess the performance of indoor localization, a variety of machine learning classifiers such as random forest, Bayes network, and SVM are used.

Figure 3. Classification of Machine Learning

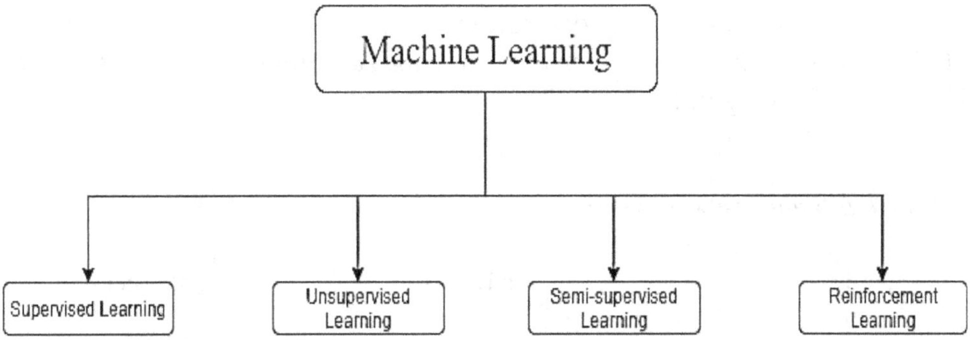

ML can achieve learning-based adaptive network setup by identifying behavioural patterns and adapting quickly and flexibly to varied scenarios, for example, forecasting traffic and planning rather than reacting directly to unforeseen occurrences (Wang et al., 2020). The most essential application of AI in 5G networks will be to apply machine learning to sophisticated radio-resource management (RRM) algorithms (Calabrese et al., 2018), such as power control, connection adaption, decision handover, or admission control. Machine-learning radio access should be able to perceive an optimal communication procedure based on computed communication.

The use of machine learning in mobile communications networks is likely to begin soon. Machine learning can be used to improve existing features (such as control of radio resources, network management etc.). The innovations can easily be implemented in existing systems without the need for standardization. On improved systems, ML would be better supported, with data availability for ML purposes and specific capabilities for the same. Through the application of these methodologies, research along this path will significantly advance the state of the art in detecting open spaces, indoor venues, and through the wall, as well as execute inference tasks that are unachievable with traditional model-based signal processing. As a result, machine learning (ML) plays a critical role in the development of wireless communication

IN COMMUNICATION, THE ART OF THE NEURAL NETWORK

Neural Networks (NN) are an important part of AI because they can imitate human intelligence, replicate compound connections between inputs and outputs, find the design in data, or draw out the analytical structure in an unspecified joint probability distribution from observed data (Chen et al., 2017). They are a set of Algorithms having AI foundations that strive to identify underlying links.

Figure 4. A Simple Neural Network

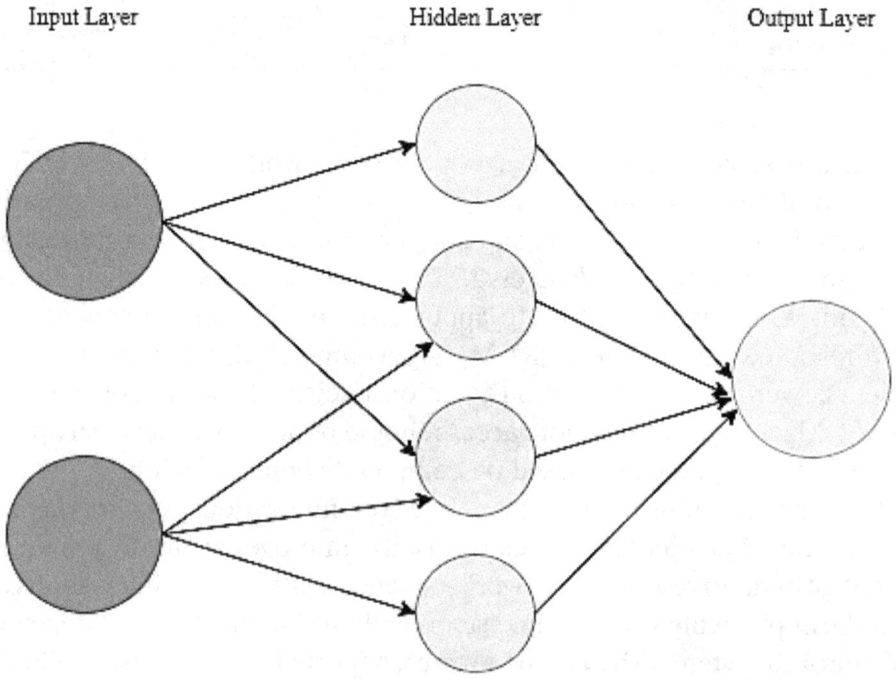

It is based on the biological working of the nervous system, and it imitates neuron behavior (Anderson, 1995), as seen in Figure 4. It resembles the brain in two ways: (1) the network acquires information through a learning process, and (2) synaptic weights, the strength of interneuron connections, are utilized to retain experiential knowledge (Haykin and Network, 2004; Charpentier and Laurin, 1999). These neurons grasp the statistical structure and can thus generate a shared probability distribution across the input data. In wireless communication systems, NN is frequently used to analyze the surroundings and automate network control.

In the realm of wireless communication, neural networks are employed in microstrip antenna analysis, adaptive beamforming, wideband mobile antenna design, Direction of Arrival (DOA) estimates, and many more applications (Haykin and Network, 2004). In a confidence-based smart routing algorithm for Delay Tolerant Networks (DTNs), the technique employs an artificial neural network to analyze and estimate the trust value from call data records, and then the results are distributed among network devices. The data flow would be more likely to transmit to nodes with higher trust scores. As a result, energy usage, calculation time, and overhead space are all lowered.

The neural network is used to achieve self-configuration and self-optimization for both radio resources and routing (Banupriya, Pandi, and Prathisha, 2018). The ability of NN to extract, forecast, and recognize common patterns from large datasets is its most essential benefit (Charpentier and Laurin, 1999). Quality of Experience (QoE) is a variable that captures both the quantitative and subjective components of a user's level of satisfaction with a particular service. A neural network is used for a range of services in order to estimate QoE. The neural networks are used to automatically determine the KPIs (key performance indicators). The QoE estimate approach for video streaming services over wireless networks is introduced (Banupriya, Pandi, and Prathisha, 2018). It is based on a feed-forward artificial neural network termed radial basis function networks. Higher-dimensional data interpolation is possible using radial-base-function networks. The main advantage of radial-basis-function neural networks is that they lower the amount of CPU time necessary to anticipate the direction of arrival. Under conditions of external intrusion, the structural stiffness of direction-finding systems based on neural networks in noise has been observed (Mishra and Patnaik, 1999a).

Neural networks have also been utilized in conjunction with a spectral-domain technique dubbed the Neurospectral Approach for microstrip antenna research (Mishra and Patnaik, 1999b, 2000; El Zooghby, Christodoulou, and Georgiopoulous, 2000). Multiple source tracking antennas based on smart neural networks are another important application of the neural network in wireless communication (Yamazaki, Asakura, and Ohuchi, 2020). Because of their sheer flying nature, UAVs (unnamed aerial vehicle) can manage human activities and gather data from any range, at any time, and from any location, such as user and vehicle data, creating an excellent environment for the deployment of neural network approaches.

With the recent boom in the use of neural network techniques, various new ways to meet the needs of wireless communication have emerged.

FUTURE AND BEYOND

CAI-AI will have a significant impact on the future of wireless communication. Wireless communication is predicted to increase data transfer speeds, and traffic is expected to increase in comparison to past records (Sun et al., 2019). In the wireless network, AI functions for privacy and reduced network traffic should be added and deployed in a distributed manner (Li et al., 2017). CAL-AI should enable 5G system operators to provide intelligent services and seamless local apps to mobile consumers (David and Berndt, 2018). AI technology may play a crucial role in allowing the end-to-end design and operation of data management in 6G wireless networks. CAL-AI networks are built to provide cutting-edge services based on modern human-centered principles (Luo, 2020). Broadband cellular telecommunication will benefit from a significantly more diversified topology of the wireless-access network. AI is expected to play a key role in identifying the intelligence of the transition from human-based network control to automated and autonomous network operations, which will be possible in the future. As a result of the integration of CAL-AI into wireless networks, current high-performance service arrangements have been reformed and upgraded.

CONCLUSION

We hope to present thorough information on the world of Computer Assisted Learning-Artificial Intelligence (CAL-AI) in Wireless Communication in this chapter. On the connectivity side, we've presented a latest configuration summary of Machine Learning. With regard to LTE, Fuzzy Logic advances as well as Fuzzy Logic controllers are also highlighted. A sweeping picture of the basic structure and use of Neural Network in the wireless network was also shown.

REFERENCES

Anderson, J. A. (1995). *An introduction to neural networks.* MIT press.

Andrieu, C., De Freitas, N., Doucet, A., & Jordan, M. I. (2003). An introduction to MCMC for machine learning. *Machine Learning, 50*(1), 5–43. doi:10.1023/A:1020281327116

Banupriya, D., Pandi, S. P., & Prathisha, R. R. (2018). A study on use of artificial intelligence in wireless communications. *Asian Journal of Applied Science and Technology*, *2*(1), 354–360.

Calabrese, F. D., Wang, L., Ghadimi, E., Peters, G., Hanzo, L., & Soldati, P. (2018). Learning radio resource management in RANs: Framework, opportunities, and challenges. *IEEE Communications Magazine*, *56*(9), 138–145. doi:10.1109/MCOM.2018.1701031

Charpentier, E., & Laurin, J. J. (1999). An implementation of a direction-finding antenna for mobile communications using a neural network. *IEEE Transactions on Antennas and Propagation*, *47*(7), 1152–1159.

Chen, M., Challita, U., Saad, W., Yin, C., & Debbah, M. (2017). Machine learning for wireless networks with artificial intelligence: A tutorial on neural networks. arXiv preprint arXiv:1710.02913, 9.

<eref>Cintula, P., Fermüller, C. G., & Noguera, C. (2021). Fuzzy logic. Stanford Encyclopedia of Philosophy. https://plato.stanford.edu/entries/logic-fuzzy/</eref>

Collobert, R., & Weston, J. (2008, July). A unified architecture for natural language processing: Deep neural networks with multitask learning. In *Proceedings of the 25th international conference on Machine learning*, (pp. 160-167). doi:10.1145/1390156.1390177

David, K., & Berndt, H. (2018). 6G vision and requirements: Is there any need for beyond 5G? *IEEE Vehicular Technology Magazine*, *13*(3), 72–80.

Dhaya, R., & Kanthavel, R. (2021). Cloud—Based multiple importance sampling algorithm with AI based CNN classifier for secure infrastructure. *Automated Software Engineering*, *28*(2), 1–28. doi:10.100710515-021-00293-y

El Zooghby, A. H., Christodoulou, C. G., & Georgiopoulos, M. (2000). A neural network-based smart antenna for multiple source tracking. *IEEE Transactions on Antennas and Propagation*, *48*(5), 768–776.

Erman, M., Mohammed, A., & Rakus-Andersson, E. (2009, July). Fuzzy Logic Applications in Wireless Communications. In *IFSA/EUSFLAT Conf*, (pp. 763-767).

Freeman, W. T., Pasztor, E. C., & Carmichael, O. T. (2000). Learning low-level vision. *International Journal of Computer Vision*, *40*(1), 25–47. doi:10.1023/A:1026501619075

Haykin, S., & Network, N. (2004). A comprehensive foundation. *Neural Networks*, *2*, 41.

He, H., Wen, C. K., Jin, S., & Li, G. Y. (2018). Deep learning-based channel estimation for beamspace mmWave massive MIMO systems. *IEEE Wireless Communications Letters*, *7*(5), 852–855. doi:10.1109/LWC.2018.2832128

Li, R., Zhao, Z., Zhou, X., Ding, G., Chen, Y., Wang, Z., & Zhang, H. (2017). Intelligent 5G: When cellular networks meet artificial intelligence. *IEEE Wireless Communications*, *24*(5), 175–183.

Luo, F. L. (Ed.). (2020). *Machine learning for future wireless communications*.

Mishra, R. K., & Patnaik, A. (1999a). Neurospectral computation for input impedance of rectangular microstrip antenna. *Electronics Letters*.

Mishra, R. K., & Patnaik, A. (1999b). Neurospectral computation for complex resonant frequency of microstrip resonators. *IEEE Microwave and Guided Wave Letters*, *9*(9), 351–353.

Mishra, R. K., & Patnaik, A. (2000, July). Neurospectral analysis of coaxial fed rectangular patch antenna. In IEEE Antennas and Propagation Society International Symposium. Transmitting Waves of Progress to the Next Millennium, 2, (pp. 1062-1065). IEEE

Nguyen, D. C., Cheng, P., Ding, M., Lopez-Perez, D., Pathirana, P. N., Li, J., Seneviratne, A., Li, Y., & Poor, H. V. (2020). Enabling AI in future wireless networks: A data life cycle perspective. *IEEE Communications Surveys and Tutorials*, *23*(1), 553–595. doi:10.1109/COMST.2020.3024783

Niemi, A., Joutsensalo, J., & Ristaniemi, T. (2000, September). Fuzzy channel estimation in multipath fading CDMA channel. In *11th IEEE International Symposium on Personal Indoor and Mobile Radio Communications, Proceedings*, 2, (pp. 1131-1135). IEEE. doi:10.1109/PIMRC.2000.881596

Pang, B., Lee, L., & Vaithyanathan, S. (2002). *Thumbs up? Sentiment classification using machine learning techniques. arXiv preprint cs/0205070. Bishop, C. M., & Nasrabadi, N. M. (2006). Pattern recognition and machine learning, 4(4).* Springer.

Sebastiani, F. (2002). Machine learning in automated text categorization. [CSUR]. *ACM Computing Surveys*, *34*(1), 1–47. doi:10.1145/505282.505283

Silva, J. F., & Pinto, S. F. (2018). Linear and nonlinear control of switching power converters. In *Power Electronics Handbook* (pp. 1141–1220). Butterworth-Heinemann., doi:10.1016/B978-0-12-811407-0.00039-8

Stone, P., & Veloso, M. (2000). Multiagent systems: A survey from a machine learning perspective. *Autonomous Robots*, *8*(3), 345–383. doi:10.1023/A:1008942012299

Sun, Y., Peng, M., Zhou, Y., Huang, Y., & Mao, S. (2019). Application of machine learning in wireless networks: Key techniques and open issues. *IEEE Communications Surveys and Tutorials*, *21*(4), 3072–3108.

Varela, F. J., & Bourgine, P. (Eds.). (1992). Toward a practice of autonomous systems: Proceedings of the First European Conference on Artificial Life. MIT press. Hydher, H., Tennakoon, P., & Jayakody, N. K. Recent Results of Machine Learning InspiredWireless Communications. ETIC.

Viterbi, A. J. (1995). *CDMA: principles of spread spectrum communication*. Addison Wesley Longman Publishing Co., Inc.

Wang, C. X., Di Renzo, M., Stanczak, S., Wang, S., & Larsson, E. G. (2020). Artificial intelligence enabled wireless networking for 5G and beyond: Recent advances and future challenges. *IEEE Wireless Communications*, *27*(1), 16–23. doi:10.1109/MWC.001.1900292

Yamazaki, S., Asakura, R., & Ohuchi, K. (2020). Throughput Analysis of Dynamic Multi-Hop Shortcut Communications for a Simple Model. IEICE TRANSACTIONS on Fundamentals of Electronics. *Communications and Computer Sciences*, *103*(7), 951–954.

ADDITIONAL READING

Charrada, A., & Samet, A. (2016). Joint interpolation for LTE downlink channel estimation in very high-mobility environments with support vector machine regression. *IET Communications*, *10*(17), 2435–2444. doi:10.1049/iet-com.2016.0132

Karthik Ganesh, R., Kanthavel, R., & Dhaya, R. (2020). Development of video compression using EWNS linear transformation and un-repetition simulated contrary based resurgence procedure. *Multimedia Tools and Applications*, *79*(5), 3519–3541. doi:10.100711042-018-6008-3

Mudassir, A., Akhtar, S., Kamel, H., & Javaid, N. (2016, July). A survey on fuzzy logic applications in wireless and mobile communication for LTE networks. In *10th International Conference on Complex, Intelligent, and Software Intensive Systems (CISIS)*, (pp. 76-82). IEEE.

Patnaik, A., Anagnostou, D. E., Mishra, R. K., & Lyke, J. C. (2004). Applications of neural networks in wireless communications. *IEEE Antennas & Propagation Magazine*, *46*(3), 130–137. doi:10.1109/MAP.2004.1374125

Sangeetha, S. K. B., Dhaya, R., & Kanthavel, R. (2019). Improving performance of cooperative communication in heterogeneous manet environment. *Cluster Computing*, *22*(5), 12389–12395. doi:10.100710586-017-1637-2

Chapter 3
The Influence of AI-Assisted Learning on CAL:
A Blueprint

Karthik Ganesh R.
SCAD College of Engineering and Technology, India

ABSTRACT

Reading, creating, hearing, witnessing, analyzing, testing, and other activities are all part of a diverse, multilayered, and dynamic learning experience. These layers combine to make learning a unique and personal experience for each individual. Understanding the factors that influence how people learn has a lot of power. When that expertise is combined with artificial intelligence (AI), the authors can develop learning experiences that are beneficial to all students. AI-assisted learning is a learning experience that is adaptive and enhances our natural learning style with machine intelligence (AIAL). AI can recognize trends and make decisions that are beneficial to users. There are numerous different tendencies in memory as it relates to humans in this study. This chapter explains how AI-assisted learning takes into account aspects including a student's background, the subject, modalities, and environment to produce an integrating teachable moment.

DOI: 10.4018/978-1-6684-5058-1.ch003

INTRODUCTION

Recognizing multiple learning strategies is crucial since it will aid in the development of Algorithms to support them, which is what AI-assisted learning aims to do. Behavioral disciplines research how people learn in a variety of settings, such as school or at home. It poses the questions, "How do we learn?" and "How do we teach?" And how do we put what we've learned into practice? (Bobrow, 1964). There are numerous approaches to learning new. A college student learning math theory, for illustration, may opt to read about it in a book. The issue is that there is usually an abundance of materials, making it difficult to choose the best ones. When a person can't relate to or identify with the content, reading alone isn't always enough (Wexler, 1970).

In this case, AI-powered programs can measure how the learner interacts with the content, including where they stopped on a page and how long they spend reading about specific topics (Simmons and Silberman, 1967). Over time, the machine will be able to make an assessment on their comprehension levels and match them with material that is more relevant and purposeful. Video knowledge can be approached in the same way (Kellogg, 1968). Similar algorithms can monitor a user's clicks, likes, and comments in order to display them videos that are more appropriate for their educational experience. Hands-on practice problems will almost certainly be more beneficial than researching about algebra for a high school senior (Weizenbaum, 1966). Algebra is made up of components that stack on top of each other, therefore it's crucial to grasp the basics before going on to the next. AI-assisted learning is ideal for material that must be taught in small chunks. (Potamianos et al. 2007).

LEARNING ASSISTED BY ARTIFICIAL INTELLIGENCE

Machine learning algorithms may take data like homework and exam outcomes and group individuals who did similarly, as well as offer supplemental material that has previously aided individuals with a similar profile, such as the relevant equations to employ and how to apply them. As the system learns, it will be able to generate the most relevant practice problems and coach students through them directly.

Adaptive gamified systems that keep students focused and engaged are another method AI-assisted learning systems might help students learn. These technologies also make it easier to learn dense content. Models that use facial expressions and task information to assess the user's emotions and forecast their performance have been developed (Swets and Feurzeig, 1965).

Researchers are looking into how common characteristics like personalities and learning styles interact with them, despite the restrictions. When it comes to younger children learning basic math principles, the systems might employ face recognition characteristics to recognize when they're having trouble and guide them to information that's more suited to their learning style (Taylor, 1968).

In education, the possibilities for AI-assisted learning are limitless. It has the potential to make our unique ways of absorbing and remembering information work in our advantage rather than against us when it comes to learning. Because of its ability to detect patterns and adapt at scale, it is a tool that can be used by anyone (Simmons, 1970).

As robots become smarter, they will be able to derive insights that will provide critical information to instructors and leaders, such as how effective different teaching approaches are in different areas or what content to recommend to pupils. Students may eventually be able and encouraged to pursue learning in their own unique way. As AI-assisted learning is improved, education can become more individualized and accessible, giving students the freedom to learn at their own speed and style (Collins and Quillian, 1969).

COMPUTER-ASSISTED INSTRUCTION (AI)

The three essential components of intelligent computer-assisted instruction (ICAI) are real concern competence, a learner model, and a teaching component. This type of system presents some information from the problem-solving expertise component to the student. This is the knowledge base of an AI software of this nature. The learner responds to the material delivered sometimes in way, either by answering questions or by exhibiting his or her awareness in any other way. The student model examines the responses of the students before deciding on a plan of action. This usually entails either giving the student some refresher information or permitting them to progress to the next level of knowledge presentation. Depending on the student's knowledge of the content, the tutoring module may or may not be used at this time. The system prevents the pupil from progressing beyond his or her current level of excellence (Quillian, 1969).

The majority of ICAI programs in use today follow a fixed pattern of presenting new content, evaluating responses, and employing tutorials (if necessary). Engineers at Yale Law school, on the other hand, have developed software that teaches in a more Socratic manner (Rockart et al., 1970). These programs promote exploration and frequently do not react directly to a student's inquiries about a particular subject. The core assumption of computer-assisted learning is that new content is presented only when a learner requires it (Carbonell, 1969). The brain is at its most ready to accept and remember information during this time. This is the ideal scenario for most teachers: pupils who become skilled self-educators, eagerly seeking the wisdom and truth that matters to them. However, the expense of these programs might be prohibitively expensive for many public schools. As a result, these ICAI are generally employed in corporate training environments (Karthik Ganesh et al., 2020).

THE STATE OF COMPUTER-ASSISTED INSTRUCTION WITH AI SUPPLEMENTATION

The classic CAI approach relies on teachers to offer course materials and set the assessment criteria for students. Learners are involved in their online learning programs in today's sophisticated versions, which include a 'reactive classroom atmosphere.' The latter systems make use of AI tools and techniques to consider students' interests and performance characteristics when conducting tutorial discussions. As a result, they're called AICAI (Artificial Intelligence Computer-Assisted Instruction) System, or just ICAI for intelligent CAI (Dhaya et al., 2021).

AICAIs like this have a knowledge-based constituent, a student model which can investigate the student learning' responses and decode their knowledge levels along with preconceptions and a component that contains information on appropriate teaching strategies in various scenarios. The AICAI technologies' content of the course and user experience should ideally be conversational in nature and sound natural. The following are some of the most popular intelligent online tutoring systems:

- It offers basic facts about the subject that can be used to respond to students' queries, develop relevant questions, and assess students' responses.

- It instructs students on how to create, test, and debug hypotheses in order to solve a problem or to repair a malfunctioning piece of equipment.

DEEP LEARNING NEURAL NETWORKS HELP AI TUTORS BECOME SMARTER.

A neural network is a machine learning model that is based on human brain neurons. The study of providing computers the autodidactic ability to learn without human involvement is known as "machine learning." Allowing artificial neurons to communicate knowledge to other artificial neurons and making them smarter through perceptions and prior expert (Uttal et al., 1969).

- Deep Learning allows us to create:
    - Supervised pre-trained networks,
    - Convolutional neural networks that can analyze visual imagery,
    - Recurrent neural networks that can use their memory to process a sequence of inputs, such as handwriting recognition or speech recognition, and
    - Recursive neural networks that can make structured predictions, which can be very useful in natural language processing.
- Naturally, as our AI tutors continue to self-teach, these deep-learning neural networks can make them wiser over time. Virtual tutors and mentors with deep learning capabilities can adapt to the demands of individual students and provide personalized education in computer-assisted instruction systems (Bryan, 1969).
    - It was discovered that using virtual teaching assistants in the classroom enhanced student engagement and prompted students to create their own chatbots using the AI principles they learnt in class.

Another example of an Artificial Intelligence talking creature is Virtual Mentor version 2.0, which answers entrepreneurship-related questions based on the advice of real mentors. AI services such as Siri and Cortana can be of great assistance to students in the near future, providing personalized training according to their learning style (Sangeetha et al., 2019).

- Virtual mentors are frequently used by online courses to provide students with immediate assignment assistance by interpreting the question through natural language processing methods and processing them to extract relevant information from the resources they have access to.

The representation of knowledge so that a computer can solve issues or respond in a way that is "common sense" is one of the key goals of AI research. Few software applications, particularly those for teaching, have behavior that resembles any aspect of the collection of human abilities and knowledge loosely referred to as "common sense." However, because of the dramatic decrease in acquisition costs, it is now conceivable to develop financially viable, complex designs for software education systems that have some of the commonsense characteristics of a human tutor (Feurzeig, 1970).

ARTIFICIAL INTELLIGENCE'S PLACE IN THE FUTURE OF EDUCATION

Artificial intelligence (AI), machine learning (ML), and robots are all impacted by the rapid growth of technology, especially education. If the education industry is to realize AI's full potential for everyone, it must continue to expose the next generation to AI from an early age and use the technology in the classroom. Many kids utilize AI through social media, and as a result, they are open to its instructional uses, according to teachers (Dhaya et al., 2022). However, some educators are concerned that AI technology will one day completely replace the role of the teacher. Thankfully, it does not appear that instructors will be replaced by robots very soon. While AI algorithms can teach pupils literacy and math, the more difficult task of instilling social and emotional skills will remain in the hands of people (Dhaya and Kanthavel, 2022)

HOW IS ARTIFICIAL INTELLIGENCE BEING USED IN EDUCATION RIGHT NOW?

AI may be connected to different schools all across the world because it is computer-based.

- COVID-19 has had a tremendous impact on how technology is used in schools. Lockdowns caused many instructors around the world to teach electronically, from their dwellings, rather than in front of a classroom full of students. According to a survey conducted by the edtech startup Promethean, 86 percent of instructors believe AI should play an essential role in education (Dhaya and Kanthavel, 2022).
- AI in education has numerous advantages for both students and teachers:
- Learning resources can be accessed at any time and from any location.\
- Difficult jobs that take a long time to complete, such as maintaining records or evaluating several assignments (Sridharan and Dhaya, 2019).
- AI can automate the completion of multiple-choice tests.
- Chat bots can answer frequently asked questions; - AI tutors and chatbots can be available at any time to answer inquiries;
- Learning can be customized and adapted to each student's goals and skills through individualized programs (Pattabiraman et al., 2016).

EXAMPLES OF ARTIFICIAL INTELLIGENCE IN EDUCATION

1. **Image from the GetSmarter Blog:** AI is already being used successfully in the classroom to improve learning and student growth, as well as the performance of instructors (Dhaya and Kanthavel, 2021).
2. **Emotional well-being:** A child's emotional state has an impact on their ability to focus, engage, and stay motivated while learning. When emotion detection technology is used, virtual schools can be just as effective as face-to-face learning environments. Learning can also be made more enjoyable thanks to gamification (Yang et al., 2014). Additionally, AI can identify areas where students struggle and assist them in improving and, ultimately, excelling (Sathyaraj et al., 2022).
3. Identifying and filling gaps in teachers' presentations and educational materials: AI can detect and fill gaps in teachers' presentations and educational materials, and recommend changes where necessary (Sangeetha et al., 2021).
4. **Children collaborating with AI:** Nao is a humanoid robot that speaks, walks, and instructs youngsters on topics ranging from reading to computer programming. Nao is a fun coding lab for youngsters that

encourages them to learn about science, technology, engineering, and mathematics (STEM) disciplines (Kanthavel et al., 2022). Students can use this introduction to basic coding to program the robot to perform certain tasks, such as making hand gestures or performing choreographed dances. Students will gain experience telling a robot (or software) what to do in this manner, preparing them for a future in which humans and robots collaborate (Simmons, 1970).

APPLICATIONS IN EDUCATION USE AI TO IMPROVE LEARNING IN STUDENTS OF ALL AGE GROUPINGS

1. **Thinkster Math** is a tutoring app that combines a personalized teaching method with a math curriculum. The software utilizes AI and machine learning to illustrate how pupils think when solving a math problem (Dhaya et al., 2021). This enables the tutor to swiftly identify areas of the child's reasoning and logic that require improvement. It then helps them by providing real-time, individualized feedback (Devi et al., 2019).
2. **Brainly:** Students can use this education platform to ask homework problems and receive automatic, verified replies from their peers. Brainly uses machine learning algorithms to filter out spam, which eventually helps students learn quicker (Dhaya et al., 2021).
3. **CTI (Content Technologies, Inc.):** Deep learning is used by an AI business to produce personalized learning tools for pupils. JustTheFacts101, for example, makes it simple for teachers to import syllabi into a CTI engine. The machine then creates tailored textbooks and assignments based on basic principles using algorithms (Liang and Li, 2011). Cram101 is another AI-enhanced service, in which any textbook may be turned into a smart study guide with bite-sized knowledge that can be learned in a short amount of time. The technology even generates multiple-choice questions, which saves pupils time and aids their learning (Kanthavel et al., 2022).
4. **Gradescope:** This platform streamlines grading (teachers' grading time is lowered by 70% or more) and gives student data that can help them identify areas where they need extra help (Dhaya et al., 2020).
5. **Duolingo:** With over 120 million users around the world, Duolingo has a large audience that extends beyond the classroom. It supports 19 languages and assists users in learning a foreign language and improving

their skills over time. The program adapts to each user's abilities via quizzes and other assessments to provide new challenges (Pillai et al., 2021).

HOW WILL AI AFFECT THE EDUCATION MARKET?

According to the World Economic Forum, by 2025, a high percentage of businesses would have incorporated technology like machine learning. To fulfill the impending requirement, they strongly recommend governments and educational institutions to focus on rapidly growing related education and skills, with a focus on both Technological and – anti people skills (Dhaya and Kanthavel, 2021). Technology might replace up to 50% of established jobs in the United States alone, according to Microsoft. Technological advancements will generate big disruptions in the workforce (Banumathi et al., 2022). 13 According to the Microsoft analysis, students will need to grasp two aspects of this new environment by the time they graduate. They must be able to: - Understand how to effectively collaborate with others in a team to solve problems - Know how to use ever-changing technology, such as AI, to their advantage (Kanthavel et al., 2022).

Preparing children to work with AI in the future can begin as early as elementary school. Because many children are already familiar with digital technology before they start school, it's critical to teach them the skills they'll need to succeed in a digital environment. The future workforce is built on today's foundations (Sangeetha and Dhaya, 2022).

CONCLUSION

The Artificial Intelligence Assisted Learning paradigm for a knowledge of communication national curriculum is presented in this research. Smart learning entails a range of training settings in which both the educators and learners emphasize the use of technology. Smart learning is organized in classrooms with online instruction using a mix of software and technology. Instead of being a passive observer of the educational process, students are taught to use digital knowledge and abilities more readily, swiftly, and conveniently. Internationalization necessitates additional certifications and new abilities in particular areas of responsibility, which must be maintained for learning and company performance. Globalization necessitates additional certifications and new abilities in particular areas of responsibility, which must be maintained for training and business operations. This chapter described how AI-assisted teaching creates an integrative learning opportunity by taking into consideration a student's past, the subject, modalities, and environment.

REFERENCES

Taylor, E. F. (1967, January). Eliza Program Conversational Tutorial. [Ieee-Inst Electrical Electronics Engineers Inc.]. *IEEE Transactions on Education*, *10*(1), 64–64.

Banumathi, J., Sangeetha, S. K. B., & Dhaya, R. (2022). Robust Cooperative Spectrum Sensing Techniques for a Practical Framework Employing Cognitive Radios in 5G Networks. *Artificial Intelligent Techniques for Wireless Communication and Networking*, 121-138.

Bobrow, D. G. (1964). Natural language input for a computer problem solving system.

Bryan, G. L. (1969). Computers and education. *Computers and Automation*, *18*(3), 1–4.

Collins, A., & Quillian, M. (1969). Retrieval time from semantic memory. journal of. *Verbal Learning and Verbal Behavior, 8,*240, 247.

Devi, M., Dhaya, R., Kanthavel, R., Algarni, F., & Dixikha, P. (2019, May). Data Science for Internet of Things (IoT). In *International Conference on Computer Networks and Inventive Communication Technologies,* (pp. 60-70). Springer, Cham.

Dhaya, R., & Kanthavel, R. (2022). Energy Efficient Resource Allocation Algorithm for Agriculture IoT. *Wireless Personal Communications*, 1–23.

Dhaya, R., Kanthavel, R., & Ahilan, A. (2021). Developing an energy-efficient ubiquitous agriculture mobile sensor network-based threshold built-in MAC routing protocol (TBMP). *Soft Computing*, *25*(18), 12333–12342. doi:10.100700500-021-05927-7

Dhaya, R., Kanthavel, R., Algarni, F., Jayarajan, P., & Mahor, A. (2020). Reinforcement Learning Concepts Ministering Smart City Applications Using IoT. In *Internet of Things in Smart Technologies for Sustainable Urban Development,* (pp. 19–41). Springer.

Dhaya, R., Kanthavel, R., & Mahalakshmi, M. (2021). Enriched recognition and monitoring algorithm for private cloud data centre. *Soft Computing*, 1–11. doi:10.100700500-021-05967-z

Feurzeig, W., Papert, S., Bloom, M., Grant, R., & Solomon, C. (1970). Programming-languages as a conceptual framework for teaching mathematics. *ACM SIGCUE Outlook*, *4*(2), 13–17. doi:10.1145/965754.965757

Carbonell, J. R. (1969, September). Interactive non-deterministic computer-assisted instruction. In *Proc. Internat. Symp. on Man-Machine Syst*

Dhaya, R., & Kanthavel, R. (2022). IoE based private multi-data center cloud architecture framework. Computers & Electrical Engineering, 100, 107933.

Kanthavel, R., Dhaya, R., & Venusamy, K. (2022). Detection of Osteoarthritis Based on EHO Thresholding. *CMC-COMPUTERS MATERIALS & CONTINUA*, *71*(3), 5783–5798.

Kanthavel, R., Indra Priyadharshini, S., Sudha, D., Sundara Velrani, K., & Dhaya, R. (2022). Multi-hoped cooperative communication-based wireless underground sensor network design. *International Journal of Communication Systems*, *35*(10), e5174.

Karthik Ganesh, R., Kanthavel, R., & Dhaya, R. (2020). Development of video compression using EWNS linear transformation and un-repetition simulated contrary based resurgence procedure. *Multimedia Tools and Applications*, *79*(5), 3519–3541.

Kellogg, C. H. (1968, December). A natural language compiler for on-line data management. In *Proceedings of fall joint computer conference, part I* (pp. 473-492).

Pillai, K. G. R., Radhakrishnan, K., Ramakrishnan, D., Yesudhas, H. R., Eanoch, G. J., Kumar, R., & Son, L. H. (2021). Compression based clustering technique for enhancing accuracy in web scale videos. *Multimedia Tools and Applications*, *80*(5), 7077–7101.

Potamianos, A., Fosler-Lussier, E., Ammicht, E., & Perakakis, M. (2007). Information Seeking Spoken Dialogue Systems Part II: Multimodal Dialogue. *IEEE Transactions on Multimedia*, *9*(3), 550–566. doi:10.1109/TMM.2006.887999

Quillian, M. R. (1969). The teachable language comprehender: A simulation program and theory of language. *Commun. Ass. Comput*, 459-476.

Rockhart, J. F., Scott Morton, M. S., & Zannetos, Z. S. (1970). Associative learning project: phase I system.

Sangeetha, S. K. B., & Dhaya, R. (2022). Deep learning era for future 6G wireless communications—theory, applications, and challenges. *Artificial Intelligent Techniques for Wireless Communication and Networking*, 105-119.

Sangeetha, S. K. B., Dhaya, R., & Kanthavel, R. (2019). Improving performance of cooperative communication in heterogeneous manet environment. *Cluster Computing*, *22*(5), 12389–12395. doi:10.100710586-017-1637-2

Sangeetha, S. K. B., Dhaya, R., Shah, D. T., Dharanidharan, R., & Reddy, K. P. S. (2021, February). An empirical analysis of machine learning frameworks for digital pathology in medical science. *Journal of Physics: Conference Series*, *1767*(1), 012031.

Simmons, R. F. (1970). Natural language question-answering systems: 1969. *Communications of the ACM*, *13*(1), 15–30.

Simmons, R. F. (1971). Natural language for instructional communication. Artificial Intelligence and Heuristic Programming, Edinburgh Univ. Press, 191-198.

Simmons, R. S., & Silberman, H. F. (1967). A Plan for Research Toward Computer-Aided Instruction With Natural English. Technical Memorandum.

Swets, J. A., & Feurzeig, W. (1965). Computer-Aided Instruction: Concepts and problem-solving techniques can be learned by conversing with a programmed-computer system. *Science*, *150*(3696), 572–576. doi:10.1126cience.150.3696.572 PMID:5837095

Uttal, W. R., Pasich, T., Rogers, M., & Hieronymus, R. (1969). Generative computer-assisted instruction. In Mental Health Res. Inst. 243. Mich., Commun.

Weizenbaum, J. (1966). ELIZA—a computer program for the study of natural language communication between man and machine. *Communications of the ACM*, *9*(1), 36–45.

Wexler, J. D. (1970). A Generative Teaching System that Uses Information Nets and Skeleton Patterns. [Ph. D. dissertation]. University of Wisconsin, Madison.

Chapter 4
Instruction Process and Learning Issues in Computer-Assisted Learning:
A Detailed Review

Banumathi J.
Anna University, India & University College of Engineering, Nagercoil, India

ABSTRACT

Computer assisted learning (CAL) has grown in popularity over the past and is also known as computer based instruction (CBI), computer aided learning (CAL), or computer aided instruction (CAI). For the purpose of this study, we might tell exactly CAL as computer-assisted learning techniques and settings. However, collaboration is the key to comprehending CAL. On numerous levels, computers can help with engagement during the learning process. This chapter looks at CAI in general because CALL and CAI share many aspects. It also goes over broad learning topics like learning styles and tactics, personalized knowledge, as well as the elements that determine the consequences of gaining knowledge. Where necessary, the education learning setting is mentioned, as well as how contemporary CAI knowledge can be applied to the education learning circumstance.

DOI: 10.4018/978-1-6684-5058-1.ch004

INTRODUCTION

This chapter looks at CAI in common because CALL and CAI share many aspects. It also goes over broad learning topics like educational psychology and tactics, personalized knowledge, as well as the elements that determine the consequences of gaining knowledge (Benson, 2001). Wherever necessary, the EL ecosystem is mentioned, as well as how existing CAI learning can be applied to the EL circumstances. The term "computer-assisted learning" has been bandied around a lot in the creation and implementation of instructional technology for a diverse range of students in a wide range of circumstances. The term "CAL" was frequently used in the 1990s to allude to the establishment of a new software application or a group of related algorithms (Beatty, 2003). Traditional instructional approaches, in especially, have a long history of success have been superseded. The presentation Learning or teaching disciplines such as mathematics, science, geography, and others through software programs or e-books with subject-specific learning packages or materials is known as Computer Aided Learning (CAL). It could be of any kind.

- Technology-Enhanced Learning (TEL) is a type of learning in which technology is employed to aid the learning process. It is supposed to be as follows: "Pedagogical theory: Digital technology has enabled me". It could be, in a general context.
- E-learning is regarded to be an aspect of it. Learning with a Computer

A computer program or file created expressly for educational purposes can be characterized as the approach is employed in a number of settings around the world, from primary school to university. The learner's route across a topic area is optimized by the CAL based on his personality, cognitive qualities, and identified state of preparedness (Fotos, 2004). One of the most crucial characteristics of CALL materials is participation. It is a different communication process that stored on servers' students' engagement, machine involvement with educators, educator involvement with students, and student interaction with students (Underwood, 1984). Integration is essential in CALL because that increases participants' commitment, develops their abilities and talents, improves their linguistic competence, and encourages language development. Unfortunately, the present CALL lacks interaction and has other usability flaws (Levy, 1997). Several of the potential dangers include persons and computers - technicalities, computers and teachers design issues, professors and staff teaching issues, and learners and learner's engagement and collaborative issues (Wyatt, 1984).

A QUICK OVERVIEW OF CAI

The computer assisted instruction/learning field, like any other discipline of learning, is littered with buzzwords. The scope of a phrase's interpretation, or its accuracy, varies (Zhao, 2004). Figure 1 depicts a brief summary of some of the most commonly used words in the CAI sector.

Figure 1. CAI associated terms

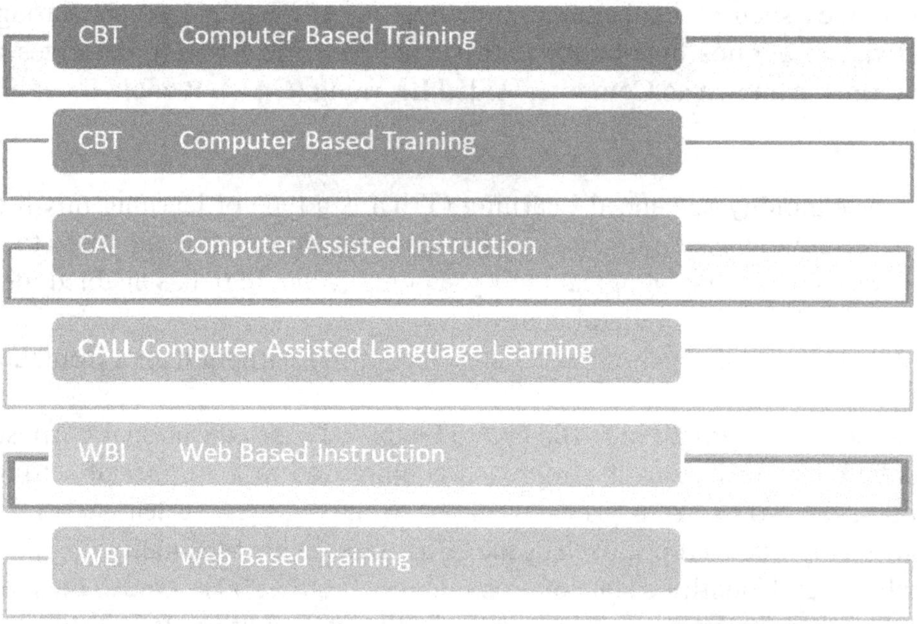

CBT Computer Based Training
CBT Computer Based Training
CAI Computer Assisted Instruction
CALL Computer Assisted Language Learning
WBI Web Based Instruction
WBT Web Based Training

The phrase CAI shall have been used as an umbrella term in this work unless otherwise stated. Some of those same principles that apply to CALL apply to CAI as well. Before diving into the CALL-specific principles, I think it's a good idea to brush up on some basic concepts (Felix, 2002). "Computer-assisted learning" refers to the use of a computer to provide instruction (CAI). The format might be anything from a simple application to teach typing to a complex system that tells trimming tools in the classroom new laparoscopic surgery approaches. CAI covers a wide range of subjects, including learning, cognition, and human-computer interaction (HCI). Many of the key concepts of CALL are reflected in the discipline of CAI (Davies, 1982).

CAI'S BENEFITS

CAI provides a number of important advantages as a classroom setting. These include self-paced learning, self-directed learning, the use of sensory cues, and the aptitude to impart material through a range of channels. So these topics will be discussed in more depth throughout this book, just a general sketch will be offered here. Although CAI has not been studied in an EL environment, most of the other parameters influencing in a standard CAI environment should also be attainable in an EL congregation (Clarke, 1989).

Learners who use self-paced learning can progress through a program at their own pace. They have the option of repeating a job or reviewing content as many times as they wish. The program will not get tired of repeating itself. If material is already known, learners can skip over a topic, increasing the efficiency of the learning process (Chapelle and Hegelheimer, 2004).

Self-directed knowledge allows students to pick whatever they want to learn and in what order they would want to learn it. Learners have a variety of learning styles and use a variety of learning strategies. The learning process is more effective when students study in a style that suits them, according to several research (Coniam and Wong, 2004).

CAI SPECIES

CAI systems can function as both tutors and tools. Computer tutors are commonly referred to as "CAIs." In the instructor categorization, the computer has the knowledge to be learned and controls the learning environment. When people utilize CAI tools, they learn more quickly because they concentrate on a single learning activity and aim to better it (Diana, 1993).

- Drill and practice, tutorials, simulations, and games are the four modes within the tutor classification. Drill and practice, with repeated exercise on lower-level cognitive skills, is well-suited to the behaviorist model.

- It can be advantageous in certain situations, despite the fact that it is frequently frowned upon. Within CAI, the tutorial mode is undoubtedly one of the most popular.

IS CAI EFFECTIVE?

In many situations, it is still uncertain which form of instruction is appropriate or preferred. Several CAI conclusions, on the other hand, are widely accepted. Students at CAI have a more positive attitude towards learning. Students that used CAI outperformed the control group by a little margin, finish their tasks in approximately a third of the time (Chapelle, 2001). According to the latest research, CAI is just as successful as traditional classroom instruction. The foregoing has been some of the advantages of CAI that have been identified: But the use of instructional technology for drill and practice of basic skills in CAI programs, students are taught faster smoothly and correctly. Students have more opportunity to gain experience thanks to the various technological devices accessible. Students report enhanced consciousness and personality, as well as enhanced learning motivation (Cheon, 2003).

EVALUATION OF CAI EFFECTIVENESS

Assessment instruments are commonly used to evaluate the efficiency of CAI. This comprises evaluating the impact of instructional programs or approaches on student performance by comparing the results of standardized proficiency assessments. Two sets of students will be taught in the anthropometric custom: one will be studied using CAI software, and the other should be presented in a typical classroom setting.

- However, it has been said that the psychometric tradition alone can't fully measure the effectiveness of CAI because it's often too simple.
- With the help of interaction, the learner's engagement with the CAI program is observed (Davies, 1997).
- Interaction analysis can be driven by educational or psycholinguistic reasons.
- Pedagogically motivated research aims to figure out what works in the classroom. What are the resources that the learner employs?

- Is the program being utilized in the manner intended by the creator?
- The goal of psycho linguistically motivated research is to learn about learners' learning strategies.
- Strategies from other domains to the language learning domain.

CALL

Computer-assisted language learning (CALL) is a method of teaching and learning in which material to be learnt is presented, reinforced, and assessed using a computer and computer-based resources such as the Internet. It usually has a significant interactive component. It also involves the search for an investigation of language teaching and learning applications. Except for self-study software, CALL is intended to supplement rather than replace face-to-face language training (Davies, 2005). CALL has also been called technology-enhanced language learning, computer-assisted language instruction, and computer-aided language learning, but the field remains the same. The technologies utilized in CALL training are divided into two categories: software and Internet-based activities.

1. **Software:** Software used in a CALL environment can be specifically built or adapted for foreign/second language teaching (Davies et al., 2005). Most language textbook publishers provide educational software, whether it's to supplement a paper textbook or to be used independently for self-study. The majority of language learning programs are tutorials. These are often drill programs that include a brief introduction followed by a series of questions to which the student responds and to which the computer provides feedback. The material to be learnt may already be programmed in by the publisher, which is more frequent, or the instructor may be able to program in the material to be learned with these types of programs. Authoring programs enable an instructor to program a portion or all of the content to be learnt, as well as a portion or all of the learning methods (De Szendeffy, 2005). Cloze master, Choice master, and Multitester are some examples of these apps. The format is pre-programmed in these, and the instructor simply adds the content. Although general authoring systems such as Macromedia Director can be used to create a full course, most professors lack the time or technical expertise to do so.

2. **Internet-based:** In 1992, the World Wide Web was developed, and by 1993, it had reached the general public, bringing up new possibilities for CALL. Online versions of software (where the student interacts with a networked computer), computer-mediated communication (where the learner interacts with other people via the computer), and apps that mix these two components are all examples of Internet activities. Nowadays, there are so many and various websites that cater to foreign-language learners, particularly those learning English, that it can be difficult to know where to start. Dave's ESL Café (www.eslcafe.com) and LLRC Recommended Sources are two meta-sites dedicated to providing a starting point. Many of these websites are drill-exercise-based, although some also feature games like Hangman.
3. **Computer-Mediated communication (CMC)** has been in some form or another since the 1960s, but it was only in the early 1990s that it became widely available to the general public. There are two types of CMC: asynchronous (such as email and forums) and synchronous such as videoconferencing, text and voice chat. Learners can communicate in the target language with other real speakers for a low cost, 24 hours a day, with these. Learners can chat one-on-one or in groups, and audio and video assets can be shared. CMC has had the greatest impact on language education as a result of all of this (Egbert and Petrie, 2006).

CALL INSTRUCTION'S PROBLEMS AND COMPLAINTS

CALL has had a limited impact on foreign language instruction. This could be due to a variety of factors. For starters, there are physical and functional constraints imposed by the technology. Cost and accessibility to technology resources such as the Internet, for starters, are major concerns either non-existent as can be the case in many developing country or lack of bandwidth, as can be the case just about anywhere. There may be issues with the limitations of today's computer technology. In the last three decades, computer technology has advanced considerably, but the demands on CALL have risen much more. One significant ambition is to have computers with which students may have actual, human-like contact, especially for speaking practice; however, the technology is still a long way from that. If the computer is not able to accurately assess a learner's speech, it is of no use at all (Egbert and Hanson-Smith, 1999).

Although most challenges with CALL have to do with instructor expectations and concerns about what computers can achieve for language learners and teachers, there are a few exceptions to this rule. Educators and administrators tend to overestimate the capabilities of computers, believing either that they are dangerous or of little value (Felix, 2001).

Lack of understanding or even fear of technology can be the source of instructors' resistance. Even if instructors are offered CALL training, they may not use it until it is mandated. In the 1960s and '70s, computer technology was mostly used for scientific research, establishing a real and psychological gap between language teaching and computer technology. A common belief is that the use of computers undermines conventional reading abilities, which are primarily reliant on books, because textbooks are what they are used for. Among the reasons for this is that teachers (many of whom did not grow up with computers) and students have a large generational gap to bridge, who did grow up with them (Warschauer, 1996).

Teachers may also be reluctant to employ CALL activities since they are more difficult to evaluate than other types of training. A completed fill-in textbook, for example, is considered by the vast majority of Mexican teachers to be a concrete indicator of student progress. Even though students appear to be enthused by activities such as branching narratives, riddles, and logic games, these activities do not give a systematic manner of assessing progress.

It's possible that even teachers who would benefit from CALL's implementation are discouraged by the amount of time and effort required to make it work. In the 1960s, when the audio language lab was first introduced, people who simply expected results by acquiring expensive equipment were likely to be disillusioned. To begin, students must be prepared to utilize computers by sorting through the many materials that are available. If pupils are unfamiliar with a resource, the instructor will need to spend time teaching it to them before they can use it in class. Another problem with CALL is that there isn't any solid empirical evidence to support the use of computers in language teaching, and a lack of coherent theoretical foundation. Creating CALL-based assignments is difficult for most teachers because to a lack of time or knowledge, so they rely on commercially supplied materials, which may or may not be pedagogically competent.

LEARNER-CENTRED CALL

Designing educational materials with the student in mind is a critical part of the educational process. Focusing on the learner's needs and motivations is what it meant by this phrase and emphasizes learner-centered education, which she defines as putting the student and the learning process at the center of decision making. Learning-centered curriculum and syllabus design is a crucial part of the educational process.

Several authors have offered concepts centered on the learner. The following are five guiding ideas for a CALL focused on students.

1. Using a socio-cultural method is a good place to start.
2. Second, learner-centered features include the ability to recognize features and their tendency to change. An individual's learning style, for example, may have a greater or lesser ability to be changed, depending on the extent to which it can be altered.
3. It's imperative that students understand how to take charge of their own learning environment
4. The task-based framework is a suitable option.
5. Using SLA and CALL as good practice models is a must.

BENEFITS OF CALL

CALL has many advantages, including the following: In the literature, learner-controlled programs are praised for their advantages. Learners are more motivated when they are in control of their own education. Boredom, anxiety, and frustration can be alleviated, and learner focus maintained by giving students more control over their learning. Higher levels of satisfaction are reported by students.

Is There a Benefit?

The subject of whether or not learner control improves learning has elicited conflicting results in various research. It is logical to think that the flexibility to customize a software to one's own style preferences will lead to better learning. Learner control programs have been found to have a detrimental effect on student learning. This is known as the Dilemma of Learner Control.

However, the improved adaptability and customization provided by learner-controlled systems is well-suited to the "each learner is a unique person" philosophy as well as the concept of learner autonomy on the one hand. In some cases, a shift to a learner-centered strategy does not pan out as expected. What's the reason for this? Wouldn't it be better for students to be able to choose what they learn, when and in what order?

The student may not know how to learn. Higher-ability students may benefit from such an approach, but lower-ability students may not. Instead of seeing it as either/or, the locus of control should be seen as a spectrum. As an example, a CAI software might be thought of as allowing learners more or less control. When working with students who have lower levels of ability, the presentation of more material and tasks should be the default setting. As a result, the application should lead the user through the system in a "fuller" of more information mode rather than a "leaner" of less information mode, because users tend to stick with default settings at least initially (Fitzpatrick, 2004).

WHAT AFFECTS THE LEARNING PROCESS' EFFICIENCY?

Several studies have found that a wide range of factors influence how students learn. Such elements include courseware characteristics such as the way of presentation and the locus of control, as well as student characteristics such as their age, gender, and ethnicity, gender, attitude and learning style (Fotos and Browne, 2004). Computer factors and learner factors can be divided into two categories. A summary of the most important criteria is shown in Figure 2 and 3

Figure 2. Computer factors involved in the learning process

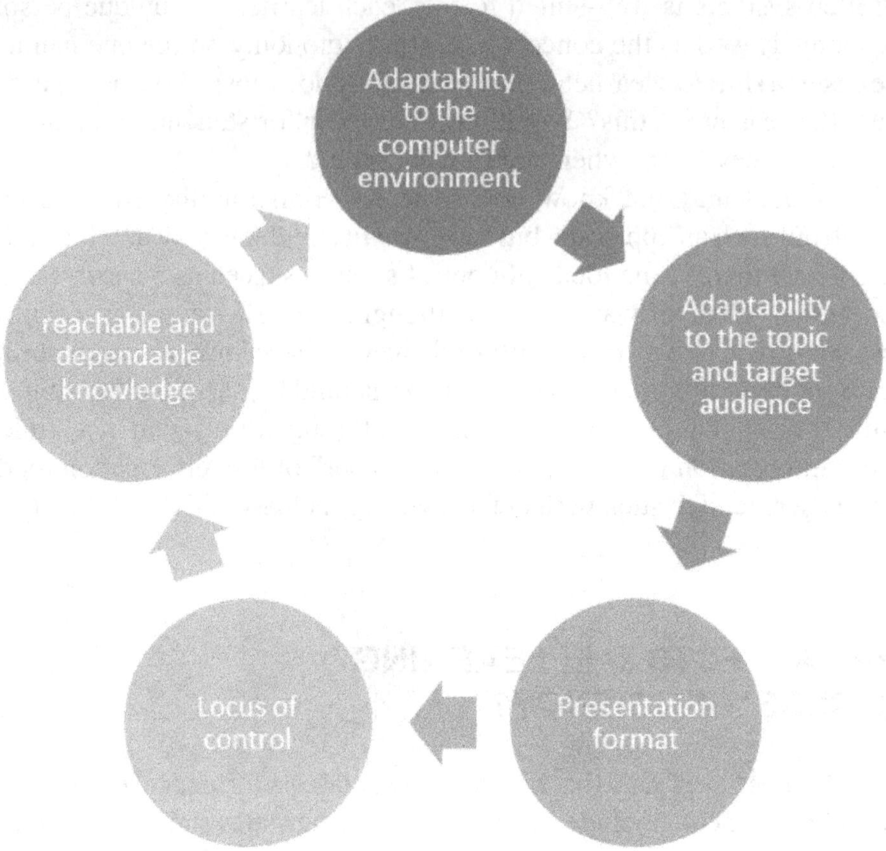

Figure 3. Learners' factors involved in the learning process

Computers Play a Role

Computer-related issues must be taken into account when developing the topic. CAI applications are best suited to tasks that need a lower cognitive level (e.g., simple exercises) since they reinforce basic fact-oriented learning. It's critical that the CAI software's intended audience is a good match. CAI tends to benefit lower-income and less-achieved students. This is because CAI applications have features that cater to these types of learners, such as drill and practice, privacy, and immediate feedback and reinforcement, all of which are important to these types of learners. The template's intended audience is likely to be composed of people who share these traits.

Diverse presentation and multimedia formats should be employed to meet the needs of students with various learning styles. Students in developed countries who are accustomed to traditional teaching techniques may prefer CAI materials that include text information as well as visual and audio features. EL residents, on the other hand, may have limited literacy, making text material less appealing to them. Furthermore, different cultures may have different presentation styles, with some preferring a lot of information on the screen, while others prefer a more spacious presentation style with less information on the screen (Liu and Chen, 2007).

CAI allows the learner to take control of their own education. The learner's degree of freedom or control must be taken into account. The low-ability student must be given adequate assistance. There is no way to presume that people of the EL population are familiar with learner-controlled programs, given the minimal educational exposure they have. Because of this, it is critical to provide instructions on how to use CAI resources. In this case, it's critical to take into account cultural differences. A "try-it-and-see" approach may be preferable to more thorough instructions in some cultures, whilst others may prefer to just follow rules.

The CAI program must be easy to use and trustworthy in a CAI setting. Although students initially understand that aCAI software would have issues, research shows that when the "wow" impact fades, students' tolerance for computer-related issues decreases. 'Techno-savvy' students may like the challenge, while less 'techno-savvy' pupils are more likely to have negative feelings as a result. Accessible and dependable technology is a must in educational settings. Anything that could make students feel unsafe, such as the computer malfunctioning or crashing, should be avoided at all costs if possible (Li et al., 2009).

FACTORS RELATED TO THE LEARNER

Motivation, attitude, stress management, and prior knowledge all play a role in student success. The likelihood of a successful learning outcome increases if the student is highly motivated and has a positive attitude. As long as the learner can handle the stress of the process, it should not have an adverse effect on the outcome of the learning. Obviously, one's prior knowledge might have an impact on one's ability to learn. Motivation in an EL setting may be different than motivation in a non-EL setting, and this may necessitate additional efforts on the part of the teacher In spite of their lack of linguistic and cultural expertise, people of the ESL community may possess secret information about the ESL through terminology for plants, animals, and places (Hubbard, 2003).Languages spoken in the area are likely to incorporate phrases and structures from other languages.

It's been established that different people receive information in different ways and learn in different ways. It's also possible that alternative approaches are more effective depending on the circumstances. The learning process will be more effective if information is delivered to people in a way that suits their learning style. It has been found that teaching and learning styles have a considerable impact on students' learning outcomes (Warschauer and Healey, 1998) As a result, it is critical to accommodate a variety of learning styles so that as many students as possible can succeed.

An important aspect of improving one's ability to learn is having a firm grasp of various teaching methods and knowing how to use them effectively. According to (Son, 2004), more proficient students are familiar with a wider range of learning strategies and how to apply them effectively. Strategy utilization can be taught to students. There's a good chance that EL community members aren't aware of learning methodologies, so it's important to make them clear.

The computer/web learning environment does not work for everyone. It's important to identify students who think they're high-ability learners and who say they're happy with a CAI system. Although they have a high level of ability, those who are dissatisfied express their displeasure. Maladaptors, despite their lack of skill, seem happy. Low-ability students who have expressed displeasure are the last group of fanatics (Hubbard, 2005). In spite of the limitations of CAI, it should consider the different ways people adapt to new situations. There is a need for further investigation into why learners adapt in different ways and what can be done to support those adaption patterns.

Computer literacy is required to utilize CAI software. A basic understanding of the keyboard and mouse is essential. People who have become accustomed to using a computer may underestimate the level of fear and frustration experienced by learners who are new to computers (Piper, 1986). This has two major drawbacks. There are two primary reasons why some students' fear may impede their ability to learn: As a second step, they must devote mental energy to using the computer as intended (for example, wondering how to select an option as opposed to considering which is the correct option). These resources, consequently, are inaccessible to the current topic's processing requirements. This is particularly relevant in the case of Endangered Languages, where literacy rates may be quite low. As a result, greater attention must be devoted to the clarity and presentation of all information, including that which is not written down (Hubbard, 2006).

ENRICHING ASPECTS

CAI has primarily been investigated in a Western context, albeit not completely. In contrast to other CAI applications, culture and language acquisition are intrinsically interwoven. To understand the benefits and effectiveness of CAI, it is important to remember that it is a Western cultural phenomenon. To be clear, this does not mean that they won't work in non-Western cultures, but rather that they may require some tweaking (Hubbard and Levy, 2005). As a claimed benefit of CAI, the student can work at his or her own pace and in a manner that works best for him or her. That's a good fit with the Western democratic ethos, no?

This point is illustrated by two non-Western cases. Students from Asian countries such as those from China or Japan are used to learning in which the student is a passive participant. Learner control is an important part of the CAI program if it was established from a Western perspective, and Asian students will need to learn how to use it, potentially on a gradual basis. As a result, when a student is asked to select the odd word from a group of four (woman, man, dog, bird), select the man, rather than the bird, because of their cultural epistemology. When students answer wrong, this has repercussions for how feedback is offered (Mills, 1996).

CAI and Endangered Languages information is poor, as well. However, while ELs have many features with LCTLs, their lack of formal education, as well as their often poor social and economic status, separates them from mainstream CALL learners. As a result of a lack of formal education, learners may not be able to traverse the system on their own and may require assistance. Despite the disdain of some educators, drill activities are useful for students who lack self-assurance and benefit from a clearer testing technique. The lack of exposure to foreign or second language acquisition might be a disadvantage for people who have never had the opportunity to acquire a second language. As a result, it would be beneficial for them if learning approach information was made available in an explicit manner (Liu and Chen, 2007).

The importance of student autonomy in the learning process has been recognized. It is, nevertheless, a challenge to cultivate and attain among students. Due to the fact that they have been used to passive learning in their past educational environments, learners find it challenging to take control of their own learning (Jarvis, 2005). This is just a theory, but it may be possible for learners with little formal schooling to acquire Learner Autonomy. This is owing to the fact that they've taken responsibility of their own education by default due to the lack of formal or directed learning. Persons from low-income origins and Pipil community members in El Salvador are more likely to ask questions and be more open to the non-formal learning process than people from more affluent backgrounds. It's an interesting question whether or not this would apply to the CAI learning environment (Levy, 1997).

THE PROPOSED FRAMEWORK'S INFLUENCE

Research on CAI-related topics has largely focused on demonstrating that the CAI learning progress is at least equal to that of traditional methods. CAI has been found to be either advantageous or neutral when it comes to student learning outcomes. We can only hope that CAI/CALL programs can be helpful in situations when the usual technique isn't even an option (Kessler, 2006).

CAI programs' efficacy is affected by a variety of circumstances, and these considerations must be taken into account while designing a framework for an EL setting. As much as possible, the curriculum should be able to accommodate students of diverse learning styles and incorporate multimedia whenever practical. It should make an effort to lessen user anxiety by making them more comfortable with their time spent in front of a computer. Students who are not computer literate must be given special consideration to minimize the additional cognitive burden they may face as a result of their computer fear. Users expect a framework to keep things as basic and straightforward as possible (Kessler, 2007).

Teaching students about learning strategies and how to use them might be beneficial, but it would place an undue burden on the students' cognitive resources already stretched thin trying to accomplish the intended learning objective. The students aren't computer experts and haven't had much prior experience learning languages (Levy and Stockwell, 2013).

CONCLUSION

The goal of this task, as stated in this chapter, is to build a template for a CALL program for languages and dialects. It gave an overview of CALL in the context of EL. The goals (framework creation, CALL materials engineering, and language specification) were outlined, as well as the requirements for ease of use, modifiability, and CALL programme output and constraints (both technological and time-based). The development's diverse research techniques were revealed. It combines the areas of CALL, EL, and Software Engineering. CAI was introduced, along with its benefits and drawbacks, as well as a breakdown of the many CAI variants. A brief description of learning styles, as well as their favored delivery modalities, was offered by the field of educational psychology. The benefits of learning approaches and their efficiency have been demonstrated. The importance of locus of control and the possibilities of learner autonomy were explored. While learner freedom is correctly praised as beneficial to the learner, the necessity for assistance, particularly for lower-ability students, is emphasized. A review of the elements that influence learning outcomes, both computer-related and learner-related, was conducted. It also looked into the relationship between CAI, cultural difficulties, and ELs. Each of these factors' impact on the framework was discussed.

REFERENCES

Beatty, K. (2013). *Teaching & researching: Computer-assisted language learning*. Routledge. doi:10.4324/9781315833774

Benson, P. (2001). *Teaching and researching autonomy in language learning. Harlow*. Pearson Education.

Chapelle, C. A. (2001). *Computer applications in second language acquisition*. Cambridge University Press. doi:10.1017/CBO9781139524681

Chapelle, C. A., & Hegelheimer, V. (2013). The language teacher in the 21st century. In *New perspectives on CALL for second language classrooms,* (pp. 311–328). Routledge.

Cheon, H. (2003). The viability of computer mediated communication in the Korean secondary EFL classroom. *Asian EFL Journal*, *5*(1), 1–61.

Clarke, D. (1989). Design consideration in writing CALL software with particular reference to extended materials. In Computer assisted language learning: Program structure and principles, (pp. 28-37).

Coniam, D., & Wong, R. (2004). Internet Relay Chat as a tool in the autonomous development of ESL learners' English language ability: An exploratory study. *System*, *32*(3), 321–335. doi:10.1016/j.system.2004.03.001

Davies, G. (1982). *Computer, Language and Language Learning*. Centre for Information on Language Teaching and Research.

Davies, G. (1997). Lessons from the past, lessons for the future: 20 years of CALL. *New technologies in language learning and teaching, Strasbourg: Council of Europe.[Electronic resource]:*: http://www. camsoftpartners. co. uk/coegdd1. Htm/

Davies, G. (2005, June). Computer Assisted Language Learning: Where are we now and where are we going. In Keynote speech at the University of Ulster Centre for Research in Applied Languages UCALL conference:"Developing a pedagogy for CALL (pp. 13-15).

Davies, G., Bangs, P., Frisby, R., & Walton, E. (2005). languages ICT. *Setting up effective digital language laboratories and multimedia ICT suites for MFL.* CILT.

De Szendeffy, J. (2005). *A practical guide to using computers in language teaching*. University of Michigan Press. doi:10.3998/mpub.97662

Diana, L. (1993). Rethinking University Teaching: A framework for the effective use of educational technology. Routledge, London/New York, 93, 94.

Egbert, J., & Hanson-Smith, E. (1999). CALL environments: Research, practice, and critical issues. Teachers of English to Speakers of Other Languages.

Egbert, J. L., & Petrie, G. M. (Eds.). (2006). *CALL research perspectives*. Routledge. doi:10.4324/9781410613578

Felix, U. (2001). Beyond Babel: Language Learning Online. Publications and Clearinghouse Manager, Language Australia.

Felix, U. (2002). The web as a vehicle for constructivist approaches in language teaching. *ReCALL, 14*(1), 2–15. doi:10.1017/S0958344002000216

Fitzpatrick, A. (2004). Information and communication technology in foreign language teaching and learning–An Overview. *Analytical Survey*, 10.

Fotos, S. (2013). Writing as talking: E-mail exchange for promoting proficiency and motivation in the foreign language classroom. In *New perspectives on CALL for second language classrooms,* (pp. 121–142). Routledge. doi:10.4324/9781410610775

Fotos, S., & Browne, C. M. (Eds.). (2013). *New perspectives on CALL for second language classrooms*. Routledge. doi:10.4324/9781410610775

Hubbard, P. (2003). A survey of unanswered questions in CALL. *Computer Assisted Language Learning*, *16*(2-3), 141–154. doi:10.1076/call.16.2.141.15882

Hubbard, P. (2005). A review of subject characteristics in CALL research. *Computer Assisted Language Learning*, *18*(5), 351–368. doi:10.1080/09588220500442632

Hubbard, P. (2006). A Review of Subject and Treatment Characteristics in CMC Research, PacSLRF Conference. Brisbane, Australia. www.stanford.edu/~efs/pacslrf06

Jarvis, H. (2005). Technology and change in English language teaching (ELT). *The Asian EFL Journal*, *7*(4), 213–227.

Kessler, G. (2006). Assessing CALL Teacher Training: What are We Doing and What Could We Do Better? In P. Hubbard & M. Levy (Eds.), *Teacher education in CALL*. John Benjamins. doi:10.1075/lllt.14.05kes

Kessler, G. (2007). *Formal and Informal CALL Preparation and Teacher Attitude toward Technology. CALL Journal*. Taylor & Francis.

Levy, M. (1997). *Computer-assisted language learning: Context and conceptualization*. Oxford University Press.

Levy, M. (1997). *CALL: context and conceptualisation.* Oxford University Press.

Levy, M., & Hubbard, P. (2005). Why call call "CALL"? *Computer Assisted Language Learning*, *18*(3), 143–149. doi:10.1080/09588220500208884

Levy, M., & Stockwell, G. (2013). *CALL dimensions: Options and issues in computer-assisted language learning*. Routledge. doi:10.4324/9780203708200

Li, L. C., Grimshaw, J. M., Nielsen, C., Judd, M., Coyte, P. C., & Graham, I. D. (2009). Evolution of Wenger's concept of community of practice. *Implementation Science; IS*, *4*(1), 1–8. doi:10.1186/1748-5908-4-11 PMID:19250556

Liu, G. Z., & Chen, A. S. W. (2007). A taxonomy of Internet-based technologies integrated in language curricula. *British Journal of Educational Technology*, *38*(5), 934–938. doi:10.1111/j.1467-8535.2007.00728.x

Mills, J. (1996). Virtual classroom management and communicative writing pedagogy. In *Proceedings of European Writing Conferences*. Barcelona, Spain.

Piper, A. (1986). Conversation and the computer: A study of the conversational spin-off generated among learners of English as a foreign language working in groups. *System*, *14*(2), 187–198. doi:10.1016/0346-251X(86)90008-4

Son, J. B. (Ed.). (2004). Computer-assisted language learning: concepts, contexts and practices. iUniverse.

Underwood, J. H. (1984). *Linguistics, Computers, and the Language Teacher. A Communicative Approach*. Newbury House Publishers, Inc.

Warschauer, M. (1996). Computer-assisted language learning: An introduction. In S. Fotos (Ed.), *Multimedia language teaching*. Logos International.

Warschauer, M., & Healey, D. (1998). Computers and language learning: An overview. *Language Teaching*, *31*(2), 57–71. doi:10.1017/S0261444800012970

Wyatt, D. H. (1983). Three major approaches to developing computer-assisted language learning materials for microcomputers. *CALICO Journal*, *1*(2), 34–38. doi:10.1558/cj.v1i2.34-38

Zhao, Y. (2004). Problems in Researching Dialogue in E-learning in Higher Education. In *Economic and Social Research Council/Worldwide Universities Network research seminar series 'Researching Dialogue and Communities of Enquiry in E-learning in Higher Education.'*

Chapter 5
Computing the Cloud Storage for Computer-Aided Learning Access

K. Juliana Gnanaselvi
Rathinam College of Arts and Science, India

ABSTRACT

Computer-assisted learning is a type of educational practice that involves the use of computer systems and other technology. It can take many different forms, and it involves a variety of tools and devices, including smartphones, tablets, personal computers, and others, despite its reputation. Different types of software and procedures are used in CAL. It can be used in a variety of subjects, including language acquisition and math. It is also used at all stages of education by then and now booming sectors in the coronavirus pandemic situation, particularly K to 12 programs, distance programs, skills and vocational training institutes, corporate training programs sometimes by individual broadcast trainers. Computer-assisted learning improves the teaching and learning process, resulting in higher levels of engagement and results. However, there are certain disadvantages to CAL. The authors look into the storage purpose of the CAL sessions as well as conversations. This is the time, the authors have to focus on the storage aspect of the CAL sessions, as much as the chats.

DOI: 10.4018/978-1-6684-5058-1.ch005

INTRODUCTION

Using a lot of technology is considered to be a good thing. Because of the human labor involved in assessing and evaluating achievement, this is odd. The widespread acceptance of the extensive use of electronic resources in education has increased the number of applications. As a result, the use of technology in education, which is employed at all stages of life, cannot be denied. Computers are filling a critical gap in a number of subjects where traditional education in this country's equipment and technologies are inadequate. Many tasks that would be difficult or even impossible in traditional education can be completed with computer systems.

In computer-assisted education, the computer has an application area where it can be used to supplement other methods and strategies, either with the educator or alone. As a result, computer-assisted learning (CAL) is regarded as the most promising of the educational methods. It has been shown that using a virtual lab in engineering education has a positive impact on factors such as learners participation in studies (Buyukbayraktar, 2006), order to provide learner with an independent learning environment (Bayam, Unal, and Ekiz, 2003), allows learners to gain a diverse set of experiences concerning various approaches, as well as facilitates in learning in an engaging and effective manner (Yuen, 2006).

In CAL environment, the trainer can equip the teaching atmosphere, recognizes the educator's skillset, and carries out activities such as reiterating, practicing, guiding, and customization based on the abilities of the learners, necessarily requires the use of the computer in various locations, times, as well as ways in accordance with the learning objectives that are determined in accordance with the structure of the teaching matter (Gorelik, 2013).

Figure 1. Flowchart of CAL System

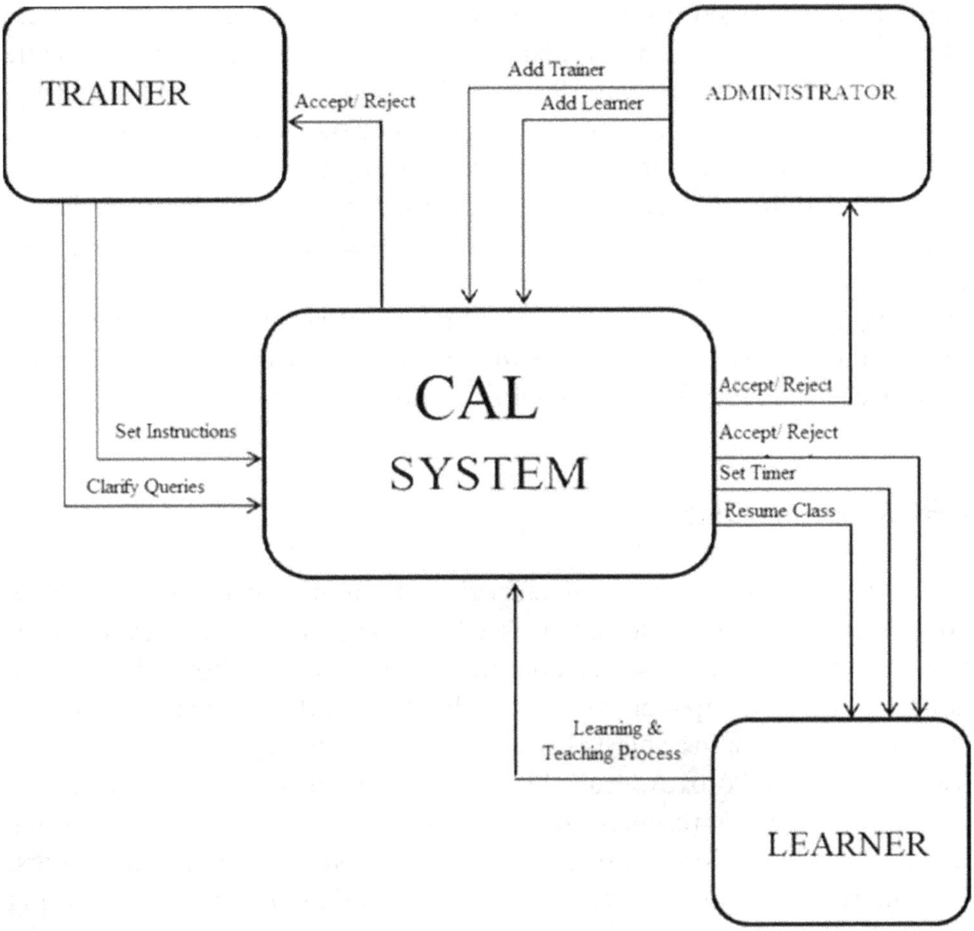

Cloud Storage Concepts

When the client can store and manage data at a low cost through the usage of cloud, the concept of cloud storage isn't worth it. As a result, the cloud should be built to be cost-effective, autonomous, computable, multi-tenant, scalable, available, controllable, and efficient. Cloud storage, that keeps data safe, manages and backs it up offsite, and makes it accessible to users over the internet. There is a slew of cloud storage companies to choose from. Most companies offer free storage up to a specified number of gigabytes (Parsi and Laharika, 2013). If a user exceeds the free storage limitations, they must pay the full amount specified in the plan. Maximum file size, auto backup, bandwidth, and upgrading for restricted space change from one provider to the next. Users do not need to invest in storage devices, and technical support is not required for maintenance, backup, or disaster recovery while using cloud storage services (Rajan, 2012).Roles and duties for storing, recovering, and information security are defined by cloud storage standards. This also provides a common inspection method, ensuring that calculations are performed consistently. Cloud storage providers, cloud storage subscribers, cloud storage developers, and cloud storage brokers can all benefit from this. Cloud storage subscribers can quickly locate providers that meet their needs by using Cloud Data Management Interface. Furthermore, the Cloud Data Management Interface provides a common interface for providers to advertise their specialized capabilities, allowing subscribers to quickly identify providers.

RELATED WORK

In terms of smart classroom characteristics and significance, research (Chen, 2015) indicated smartphone-based discussion can be done for the development of learning and social skills. According to the research (Zhou, Li, and Sun, 2017) learners' participation in classroom learning can be improved with the use of wireless devices. In a smart classroom-based teaching terminal can clarify learners' queries (Porozovs et al., 2015), determine current teaching activities, recommend learning resources to fulfill n their needs, and support effective real-time collaboration and resource sharing between trainers and learners. The smart classroom activities not only focus on the knowledge gathering and examination scores, but it also cultivates their wisdom (Oliveros, Garcia, and Valdez, 2015). In terms of resource quality improvement and teaching method optimization, literature (Liu et al., 2020) rebuilt and improved the blended learning and proposed a transition from such a blended learning to something like a smart classroom.

Literature (Reisenwitz, 2016) believes that wisdom learning occurs in a contextual environment, providing students with a wide range of learning resources and promoting new learning paradigms for educational development. The conceptual framework of wisdom learning is built on the basis of analyzing the intellectual learning interpretation, and introduced 4-wisdom learning models, according to document (Shang et al., 2021). As per the research (Garofalo et al., 2017), the technical properties of the wisdom class have led to the development of a learning model based on the wisdom class, as well as the application study of the learning model. In (Gong, 2016) authors have suggested a structural model which consists of 3-Sections and 10-Steps by comparing traditional classroom teaching models. This work (Zhao, 2015) has enhanced the classroom environment from software and hardware to LMS. ITLA called the Integrated Teaching and Learning Assistance system has been introduced in (Tran, 2015). It looked into key aspects that influence the wisdom class's ability to develop effectively. The HiTeach Interactive System, when contrasted to traditional classrooms and wisdom classroom instruction, supports literature (Wu et al., 2015) which explores the positive relevance of teaching in teaching. Evaluation of wisdom in the classroom. The reaction to the wisdom classroom teaching strategy in the network learning space is shown in literature (Willis et al., 2016), which also presents the teaching strategy of the trainer and the learner behavior for teaching assessment.

CLOUD DESIGN FOR CAL

The final goal of Open Education Information is to build a public service platform, achieve system integration, multilevel information sharing, and combine with the features of the Radio and Television University System: broad regional reach, numerous levels, and ideal network. Which is satisfied with the cloud computing's ultimate goals. As a result, this article proposes a cloud-based architecture called "Cloud Education," as depicted in Figure 2. The Physical hardware layer, virtualization layer, education middleware layer, application program interface layer, management system, and security certification system are all included in the model.

The *"physical hardware layer"* is a fundamental platform in the concept, consisting of servers, storage devices, and network devices. This layer is supported by the provincial radio and television university, which provides high performance physical hardware server, large capacity of memory, and high-speed network from an architectural standpoint, linking with the radio and television university actuality. As a result, the cloud CAL architecture is distributed computing and scalable.

Figure 2. CAL Cloud Design

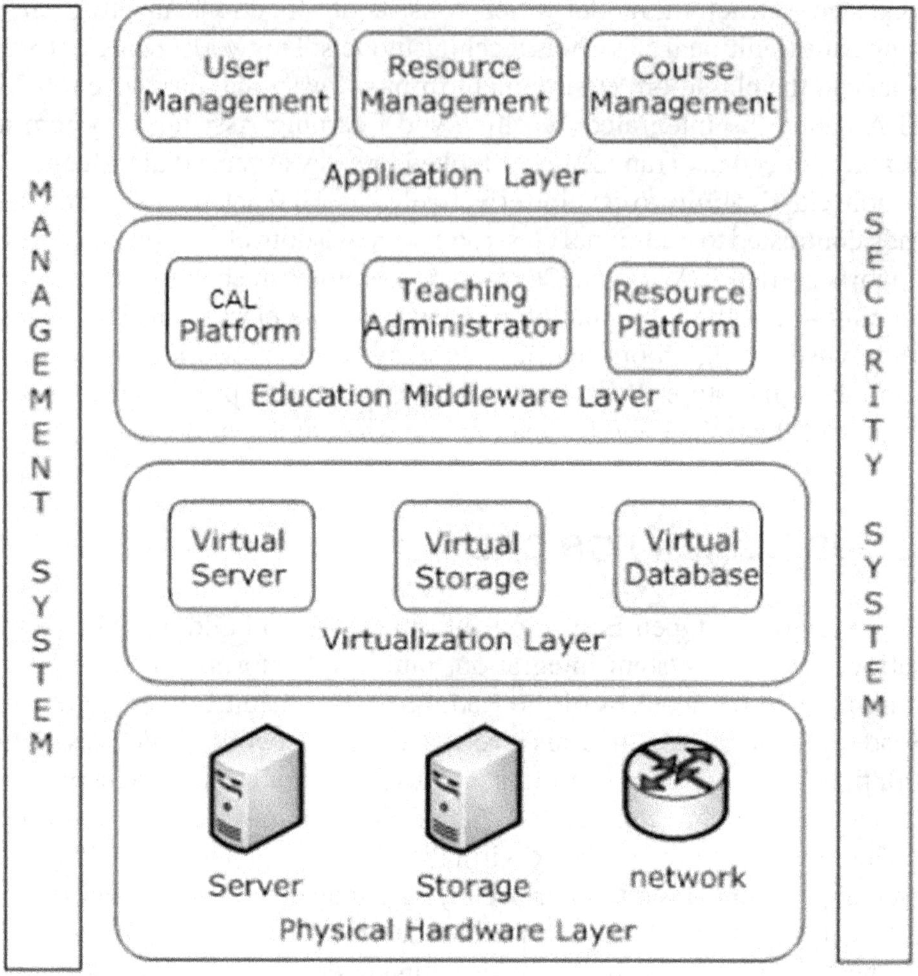

The five characteristics of cloud computing are achieved through the "*virtualization layer*", which has the following features: dynamic setup, dispersed deployment, and cost assessment. The purpose of the virtualization layer is to totally decompose regional economic data blocks using distributed technology and virtualization technologies. Virtual servers, virtual storage areas, and virtual databases are all elements of this tier. Virtual Databases allow users to query a set of data using Online services. VM databases are not standard relational database systems, but rather high-availability storage engines that assure eventual consistency as a requirement, as well as increased system availability and extendibility.

Because it is the main business platform, the *"CAL middleware layer"* is the core layer. This tier is distinct from others in that it stores any information on several computer nodes, even regular files and databases. As a result, all application systems on the middleware layer have the following characteristics: distributed, fault-tolerant, and extensible.

The adaptability of a system could be ensured through the *"Application program interface layer"*. Due to the obvious multiplicity of contemporary software applications, no single application system can meet all of a customer's needs. This layer must also provide the appropriate interface, as well as the ability to provide hosting services.

Physical state, virtualization software, hardware and software, and open API are all monitored by the *"Management system"*. Authentication mechanisms, single point login, virtualization software and hardware access control and audit, CAL gateway, and open API access control are all part of the *"security system"*.

CAL CLOUD STORAGE AND BIG DATA MINING

CAL Cloud storage, as a new type of service, could be a viable answer to these problems. The use of cloud storage to integrate CAL users' information resources not only saves money, but it also simplifies difficult setup and management activities. Putting resources in the cloud also allows for easier access to resources from more locations, allowing for the exchange of CAL records. We need to create a cloud storage environment where learners' and trainers' records, marks, and other information records are communicated over the network. Information is merged into a comprehensive database of CAL information after data preparation. Data storage can be dynamically increased with resource storage virtualization to accomplish information synchronization and sharing. Furthermore, one of the most significant considerations of the design is information security. All operational behavior of the document can be recorded, and a log-in authentication method is required, as well as high-security encryption of file data kept on the platform.

The foundation for CAL data analysis and big data mining is a comprehensive database of patient information based on cloud storage structure. Through data analysis, trainers can gain a better understanding of the learner's status and learning efficacy, allowing them to make more accurate training, laying the groundwork for the construction of an efficacy evaluation system.

Researchers using a range of data mining and information modeling techniques can better understand and identify the teaching methodologies as well as provide direction for future research. Through statistical analysis of the data platform, CAL Management and related departments may make the right analyses and decisions.

Table 1. CAL big data mining processes

Sr.No	Module Name	Purpose of the Mining Module
1	CAL Database Management Module	Acquiring and Maintaining CAL related records
2	CAL Data Preprocessing Module	Data cleaning, Integration, Translation of CAL records
3	CAL Mining Operation Module	CAL Pattern Recognition
4	Model CAL Evaluation Module	Result and Model assessment
5	Knowledge CAL Output Module	Knowledge based CAL Data output

CAL CLOUD STORAGE ESTIMATION

When calculating backup storage capacity, we should notice that the size of the CAL data source that will be backed up to the cloud, as well as the space that will be required when data is added each time a backup runs, which will be determined by the job's retention scheme. As a rule of thumb, allot 150GB of storage for every 100GB of source material backed up.

Backup's source data 100GB 200GB 500GB 1TB 1.5TB
Cloud storage allowance 150GB 300GB 750GB 1.5TB 2.25TB

For example, if you have a 200GB data source, you should expect to need 300GB of storage capacity over time. This provides for 20 backup revisions with an overall average shift of 5percent of total backup, as well as space planning. These calculations take into account the fact that streamlining, and compression will save a lot of space.

CONCLUSION

With the maturation and advancement of cloud computing technology, cloud computing now provides an ideal lesson plan for implementation of the information building in CAL. It can assist us in lowering educational costs, sharing superior resources in schools and industries, and providing a new teaching of CAL paradigm. We also prescribed the modules for CAL big data storage and access with mining methods, cloud storage calculation also considered one of the sections for CAL distance access.

ACKNOWLEDGMENT

First, our appreciation goes to parents and family for their sacrifice, commitment, and overalls, their support and consistent encouragement. I wish to express my sincere thanks to our Prestigious Institution.

REFERENCES

Bayam, Y., Unal, H., & Ekiz, H. (2003). Distance education application on logic circuits [Mantıksal devreler üzerinde uzaktan eğitim uygulaması.]. *The Turkish Online Journal of Educational Technology*, *2*, 92–94.

Büyükbayraktar, M. (2006). *The effect of computer-aided application of logic circuit design on student success. [Lojik devre tasarımının bilgisayar destekli olarak uygulanmasının öğrenci başarısına etkisi]* [Doctoral dissertation]. Sakarya Universitesi, Turkey.

Chen, S. L. (2015). Research on fuzzy comprehensive evaluation in practice teaching assessment of computer majors. *International Journal of Modern Education & Computer Science*, *7*(11), 12–19. doi:10.5815/ijmecs.2015.11.02

Garofalo, F., Mota-Moya, P., Munday, A., & Romy, S. (2017). Total extraperitoneal hernia repair: Residency teaching program and outcome evaluation. *World Journal of Surgery*, *41*(1), 100–105. doi:10.100700268-016-3710-z PMID:27637604

Gong, G., & Liu, S. (2016). Consideration of evaluation of teaching at colleges. *Open Journal of Social Sciences*, *4*(07), 82–84. doi:10.4236/jss.2016.47013

Gorelik, E. (2013). *Cloud computing models.* [Doctoral dissertation]. Massachusetts Institute of Technology, Massachusetts.

Liu, L., Feng, J., Pei, Q., Chen, C., Ming, Y., Shang, B., & Dong, M. (2020). Blockchain-enabled secure data sharing scheme in mobile-edge computing: An asynchronous advantage actor–critic learning approach. *IEEE Internet of Things Journal*, *8*(4), 2342–2353. doi:10.1109/JIOT.2020.3048345

Oliveros, M. A., García, A., & Valdez, B. (2015). Evaluation of a teaching sequence regarding science, technology and society values in higher education. *Creative Education*, *6*(16), 1768–1775. doi:10.4236/ce.2015.616179

Parsi, K., & Laharika, M. (2013). A Comparative Study of Different Deployment Models in a Cloud. *International Journal of Advanced Research in Computer Science and Software Engineering*, *3*(5), 512–515.

Porozovs, J., Liepniece, L., & Voita, D. (2015). Evaluation of the teaching methods used in secondary school biology lessons. *Signum Temporis*, *7*(1), 60–66. doi:10.1515igtem-2016-0009

Rajan, A. P. (2013). Evolution of cloud storage as cloud computing infrastructure service. *arXiv preprint arXiv:1308.1303.*

Reisenwitz, T. H. (2016). Student evaluation of teaching: An investigation of nonresponse bias in an online context. *Journal of Marketing Education*, *38*(1), 7–17. doi:10.1177/0273475315596778

Shang, W. L., Chen, J., Bi, H., Sui, Y., Chen, Y., & Yu, H. (2021). Impacts of COVID-19 pandemic on user behaviors and environmental benefits of bike sharing: A big-data analysis. *Applied Energy*, *285*, 116429. doi:10.1016/j.apenergy.2020.116429 PMID:33519037

Tran, N. D. (2015). Reconceptualisation of approaches to teaching evaluation in higher education. *Issues in Educational Research*, *25*(1), 50–61.

Willis, E. A., Szabo-Reed, A. N., Ptomey, L. T., Steger, F. L., Honas, J. J., Al-Hihi, E. M., Lee, R., Vansaghi, L., Washburn, R. A., & Donnelly, J. E. (2016). Distance learning strategies for weight management utilizing social media: A comparison of phone conference call versus social media platform. Rationale and design for a randomized study. *Contemporary Clinical Trials*, *47*, 282–288. doi:10.1016/j.cct.2016.02.005 PMID:26883282

Wu, P., Low, S., Liu, J. Y., Pienaar, J., & Xia, B. (2015). Critical success factors in distance learning construction programs at Central Queensland University: students' perspective. *Journal of Professional Issues in Engineering Education and Practice, 141*(1).

Yuen, A. H. (2006). Learning to program through interactive simulation. *Educational Media International*, *43*(3), 251–268. doi:10.1080/09523980600641452

Zhao, H. (2015). College physics teaching model design and evaluation research of students' seriousness. *The Open Cybernetics & Systemics Journal*, *9*(1), 2017–2020. doi:10.2174/1874110X01509012017

Zhou, L., Li, H., & Sun, K. (2017). Teaching performance evaluation by means of a hierarchical multifactorial evaluation model based on type-2 fuzzy sets. *Applied Intelligence*, *46*(1), 34–44. doi:10.100710489-016-0816-9

KEY TERMS AND DEFINITIONS

CAL: Computer Assisted Learning
CDMI: Cloud Data Management Interface
ITLA: Integrated Teaching and Learning Assistance
LMS: Learning Management System

Chapter 6
An Overview of the Big Data Technology for Computer-Assisted Learning

Sivaranjani R.
Hindusthan College of Arts and Science, India

ABSTRACT

Education has gradually gotten rid of old teaching methods and their limits as society has progressed under the impact of high technology such as big data, cloud computing, network technology, and mobile Internet. This study uses data mining technology to implement educational reforms, creates a computer-aided learning system (CAL) based on data mining, and creates teaching system functions based on real-world data with big data techniques. Many strategies for data analysis are available through data mining. Without the use of automated analytic techniques, the big data now in student databases exceeds the human ability to examine and extract the most important information. Data analytics for CAL will be helpful in evaluating teaching and learning processes, and measures will be taken based on the findings to improve the process.

DOI: 10.4018/978-1-6684-5058-1.ch006

INTRODUCTION

Through this work, we have focused on the seamless data storage and analytics of Computer Assisted Learning. To do this, CAL principles were first presented to provide a better understanding of the notion, followed by big data and its storage strategies. In the following section, related research works on big data storage are offered, demonstrating the addressed concerns and the recommendations made by researchers in order to fix the bugs in CAL storage. We've spoken about the different forms of analytics and the life cycle of analyzing CAL data in big data analytics. Data mining-based algorithms that have been suggested can be useful for analytics. Only a few of the obstacles and issues have been discussed.

Computer Assisted Learning

The practical paradigm of learning is related to computer-assisted learning (CAL). Experiential learning proponents are emphatic about the way we perceive. Learning is rarely done by rote. We learn because we immerse ourselves in a setting that requires us to execute. Learners can fall into various categories like students, employees and so on. Because they have to learn new things based on requirements. The manner in which trainers strive to assist learners in acquiring skills and knowledge has nothing to do with how students actually learn. Lectures, examinations, and memorization are used by many educators. We undoubtedly learn by doing, failing, and practicing until we get it correctly. The purpose of computer-assisted learning is to concept understanding and problem solving (Arsham, 1994). Users from various educational institutions can access educational packages. Probably the majority of consumers can afford computers and software packages that aid in the application of CAL. Visual components such as photographs, Animated movies, and text, which are used extensively in CAL. Digital effects, such as sound effects for blind users or visual representations for deaf users, are useful for impaired learners whereas, most of the organizations find the use of CAL to be beneficial, the gear & technology required to implement the program can indeed be costly. The cost of maintaining CAL can be exorbitant because the programs must be altered over time, requiring the tutors to have advanced programming skills (Gunawardhana, 2020). Nevertheless, CAL usually focuses on a single topic and is not personalized to individual needs. A CAL system is designed to meet the demands of a company, which may differ from the needs of the employee (Rogers, Sharp, and Preece, 2002). CAL serves as an instructional portal that can store large amounts of data. Computer systems are fantastic training tools because they can display information, questions, examples, and simulations for students to explore. CAL programs can create simulations and walk a user through a subject in a specific setting (Singh and Sharma, 2008). Figure 1 has discussed a few of the modalities of CAL which can be used for betterment of teaching and learning.

Figure 1. Modes of CAL ("Computer Assisted Instructions (CAI)", 2017)

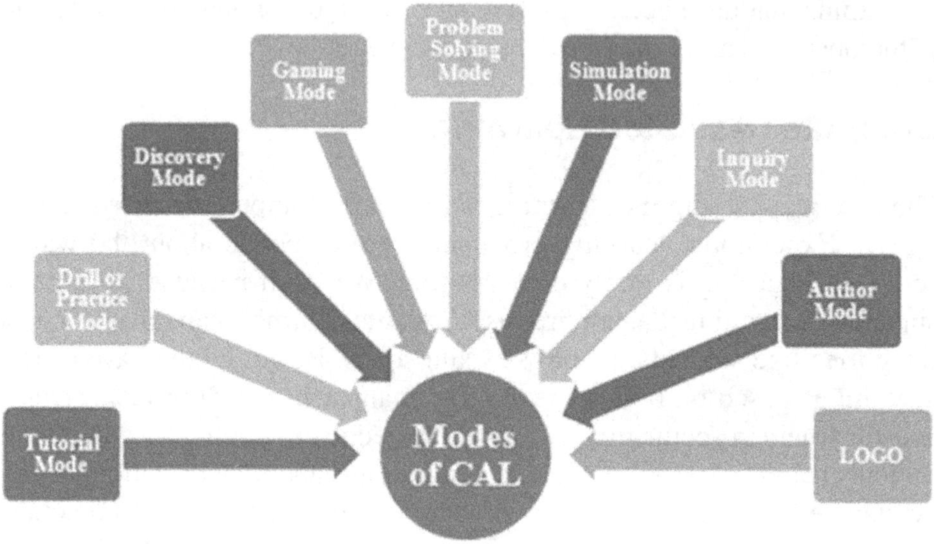

Basic Storage Versus Big Data Storage

CD-ROMs, Discs, movies and other media materials must be properly cared for and stored when software for computer-assisted instruction is used. In the event that the material is lost or damaged, backup copies of the software should always be retained. Extreme temperatures or magnetic surfaces should not be exposed to software, CD-ROMs, or VHS films. DVDs, or digital video discs, look to have a better chance of lasting longer than Disc or videotapes. For the appropriate management of multimedia, robust security is required. Because educational multimedia is so expensive, it must be safeguarded from theft and loss. Web-based learning necessitates adequate computer care and maintenance, including Internet browser updates, hardware upgrades as needed, and file management. In today's world, data generated by devices and users is large in volume and has a complex structure. Big Data, as a whole, is challenging to store and process with typical processing techniques. Conventional file storage systems focus on physical servers or the cloud, which adds to the cost and complexity of the system. Contemporary Big Data tools are Google File System, Hadoop Distributed File System, BigTable, HBase, Hypertable, MongoDB, Terrastore, Qizx, HyperGraphDB, InfiniteGraph, Rocket U2, Scalaris, DynamoDB, RethinkDB, Aerospike, Cassandra, Voldemort, SimpleDB, MemcacheD and CouchDB.

RESEARCH DIRECTIONS

The focus has been on the role and importance of computers, the Internet, and other similar technologies in assisting for learning, which has been covered more briefly, as well as the impact of computer-assisted training on language learning.

The primary study direction in the deep application stage of CAL research is storage, which has been considered here. Various systems experimented with various strategies in order to build an efficient data storage system. We conducted a comparison study between several Storage Management Systems based on some distinguishing parameters.CAL with Big Data based technologies undoubtedly play a beautiful role in learning and teaching routine. Big data storage is a crucial challenge in most organizations, which is why many researchers have attempted to address it in a variety of methods. Here is a discussion of a few works in Table 1.

Table 1. Research of big data storage

Sr.No	Literature	Addressed Issues regarding Big Data Storage
1	(Putnik et al., 2013)	Optimizing storage based on volumes.
2	(Gani et al., 2016)	Increasing storage requirements based on future use.
3	(Bohlouli et al., 2013)	Quick access to data storage resources.
4	(Wang et al., 2014)	Increasing big data retrieval efficiency.
5	(Hilker, 2012)	Node failure of distributed storage systems
6	(Cattell, 2011)	Predefined Schema for different data structures

BIG DATA ANALYTICS OF CAL

Big Analytic is the study of enormous concentrations of different data kinds, or Big Data, in order to identify underlying patterns, unknown relationships, as well as other important details. Although CAL data should be analyzed in the same manner. In fact, certain well-known algorithms for data analysis in Data Warehouse may not scale, necessitating parallelization and distribution strategies. Big Analytics necessitates not only new database structures, but also new data analysis methods. It then entails either new formulation or fresh application of traditional data mining methods, as well as the creation of entirely new approaches (Kelly, 2014).

Typology

Descriptive Analytics

This summarizes previous data in an easy-to-understand format. This aids in the creation of reports such as test reports, attendee tracking and other management related to CAL. It also aids in the tally of social media metrics.

Diagnostic Analytics

This is created in order to figure out which one created the issue. Data mining, Data Recovery and Drill-down are all instances of techniques. Diagnose analytics are used by the CAL environment because they provide a detailed understanding of a problem.

Predictive Analytics

This sort of analytics examines past and current data in order to create predictions about the future. Predictive analytics develops comprehensive data and makes predictions about the future using data analysis, AI, and ML. It predicts study content, trainer data, among other things.

CAL Data Analytics Life Cycle

We have gone over the data analytics life cycle of CAL in detail, breaking it down into eight stages.

- *Stage 1* -The Big Data analytics life cycle begins with the examination of a CAL use case, which describes the purpose and goal for the study.
- *Stage 2* - Identification of data sources - This step identifies a wide range of data sources which have been utilized by the CAL environment.
- *Stage 3* - CALData filtering - All of the previously detected data is filtered here to remove any corrupted data.
- *Stage 4* - CAL Data extraction - Data extraction - Incompatible data is extracted and then transformed into a format that is compatible with the tool.
- *Stage 5* - CAL Data aggregation - Data from several datasets with the same fields are combined in this stage.
- *Stage 6* - CALData analysis - To find meaningful information, data is analyzed utilizing analytical and statistical methods.
- *Stage 7* - Data visualization - Big Data researchers may create graphic visualizations of their analysis using technologies like Power BI, QlikView and Tableau.
- *Stage 8* -Final analysis result of CAL - At this point in the Big Data analytics lifecycle, the final analysis results are made available to learners and trainers who will act on them.

Data Mining Algorithm

Data mining algorithm for CAL data analytics

```
Input CAL Data d
Set predefined measurement m
Initialize Rules r, Candidate Rules Cr
        IF Termination criteria meet
                cd= Scan (d)
v=Construct(d,r,m)
r= update (Cr)
END
Output Rules r
```

The initialization, data input and output, data scan, rules generation, and rules update operators are all present in most data mining methods. In algorithm 3.1, d stands for CAL data, m for predefined measurement, r for rules and Cr for Candidate Rules. Until the termination requirement is reached, the scan, construct, and update operators will be repeated. The use of the scan operator is dependent on the data mining algorithm's design; consequently, it can be considered an optional operator. This algorithm depicts the majority of data algorithms, as well as how the typical algorithms—clustering, classification, association rules and sequential patterns—will use these operators to discover the hidden data.

THE OPEN ISSUES

Even though analytics may be ineffective for CAL big data presently environmental factors, systems, structures, and perhaps even problems that are quite different from traditional mining problems, a few characteristics of big data as well arise in conventional data data analysis. A few issues and challenges caused by CAL big data are addressed here as platform/framework and data mining perspectives of big data. Here are some of the outstanding issues:

Input and Output Based Issues

Big data analytics of CAL is undoubtedly useful and has numerous potential that can help us better comprehend the so-called "things" from a pragmatic standpoint. Most studies of big data analytics of CAL, on the other hand, have suggested that while the results of big data are valuable, the business models of most big data analytics are unclear.

Communication Systems Issues

Because most big data analytics systems are designed for parallel computing and typically work on other systems (– for example, cloud service) or with other systems (e.g., search engine or knowledge base), communication between big data analytics with trainer and other systems will have a significant impact on the overall performance of Knowledge discovery in databases in CAL environment (Tsai et al., 2015).

CONCLUSION

We reviewed studies on data analytics from the traditional data analysis to the recent big data analysis. Traditional data analytics, on the other hand, may not be able to handle such enormous amounts of data. This work will concentrate on a few methodologies that were combined with Computer Assisted Learning storage. Data Mining with the combination Data Analytics can make good storage and access with feasibility. Using this strategy in the CAL concept, we were able to build fluid teaching and learning programs. The relationship between the trainer and the learner can be improved by combining these technologies.

ACKNOWLEDGMENT

First, our appreciation goes to parents and family for their sacrifice, commitment, and overalls, their support and consistent encouragement. I wish to express my sincere thanks to our Prestigious Institution.

REFERENCES

Arsham, H. (1994 February 25). Computer-assisted Learning Concepts & Techniques. UBalt. http://home.ubalt.edu/ntsbarsh/business-stat/opre/partX.htm#rLPSotGuide

Bohlouli, M., Schulz, F., Angelis, L., Pahor, D., Brandic, I., Atlan, D., & Tate, R. (2013). Towards an integrated platform for big data analysis. In *Integration of practice-oriented knowledge technology: Trends and prospectives* (pp. 47–56). Springer. doi:10.1007/978-3-642-34471-8_4

Cattell, R. (2011). Scalable SQL and NoSQL data stores. *SIGMOD Record*, *39*(4), 12–27. doi:10.1145/1978915.1978919

Gani, A., Siddiqa, A., Shamshirband, S., & Hanum, F. (2016). A survey on indexing techniques for big data: Taxonomy and performance evaluation. *Knowledge and Information Systems*, *46*(2), 241–284. doi:10.100710115-015-0830-y

Gunawardhana, L. P. D. (2020). Introduction to Computer-Aided Learning. *Global Journal of Computer Science and Technology*.

Hilker, S. (2012). Survey Distributed Databases—Toad for Cloud.

Kelly, J. (2014). Big data: Hadoop, business analytics and beyond. *Wikibon, 5*(2).

Putnik, G., Sluga, A., ElMaraghy, H., Teti, R., Koren, Y., Tolio, T., & Hon, B. (2013). Scalability in manufacturing systems design and operation: State-of-the-art and future developments roadmap. *CIRP Annals, 62*(2), 751–774. doi:10.1016/j.cirp.2013.05.002

Rogers, Y., Sharp, H., & Preece, J. (2002). *Interaction design: Beyond human-computer interaction.* Jon Wiley & Sons. Inc.

Singh, A., & Sharma, S. (2008). *Skilled labour shortage threatens expansion in India.* Deccan Herald.

Tsai, C. W., Lai, C. F., Chao, H. C., & Vasilakos, A. V. (2015). Big data analytics: A survey. *Journal of Big Data, 2*(1), 1–32. doi:10.118640537-015-0030-3 PMID:26191487

VBCED. (2017). *Computer Assisted Instructions (CAI).* Viswa Bharathi College of Education for Women, Veerachipalayam, Sankari West, Salem District. https://drarockiasamy.wordpress.com/computer-assisted-instructions-cai/

Wang, H., Li, J., Zhang, H., & Zhou, Y. (2014, March). Benchmarking replication and consistency strategies in cloud serving databases: Hbase and cassandra. In *Workshop on big data benchmarks, performance optimization, and emerging hardware,* (pp. 71-82). Springer, Cham. 10.1007/978-3-319-13021-7_6

KEY TERMS AND DEFINITIONS

CAL: Computer Assisted Learning
GFS: Google File System
HDFS: Hadoop Distributed File System

Chapter 7
Analyzing the Novel Approaches for Intelligent Computer-Aided Learning (ICAL)

Shaheen H.
https://orcid.org/0000-0003-3544-5424
MVJ College of Engineering, India

ABSTRACT

Beyond the spread of the disease and efforts to treat, the coronavirus pandemic has far-reaching implications. It is crystal clear that the pandemic wreaked havoc on critical fields such as healthcare, business, and academic. In terms of academics, one direct outcome of the pandemic's spread was the decision to suspend traditional in-person classroom courses in favor of remote learning and home-based schooling through the use of computer assisted learning technologies, but these technologies confront numerous hurdles. The majority of these issues revolve around the effectiveness of these delivery modalities, as well as engagement and knowledge testing. These difficulties highlight the need for an advanced smart educational system that aids all types of learners, gives teachers a variety of smart new tools, and enables a more flexible learning environment. The internet of things, artificial intelligence and virtual reality is a blooming sector, and IoT-based devices have ushered in a revolution in electronics and information technology.

DOI: 10.4018/978-1-6684-5058-1.ch007

INTRODUCTION

The concept of Computer-Assisted Learning (CAL) was introduced in 1960 itself in the PLATO Project, initiated by Illinois University. It is developed in each decade till now. CAL's present theory emphasizes student-centered skills that enable students to work independently (Wikipedia contributors, 2022). As the name suggests, computer assisted learning (CAL) is the use of electronic devices/computer devices to deliver educational instructions to educate people. Computer-Assisted Learning can be applied in almost any field of education, from kindergarten children's Television based game programs earlier and computer-based programs nowadays also medical people studying quad bypasses treatment methods. Knowledge from all domains of education/learning, Human-Computer Interaction (HCI), and cognitive has been combined to create CAL (Wang and Wu, 2020).

These resources might be structured or unstructured, but they usually include two key elements: participatory training and personalized learning. CAL is essentially a technology that aids teachers in making the language learning process easier for students. It can be used to reinforce what students have also already learnt in class or as a remediation tool for students who need more help. CAL products are made with language education and method in mind, which can be taken from a range of instructional concepts (e.g., cognitive, behaviorist, constructivist) and second-language development theory. The definition of blended learning is the combo of CAL and face to face learning (Gunawardhana, 2020).

Typology

There are many CAL methods identified once it starts to bloom. The Scientists Warschauer and Healy (1998) outlined there are three phases to determine the CAL types from the 1960s as shown in the figure 1. In Type-1 approach Students' inputs will be analyzed and feedback will be provided, and more advanced algorithms would react to errors by diverging to assistance screens as well as corrective tasks. Since such programmes and their underlying methodology still exist today, most language teachers reject behavioristic effects on language acquisition, and the rising power of new technologies has driven CAL to explore other options. The Next type is communicative strategy The emphasis is on communication rather than analysis, and grammar is taught implicitly rather than formally. It also permits students' linguistic outputs to be more creative and flexible. The communicative approach coincided with the introduction of the personal computer, which made computers considerably more accessible and resulted in a surge in the creation of linguistic programs. In the final type attempts were made to address concerns of the communicative approach by incorporating language ability instruction into tasks and assignments to offer direction and coherence. It also happened to be about the same time as the invention of multimedia technology (textual, images, audio, and animations) and computer-mediated interaction.

Figure 1.

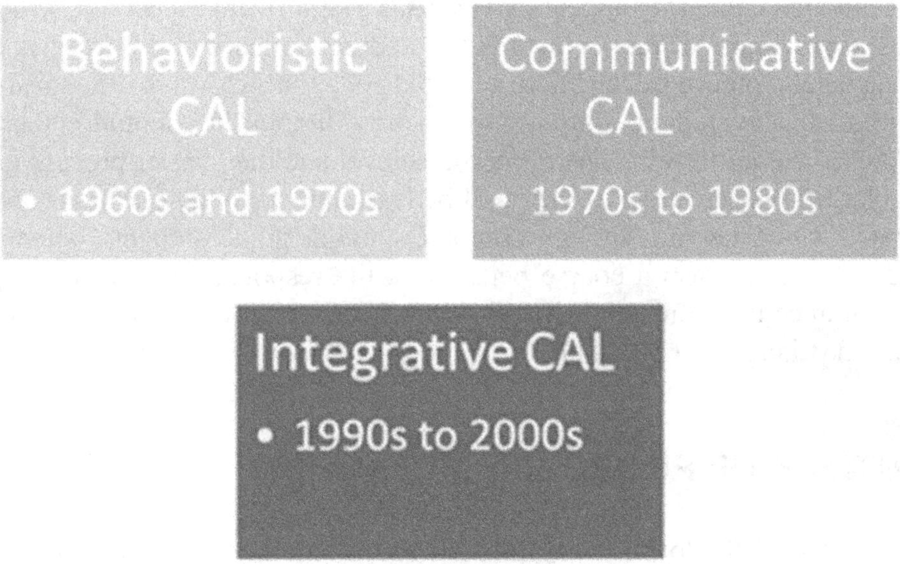

CHALLENGES AND BOTTLENECKS OF COMPUTER ASSISTED LEARNING

Learners could be unfamiliar to what will be provided to them the first-time computers are brought into the educational process, resulting in general nervousness. If the learners (especially the older ones) are still not computer proficient, the educator will have to deal with technophobia as well. In this setting, it would take a long time for pupils to become accustomed to CAL.

Learners may become overwhelmed by the amount of data they are processing in a computer-based self-assessment class where they are left on their own. As a result, excessive use of multimedia relays should be avoided while teaching CAL for the first attempt, as well as the instructor should concentrate further on the topic getting taught because learners' gaze is very often drawn to the computer.

There seems to be an unfavorable situation in which learners are so enthralled according to things shown on the computer and they fail to pay attention to what is being taught. They may become enthralled by the holographic graphics to the point where, by the end of the training, they have failed to grasp the lesson's main themes or are only roughly twice following the lectures because their mindset will be somewhere else. This is more likely to happen if the learners are younger (Yang, Yang, and Hwang, 2014).

Although delivering appealing visuals is a significant aspect of CAL, the most crucial goal of the lectures is for students to learn and grasp what is being taught; otherwise, technology would not be successful in the education process. In the student-computer interaction, the teacher should endeavor to preserve equilibrium. The trainer must evaluate the learner process on a regular basis to ensure that they will be learning by asking questions about what is being taught. Though computers might pique students' attention and help them grasp a course better, it is the responsibility of professors to guarantee that students learn and can effectively convey what they have learned (Liang and Li, 2011).

OUTLINE OF PROPOSED METHODS

The above listed reasons being the bottleneck of the CAL, it can be rectified and bring more interest to learners by adopting the current technologies which are explored below.

Internet of Things (IoT)

The Internet of Things brings a new invention that received much attention in recent science experiments and the technological revolution. The processing, gathering and analysis of provided data by IoT sensors, IoT still supports and copes up systems for the observation and control of the physical environment. The current host-to-host architecture of the World

Wide Web is unfit for handling these IoT devices, and thus may be unable to deliver adequate content to its connected devices, due to issues such as high latency, limited protection, inadequate address spacing and caching, and so on (Murali and Jamalipour, 2019). The Internet of Things also introduced the slew of additional requirements to people's lives, as well as a slew of new business opportunities for Smartphone designers, ISPs, and app developers. Global technology investment in IoT could hit trillions by 2022, according to International Data Corporation, rising at a compound annual growth rate of 13.6 percent over the 2017–2022 periods (Boussada et al., 2019) by 2030, it is expected that approximately 500 billion devices would be wired to the internet ("IDC forecasts worldwide technology spending on the internet of things to reach $1.2 trillion in 2022", 2018) Clearly, with high-quality advantages and incentives, IoT would become an indispensable aspect of human life in the not-too-distant upcoming days (Cisco, 2022).

The key aim of the proposed ideas is to let all computers intelligently interact with one another. For example, a person can learn and/or teach the content from their mobile phone or personal computer. Certain terminology and concepts, such as machine learning and deep learning, neural network and fuzzy logic must be grasped in order to adapt Artificial Intelligence technologies to IoT networks (Hoang et al., 2020). Gartner, Inc. has predicted that 6.4 billion devices that can be connected worldwide in 2016, up to 30 percent from the year 2015 which has been enlarged, and the same will reach 20.8 billion by 2020 (Lily, Chan, and Wang, 2013).

Artificial Intelligence (AI)

Artiðcial Intelligence is the knowledge of imparting intelligence in devices that can act like the human mind that used to be capable of doing tasks. AI built systems are developing promptly in the ways of applications, alteration, process speed and competences. Machines are progressively getting skilful of taking on tasks with less routine. While human intelligence mostly seems to make decisions perfectly also, Artificial Intelligence is just about 'selecting' a correct choice at the right time. To put it simply, Artificial Intelligence lacks the imagination in decision-making that humans possess. It could be noted that creativity will still alter the function with effective work, but Intelligence systems have expertly minimized manual intervention, duplication and can give results in a very short amount of time (Câmara, D., and Nikaein, 2016). To examine applied Artificial Intelligence to the IoT is mostly to make things more capable. In the past, there were many ideas and techniques projected about applied Artificial Intelligence to the IoT. Machine sometimes referred to as 'Things' will be more intelligent once it will tie up with 'intelligence' rather than human but with a machine connected via 'network' also called the Internet (Ghosh, Chakraborty, and Law, 2018). This concept is shown in Equation (1).

$$\text{Things} \cap \text{Intelligence} \cap \text{Network} = \text{Internet of Things (IoT)} \quad (1)$$

Artificial intelligence and the internet of things combination has resulted in smart speakers and robots, as well as IoT technologies and/or computers that make human tasks easier [15]. Image recognition, face recognition, speech and gesture recognition, deep neural networks, transfer learning, computer vision, and other applications are all possible with AI-enabled smart objects. A few popular implementations include smart lighting, intelligent ovens, Skybell, and automotive AI.

Virtual Reality

Virtual Reality is bringing the concept of mimicking the real world to capture user attention in the same way that a live experience does. It is also feasible to create a better learning and teaching environment in the classroom. Across many ways, the benefits of utilizing virtual reality to accomplish academic goals were comparable to those of using a system or simulation. Educators' attention is captured and held by virtual reality. Virtual reality can further adequately describe certain characteristics, procedures, and so on over conventional methods.

ANALYZING THE NOVEL APPROACHES FOR ICAL

We devised some of the novel concepts using few of the trending techniques like Internet of Things (IoT), Artificial Intelligence, and Virtual Reality for developing power demand forecasts as well as concentrating production, transmission, and disposal. Internet of Things (IoT) is a new sector, and IoT-based devices have ushered in a renaissance in technological advancement. This section depicts technologies like IoT and virtual reality implemented with the help of artificial intelligence to attain and retain the interest of teacher and learner.

Internet of Things Based Ideas

Connected devices provide learners with better accessibility to anything from learning resources to channels of communication, as well as allowing teachers to track learner progress on a regular basis. Few of the real time IoT based applications in practice are given below. It is also important to notice there are a lot of techniques that are quite common to avoid IoT attacks which can cause the issues (Thavamani and Sinthuja, 2022).

In order to set up ICAL via Internet of Things ideas sensors, actuators can be utilized to present the live classroom environment. As shown in the figure 2, various locations students can be connected in class, or they can be also used in a live classroom with learning by doing pedagogy. Operating systems can be installed on the open platform in a variety of ways. Then, using various examples, we show how the Raspberry Pi can be used for educational purposes in the future. Depending on the content on the microSD card, Raspberry Pi can act as a full-fledged computer, media player, or play stations. Learning/teaching of computer programs, mathematics, medical, electronic subjects with these sensors will make an impact. Because IoT will make jobs like sensing, connecting, and collaborating in ICAL much easier.

Figure 2.

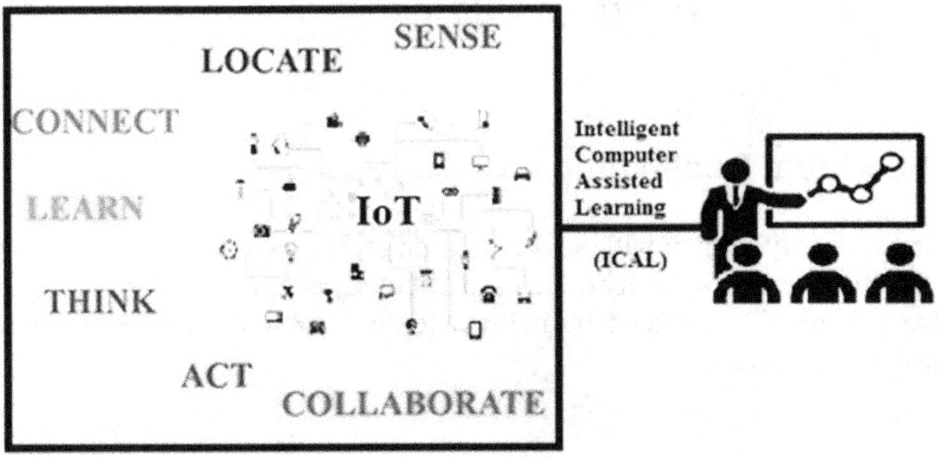

Initiative via Artificial Intelligence

This domain research includes robots, Intelligent Tutoring System, Automatic Speech Recognition, Natural Language Processing, Neural Networks, Knowledge Representation and Expert Systems. AI seeks to grasp the nature of intelligence and build a new approach to social intellectual ability like to respond via machine intelligence. We might envision that the future of AI technology products will bring the wisdom of human beings, as concepts as well as engineering mature as application fields grow.

Figure 3.

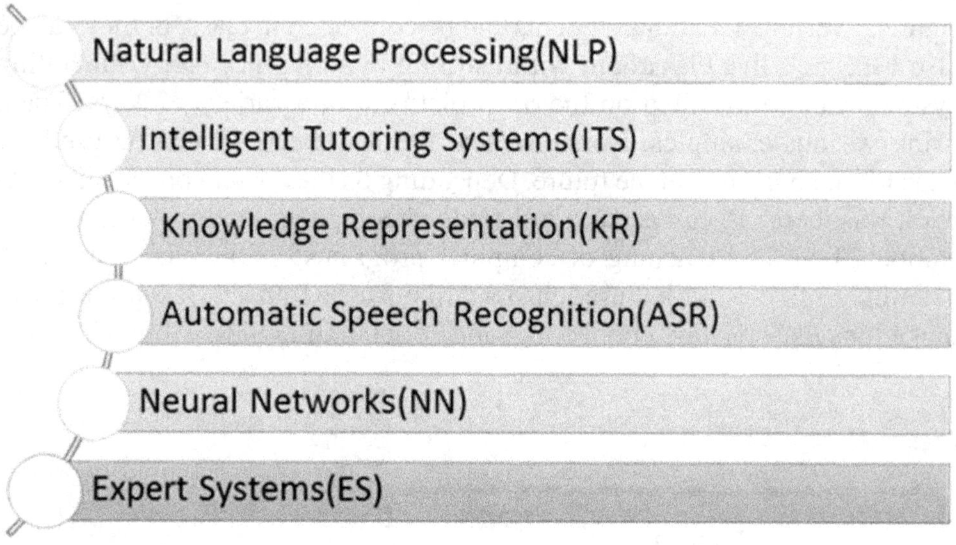

The Virtual Reality Impact

Virtual Reality, with or without the addition of Augmented Reality, can play a significant role in a variety of fields, particularly computer-based education also known as CAL. In the table below, a few examples of real-time evidence have been explored.

ICAL MARQUETTE VIA NOVEL APPROACHES

In this scenario we have considered a scenario for "Designing a smart thermometer using a microcontroller that can work without the Raspberry Pi", that could be attained via IoT, AI and also VR technologies. Step by step procedures discussed below to attain smart thermometer creation:

- Step 1: Configuring Raspberry Pi in Linux
- Step 2: Dealing with MySQL to create Database to store humidity data
- Step 3: Medium Level Programming for microcontroller to handle the sensors
- Step 4: IP address fixing to Wi-Fi / wired network
- Step 5: Testing via simulations to fetch better results.

For demonstration purposes, the suggested model is simple to put up. The concept is catapulted into action by the learners. Learners will be able to grasp any subject more quickly, and trainers will be able to communicate their perspectives. Artificial Intelligence may also be trained to detect high or low humidity swings, which will be useful in the future. In the event that hands-on instruction fails, the identical issue can be imagined using animated VR to aid comprehension.

Figure 4.

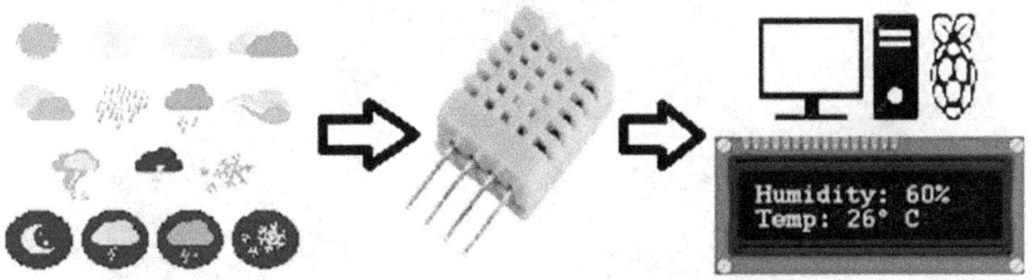

Figure 5.

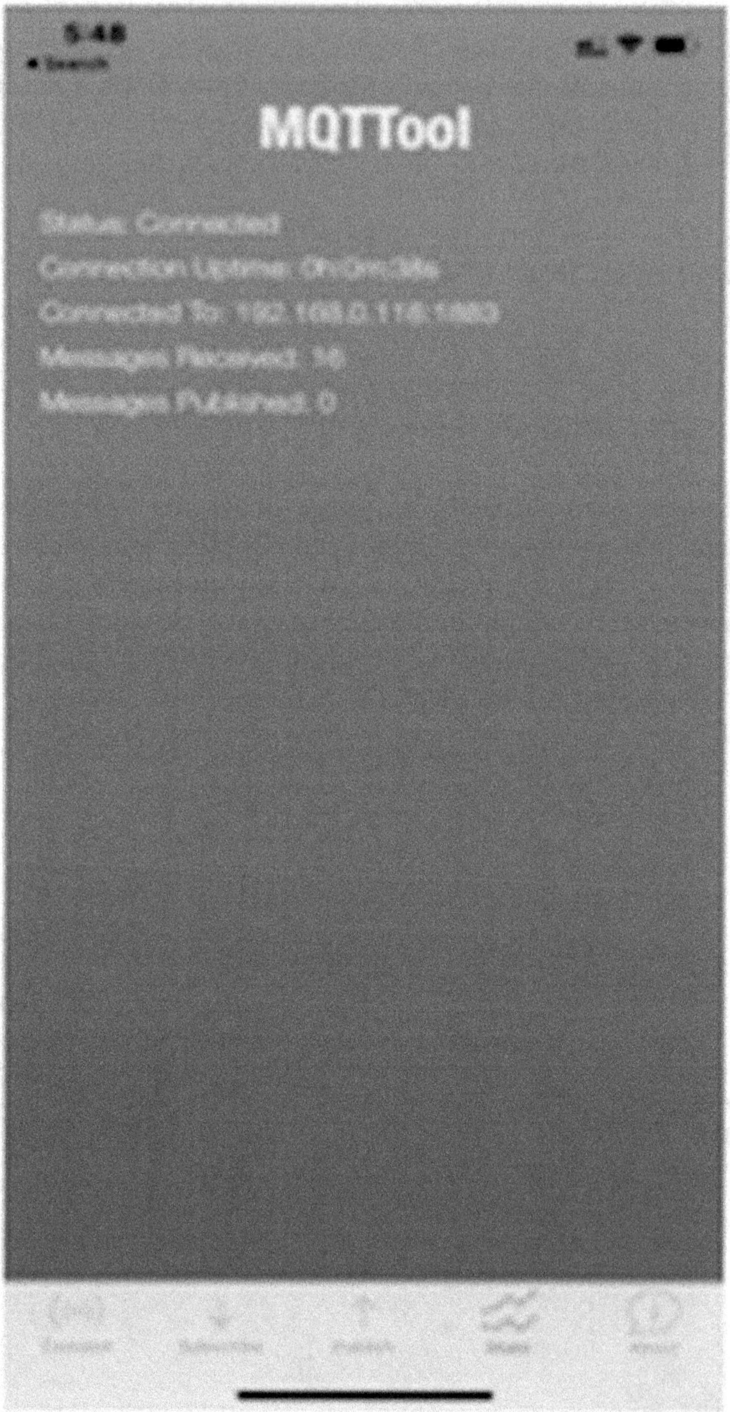

In Figure 5 there were 16 humidity messages received as per the scheduled time (38mins) in order to test the activated smart thermometer. We can also adjust the time limit as per user need. In this research one of the IoT famous protocols MQTT (Message Queue Telemetry Transport) was used in order to publish humidity data. Even MQT Tool mobile application was helpful to subscribe in order to fetch the humidity data.

CONCLUSION

This project can focus solely on a few approaches that were integrated with Computer Assisted Learning to develop the ICAL. Throughout the debate, the Internet of Things, Artificial Intelligence, and Virtual Reality were discussed, all of which are burgeoning technology. We were able to achieve smooth teaching and learning programs employing this method in the ICAL idea. Combining these technologies can improve the interaction between the trainer and the learner. Our Intelligent Computer Aided Learning System seems most important in this era, even though it creates the most vibe with tools and techniques to make learners centric. For this reason we have suggested the idea uses AI and IoT to provide information on learning, problem solving, question answering and so on. It is one of the added advantages of the method, by implementing the idea Computer Aided Learning and Teaching will become smart in future.

ACKNOWLEDGMENT

First, my appreciation goes to parents and family for their sacrifice, commitment, and overalls, their support and consistent encouragement. I wish to express my sincere thanks to our Prestigious Institution.

REFERENCES

Wikipedia. (2022, May 29). Computer-assisted language learning. In *Wikipedia, The Free Encyclopedia.*

Wang, F., & Wu, S. (2020, December). Research and Practice of Computer English Assisted Learning System. In *5th International Conference on Mechanical, Control and Computer Engineering (ICMCCE)* (pp. 1182-1185). IEEE.

Gunawardhana, L. P. D. (2020). *Introduction to Computer-Aided Learning*. Global Journal of Computer Science and Technology.

Yang, T. C., Yang, S. J., & Hwang, G. J. (2014, July). Development of an interactive test system for students' improving learning outcomes in a computer programming course. In *IEEE 14th International Conference on Advanced Learning Technologies* (pp. 637-639). IEEE.

Liang, Z., & Li, L. (2011, July). Self-assessment in autonomous Computer-Assisted Language Learning. In *2011 International Symposium on Computer Science and Society* (pp. 396-399). IEEE.

Murali, S., & Jamalipour, A. (2019). A lightweight intrusion detection for sybil attack under mobile RPL in the internet of things. *IEEE Internet of Things Journal*, *7*(1), 379–388. doi:10.1109/JIOT.2019.2948149

Boussada, R., Hamdane, B., Elhdhili, M. E., & Saidane, L. A. (2019, April). PP-NDNoT: On preserving privacy in IoT-based E-health systems over NDN. In IEEE Wireless Communications and Networking Conference (WCNC,) (pp. 1-6). IEEE.

Businesswire. (2018, June 18). *IDC forecasts worldwide technology spending on the internet of things to reach $1.2 trillion in 2022*.

Cisco. (2022, August 18). *Internet of things (IOT) products & solutions*. Cisco. https://www.cisco.com/c/en/us/solutions/internet-of-things/overview.html#~industries

Hoang, D. T., Nguyen, D. N., Alsheikh, M. A., Gong, S., Dutkiewicz, E., Niyato, D., & Han, Z. (2020). Borrowing Arrows with Thatched Boats": The Art of Defeating Reactive Jammers in IoT Networks. *IEEE Wireless Communications*, *27*(3), 79–87.

Lily, D., Chan, B., & Wang, T. G. (2013). A Simple Explanation of Neural Network in Artificial Intelligence. *IEEE. Trans on Control System*, *247*, 1529–5651.

Câmara, D., & Nikaein, N. (Eds.). (2016). *Wireless public safety networks 2: a systematic approach*. Elsevier.

Ghosh, A., Chakraborty, D., & Law, A. (2018). Artificial intelligence in Internet of things. *CAAI Transactions on Intelligence Technology*, *3*(4), 208–218.

Xu, Y., Shieh, C. H., van Esch, P., & Ling, I. L. (2020). AI customer service: Task complexity, problem-solving ability, and usage intention. *Australasian Marketing Journal*, *28*(4), 189–199.

Thavamani, S., & Sinthuja, U. (2022, January). LSTM based Deep Learning Technique to Forecast Internet of Things Attacks in MQTT Protocol. In *2022 IEEE Fourth International Conference on Advances in Electronics, Computers and Communications (ICAECC),* (pp. 1-4). IEEE.

Warschauer, M., & Healey, D. (1998). Computers and language learning: An overview. *Language Teaching*, *31*, 57–71.

KEY TERMS AND DEFINITIONS

CAL: Computer Assisted Learning
ICAL: Artificial Intelligent Computer Assisted Learning
IoT: Internet of Things
AI: Artificial Intelligence
VR: Virtual Reality

Chapter 8
Recent Trends in Nanomaterials:
Challenges and Opportunities

Kannadhasan S.
https://orcid.org/0000-0001-6443-9993
Study College of Engineering, Coimbatore, India

Nagarajan R.
https://orcid.org/0000-0002-4990-5869
Gnanamani College of Technology, India

Kanagaraj Venusamy
https://orcid.org/0000-0001-9479-8073
Rajalakshmi Engineering College, Chennai, India

ABSTRACT

Nanoscience is the analysis of phenomena and material modification at the chemical, cellular, and macromolecular scales, where properties vary greatly from those at larger scales. Nanotechnologies are the regulation of form and size at the nanometer scale in the design, characterization, processing, and deployment of materials, components, and systems. The development of efficient methods for the synthesis of nanomaterials in a variety of sizes and chemical compositions is a hot topic in nanotechnology research. There have been many changes and modifications to the methods for producing metal nanoparticles that provide greater control over the scale, form, and other characteristics of the nanoparticles. These advancements have enabled researchers to investigate quantum confinement as well as other properties that are affected by scale, form, and composition.

DOI: 10.4018/978-1-6684-5058-1.ch008

INTRODUCTION

While nanoparticle synthesis and organization are useful resources for nanotechnology, processing nanoparticles or nanopowders into bulk shapes while maintaining their nanosized is a difficult task in structural and engineering applications. Nanoparticle synthesis and assembly methods typically use liquid, solid, or gas phase precursors, chemical or physical deposition techniques, and chemical reactivity or physical compaction to incorporate the nanostructure building blocks into the final material framework (Jalali et al., 2014). The bottom-up approach to nanomaterials synthesis begins with the development of nanostructured building blocks (nanoparticles), which are then assembled into the final substance. The formulation of powder components using aerosol and sol-gel methods, followed by compaction of the components into the final substance, is an example of this method. These techniques can process nanoparticles with diameters varying from 1 nm to 10 nm, a stable crystal structure, surface derivatization, and a high degree of monodispersity (Chen et al., 2012). The production of nanoparticles in the gas phase, also known as aerosol processing, is focused on evaporation and condensation (nucleation and growth) in a sub atmospheric inert gas atmosphere, with processing methods like combustion burn, laser ablation, chemical vapor condensation, spray pyrolysis, electro spray, and plasma spray. Sol-gel production, on the other hand, is a wet chemical synthesis method that involves gelation, precipitation, and hydrothermal treatment to produce nanoparticles. Inverted micelles, polymer-matrix architecture based on block copolymers or polymer blends, and ex situ particle-capping techniques may also help monitor the size and stiffness of nanoparticles (Ali et al., 2021). Sonochemical deposition, hydrodynamic cavitation, and microemulsion processing are several other nanoparticle synthesis techniques. An acoustic cavitation is a form of acoustic cavitation that occurs in sonochemistry.

Huang et al. (2021) studied a temporary localized hot zone with extremely high temperature gradient and pressure can be created by the operation. The degradation of the sonochemical precursor (e.g., organometallic solution) and the production of nanoparticles are aided by certain abrupt temperature and pressure shifts. The method may be used to make a huge amount of content for commercial purposes. Nanoparticles are generated by hydrodynamic cavitation, which involves the formation and release of gas bubbles inside a sol-gel solution (Polachan et al., 2021). The solgel was quickly pressurized in a supercritical drying chamber and exposed to cavitation disruption and high temperature heating (Meisak et al., 2021). The approach has been combined. The nucleation, formation, and quenching of nanoparticles are all caused by the erupted hydrodynamic bubble (Zheng et al., 2012). The cavitation chamber's pressure and solution retention period may be adjusted to monitor particle size. Another critical processing method is microemulsions, which are widely used for the synthesis of metallic, semiconductor, and magnetic nanoparticles (Zheng et al., 2010). This microemulsions are generated spontaneously without the need for substantial mechanical agitation by regulating the very low interfacial tension (10.3 mN/m) by applying a cosurfactant (e.g., an intermediate chain length alcohol). The method may be used to mass-produce nanoparticles on a wide scale with reasonably low-cost hardware (Swekis et al., 2021). The top-down strategy starts with a good starting content and then sculpts features out of it. This method is close to how the semiconductor industry creates devices out of an electronic substrate (silicon) by using pattern formulation (such as electron beam lithography) and pattern-transfer processes (such as reactive-ion etching) with the necessary spatial resolution to create nanoscale structures (Thanner and Eibelhuber, 2021). This field of nanostructure formation has a lot of potential and is a major concern for the electronics industry.

One thousand millionth of a metre is a nanometre (nm). A single human hair is about 80,000 nanometers large, a red blood cell is about 7,000 nanometers wide, and a water molecule is about 0.3 nanometers wide. People are interested in the nanoscale (which we describe as being about 100nm and the size of atoms (approximately 0.2nm) since the properties of materials at this scale will vary dramatically from those at larger scales. We characterize nanoscience as the analysis of phenomena and modification of materials at the atomic, chemical, and macromolecular scales, where properties vary dramatically from those at larger scales; and nanotechnologies as the nature, characterization, processing, and deployment of structures, machines, and systems at the nanometer scale by manipulating form and size. Nanoscience and nanotechnologies are not recent in several ways. For decades, chemists have been creating polymers, which are huge molecules made up of nanoscale subunits, and for the last 20 years, nanotechnologies have been used to produce the minuscule features on computer chips (Pillai et al., 1995). However, developments in instruments that now enable atoms and molecules to be analyzed and probed with extreme precision have enabled nanoscience and nanotechnology to expand and evolve.

NANOMATERIALS

Materials may have various properties at the nanoscale for two purposes (Saravanan, Alam, and Mathur, 2003). First, as opposed to the same mass of material formed in a larger form, nanomaterials have a larger surface area. This will change the chemical reactivity of materials (in certain situations, materials that are inert in their larger form become reactive when manufactured at the nanoscale), as well as their strength and electrical properties. Second, quantum effects will start to control matter's behavior at the nanoscale, particularly at the lower end, influencing materials' optical, electrical, and magnetic properties. Nanoscale materials may be made in one dimension (for example, very thin surface coatings), two dimensions (for example, nanowires and nanotubes), or all three dimensions (for example, nanowires and nanotubes) (for example, nanoparticles).

Wang et al. (2021) found most nanotechnologies and all of nanoscience are concerned with developing new or improved materials. Nanomaterials may be created using 'top down' methods, such as etching to generate circuits on the surface of a silicon microchip, to produce very tiny structures from larger pieces of material. They may also be designed from the ground up, atom by atom or molecule by molecule. Self-assembly is one method for accomplishing this, in which atoms or molecules assemble themselves into a configuration based on their natural properties. Crystals grown for the semiconductor industry, as well as chemical synthesis of massive molecules, are examples of self-assembly. A second option is to use instruments to independently transfer each atom or molecule (Zarinwall et al., 2021). While this kind of 'positional assembly' allows for more flexibility over the construction process, it is currently too time-consuming for commercial use. Nanoscale materials are already used in sensors and active structures, for example, as extremely thin coatings (for example, self-cleaning windows). Many nanoscale components will be fixed or integrated in most applications, although others, such as those used in cosmetics and some pilot environmental remediation applications, will use free nanoparticles.

The capacity to manufacture materials to extremely high precision and accuracy (better than 100nm) has significant benefits in a variety of industries, including the manufacturing of components for the information and communication technology (ICT), automobile, and aerospace industries, to name a few. While it is difficult to forecast the timing of advances, we believe that nanomaterials can improve efficiency in a variety of products in the coming years, including silicon-based devices, screens, paints, batteries, micro-machined silicon sensors, and catalysts. We can see composites in the future that take advantage of the properties of carbon nanotubes, which are incredibly powerful and lightweight and may conduct electricity (Fresegna et al., 2021). Carbon nanotubes are rolls of carbon with one or two walls, weighing a few nanometers in diameter and up to a few centimeters in total. The challenge of manufacturing these tubes in a standardized fashion and sorting them into individual nanotubes currently limits their applications. We may also see inorganic nanosphere-based lubricants, nanocrystalline grain-based magnetic products, nanoceramics for more stable and safer surgical prosthetics, vehicle parts or high-temperature furnaces, and nanoengineered membranes for more energy-efficient water purification. Since it enables the characterization of products in terms of measurements as well as characteristics such as electrical properties and density, metrology, the science of measuring, underpins many other nanoscience and nanotechnologies. Nanoscience and nanotechnologies can benefit from increased metrology accuracy.

Nanotechnology applications in medicine are very interesting, and fields such as cancer detection, medication distribution aimed at precise locations in the body, and molecular imaging are now being researched extensively, with several drugs now undergoing clinical trials. The prefix 'nano' comes from the Greek word 'dwarf.' One billionth of a meter (10–9m) is equivalent to one nanometer (nm). The width of a human hair is approximately 80,000nm, and the width of a red blood cell is approximately 7000nm. Atoms are smaller than a nanometer, while certain compounds, like certain proteins, are larger than a nanometer. The size range that has sparked so much attention is usually from 100nm down to the atomic level (approximately 0.2 nm), since materials may have different or improved properties in this range (particularly at the lower end) as opposed to the same materials at a larger size. An expanded relative surface area and the domination of quantum effects are the two major causes of this shift in behavior. Since an improvement in surface area (per unit mass) leads to an improvement in chemical reactivity, certain nanomaterials may be used as catalysts to enhance fuel cell and battery production. Quantum effects can begin to play a part when the size of matter is decreased to tens of nanometers or smaller, and this can greatly alter a material's optical, magnetic, or electrical properties. Size-dependent properties have been used for decades in certain ways. Since the 10th century AD, gold and silver nanoparticles (particles with a diameter smaller than 100 nm) have been used as colored pigments in stained glass and ceramics. Gold particles may be red, blue, or gold in color, depending on their scale. Making all nanoparticles the same size (and therefore the same color) was a problem for ancient (al)chemists and producing single-size nanoparticles is still a challenge today.

Other factors, such as surface tension or "stickiness," play a role at the greater end of our size spectrum, affecting physical and chemical properties. Brownian motion, which explains the spontaneous movement of larger particles or molecules due to bombardment by smaller molecules and atoms, is often significant in liquid or gaseous settings. Individual atoms or molecules in these conditions are incredibly difficult to manipulate due to this impact. Nanoscience is concerned with determining these consequences and their impact on material resources. Nanotechnologies want to take advantage of these effects in order to construct materials, machines, and systems with novel properties and functions as a result of their small scale. Nanoscience and nanotechnologies are not recent in several ways. For decades, chemists have been creating polymers, huge molecules made up of tiny nanoscalar subunits. Over the past 20 years, nanotechnologies have been used to build the minuscule features on computer chips. From milk (a nanoscale colloid) to complex nanosized and nanostructured proteins, the natural universe includes numerous representations of nanoscale structures.

We divided nanomaterials, nanometrology, optics, optoelectronics, and knowledge and communication technology, and bio-nanotechnology and nanomedicine into four different categories since nanoscience and nanotechnologies span such a broad variety of fields (from chemistry, physics, and biology to medicine, engineering, and electronics). This division aids in distinguishing between advancements in various fields, though some convergence is unavoidable. We categorize potential application growth into three categories: short term (under 5 years), medium term (5–15 years), and long term (over 15 years) (over 20years). Any of the possible applications that we identify will never be realized, whereas others that are actually unknown may have a significant effect. We still see promise in terms of environmental, health and safety, ethical or social consequences, or complexities, which would be addressed in more detail in subsequent chapters.

SOURCE OF NANOMATERIALS

The ability to manipulate the shape of materials at smaller and smaller scales has been a central factor in the invention of new and better materials, from the steels of the nineteenth century to the advanced materials of today. The micro- and nanoscale composition of products as varied as paints and silicon chips determines their ultimate properties. As our knowledge of nanoscale materials and our capacity to manipulate their structure increases, there will be further opportunities to develop materials with novel properties, functions, and applications. We classify nanomaterials as those with structured components with at least one dimension smaller than 100nm, which is a general concept. Layers, such as thin films or surface coatings, have one dimension in the nanoscale (and are expanded in the other two dimensions). This category includes some of the features used on computer chips. Nanowires and nanotubes are two-dimensional nanoscale materials that can be expanded in one dimension. Particles, such as precipitates, colloids, and quantum dots, are nanoscale structures in three dimensions (tiny particles of semiconductor materials). This group also includes nanocrystalline products, which are made up of nanometer-sized grains. Many of these resources have been around for a and, while others are brand fresh. The aim of this chapter is to provide a summary of the properties of several primary nanomaterials as well as their important future applications.

Nanomaterials' properties vary greatly from those of other products due to two main factors: enhanced relative surface area and quantum effects. Properties including reactivity, power, and electrical characteristics may be altered or improved by these influences. A larger proportion of atoms are present at the surface of a particle when it shrinks in bulk, relative to those within. For example, a particle with a diameter of 30 nm has 5% of its atoms on its surface, a particle with a diameter of 10 nm has 20% of its atoms on its surface, and a particle with a diameter of 3 nm has 50% of its atoms on its surface. In comparison to bigger objects, nanoparticles have a much larger surface region per unit mass. Since growth and catalytic chemical reactions take place at surfaces, a given mass of material in nanoparticulate shape would be much more reactive than a similar mass of material made up of larger particles.

Quantum effects will begin to overpower the properties of matter when size is reduced to the nanoscale, in parallel with surface-area effects. These can have an impact on a material's optical, electrical, and magnetic properties, particularly when the structure or particle size reaches the nanoscale. Quantum dots and quantum well lasers for optoelectronics are examples of materials that take advantage of these results. Most products, such as crystalline solids, have a much larger surface region within the substrate as the scale of their structural elements decreases; this may have a significant impact on both mechanical and electrical properties. Many metals, for example, are made up of tiny crystalline grains; as the substance is strained, the boundaries between the grains slow or stop the proliferation of defects, granting it strength. The interface region inside the substance will be massively increased if these grains can be rendered very tiny, or even nanoscale in dimension. Nanoparticles are objects with a diameter of less than 100 nanometers. Nanoparticles are particles less than 100nm in diameter that show new or improved size-dependent properties as compared to larger particles with the same substance, according to our concepts of nanoscience and nanotechnologies. Nanoparticles are abundant in nature, for example, as products of photochemical and volcanic activity, as well as those generated by plants and algae. They've also been generated for thousands of years as a result of combustion and food preparation, as well as more recently from car exhaust. Metal oxides, for example, are intentionally engineered nanoparticles that are in the minority. Natural, pollutant, and engineered nanoparticles will be referred to as such in this study.

Shortly after CNTs, inorganic nanotubes and inorganic fullerene-like materials based on layered compounds like molybdenum disulphide were discovered. They have outstanding tribological (lubricating) properties, shockwave tolerance, catalytic reactivity, and strong hydrogen and lithium storage power, indicating a wide variety of potential applications. The use of oxide-based nanotubes (such as titanium dioxide) in catalysis, photocatalysis, and energy storage is being investigated. Nanowires are self-assembled ultrafine wires or linear pairs of dots. They may be constructed out of a variety of different products. Silicon, gallium nitride, and indium phosphide semiconductor nanowires have shown extraordinary electrical, mechanical, and magnetic properties (for example, silica nanowires can bend light around very tight corners). Nanowires could be used in high-density data storage as magnetic read heads or patterned storage media, as well as in electronic and opto-electronic nanodevices for metallic interconnects in quantum devices and nanodevices. Self-assembly methods, in which atoms spontaneously assemble themselves on stepped surfaces, chemical vapor deposition (CVD) onto patterned substrates, electroplating, and molecular beam epitaxy are among the advanced growth techniques used to create these nanowires (MBE). The 'molecular beams' are typically derived from elemental sources that have been thermally evaporated.

Biopolymers, such as DNA molecules, provide a lot of variability and site identification, which opens up a lot of possibilities for wire nanostructures to self-organize into even more complicated patterns. The DNA backbones could then be covered in copper, for example. They also have opportunities to combine nanotechnology and biotechnology in biocompatible sensors and lightweight, basic motors, for example. Organic backbone nanostructure self-assembly is often dominated by poor interactions, such as hydrogen bonds, hydrophobic, or van der Waals interactions (generally in aqueous environments), and therefore necessitates synthesis techniques that are very different from CNTs, for example. The combination of biopolymers and inorganic compounds in one-dimensional nanostructures opens up a slew of science and technical possibilities. Coatings with nano- or atomic-scale thickness modulation have been in use for a while, for example in MBE or metal oxide CVD for optoelectronic applications, or in catalytically active and chemically functionalized surfaces. The self-cleaning windshield, which is coated in highly active titanium dioxide and designed to be highly hydrophobic (water repellent) and antibacterial, as well as coatings based on nanoparticulate oxides that catalytically degrade chemical agents, are examples of recently established applications. Nanoscale intermediate layers (or multilayers) between the rigid outer layer and the base content greatly increase the wear and tear resistance of hard coatings. The intermediate layers improve adhesion by providing strong bonding and graded balancing of elastic and thermal properties. Improved regulation of porosity at the nanoscale and surface roughness in a variety of polymers and inorganics has allowed a number of enhanced textiles, including breathable, durable, and stain resistant fabrics.

CNTs have outstanding mechanical properties, including high tensile strength and low weight. Nanotube-reinforced composites will be an obvious application, with results superior to existing carbon-fiber composites. The challenge of structuring the tangle of nanotubes in a well-ordered way such that their power can be used is currently a barrier to CNTs being used in composites. Another difficulty is achieving solid bonding between CNTs and the matrix, which is essential for good overall composite efficiency and retention during wear or corrosion. Since CNTs have smooth, non-reactive surfaces, they appear to slide through the matrix while it is strained. Attaching chemical side-groups to CNTs, essentially becoming "anchors," is one method being investigated to avoid this slippage. Another stumbling block is the cost of CNT processing. However, the possible advantages of such a light, high-strength material in a variety of transportation applications warrant further investigation.

Data storage is another use for nanoscale-fabricated magnetic materials. Computer hard disks, for example, rely on the ability to magnetize tiny parts of a rotating disk to record data. If the region used to store one piece of information can be reduced to the nanoscale (and efficiently written and read), the disk's storage capacity can be greatly increased. The magnetic properties of these electrons, known as spin, may be used in the future to benefit devices on computer chips that already work using electron flows. In this regard, recent developments in novel magnetic materials and their nanofabrication are promising. Different hybridization states (sp, sp2, sp3) enable reactive carbon atoms to form direct covalent bonds with other carbon elements, resulting in a broad variety of carbon nanostructures such as 0D fullerene, 1D CNT and CNF, 2D GFM, and 3D carbon superstructures. Carbon nanostructures have a wide range of properties due to their varying sizes and crystallinity, implying that their future uses in wastewater treatment will be diverse. Carbon nanostructures have various surface energies depending on their scale (from bulk to nano state), which dictate their stiffness and adhesion energy. Knowing the aggregation and dispersibility of carbon nanostructures in water requires an appreciation of these energies. However, through combining 0D, 1D, and 2D carbon nanostructures, effective hybrid NMs-based water purification technologies (e.g., carbon aerogels, thin films, etc.) can be developed. Because of their well-defined pore structures and surface flexibility that promote complex surface reactions, CNTs are more common in wastewater treatment than other carbon nanostructures.

Nanomaterials and nano-manufactured products are rapidly growing fields of scientific study and industrial use. They are now a part of the manufacturing and economic landscape. The launch of these new goods, including those of other manufacturing industries, should be viewed in terms of their pollution and ecotoxicity impacts, in order to assess and monitor the social implications that environmental and health issues may have.

NANOTECHNOLOGY

Nanotechnology may be used to track and remove a variety of toxins in wastewater treatment. Since heavy metal contamination is harmful to living species, including humans, and is not biodegradable, it presents a significant danger to the atmosphere. Photocatalysis, Nanofiltration, Adsorption, and Electrochemical oxidation are only a few of the technologies that use TiO2, ZnO, ceramic membranes, nanowire membranes, polymer membranes, carbon nanotubes, submicron nanopowder, metal (oxides), magnetic nanoparticles, and nanostructured boron doped diamond to fix or significantly reduce water quality issues in the natural world. When nanoparticles are used as adsorbents, nanosized zerovalent ions, or nanofiltration membranes, pollutants are removed from water, while nanoparticles used as catalysts for chemical or photochemical oxidation allow contaminants to be destroyed. Dendrimers, metal-containing nanoparticles, zeolites, and carbonaceous nanomaterials are the four classes of nanoscale materials that are being tested as usable materials for water purification by scientists. The following are the various categories of materials that are or may be used in nanotechnology-based wastewater treatment and purification.

Random hyperbranched polymers, dendrigraft polymers, dendrons, and dendrimers are all examples of dendrite polymers. They are symmetrical and spherical macromolecules with a thick shell made up of a nucleus, branching sites, and terminal groups that shape a well-defined surface. Dendrimers come in a variety of sizes, including cones, spheres, and discs, and vary in size from 2 to 20 nm. The reaction of many dendrons with a multifunctional center yields a dendrimer structure. More than a hundred different dendrimer families have been synthesized, with more than 1000 different chemical surface modifications recorded. The catalyst was discovered to be extremely active, magnetically re-extractable, and resistant to large organic solvent concentrations; nevertheless, it was discovered to be susceptible to heavy metals (Pb, Hg). Laser-induced degradation of zeolite LTA microparticles using a pulsed laser or hydrothermal activation of fly ash may be used to make zeolite nanoparticles. Zeolites are used as metal ion ion exchange media and as efficient sorbents for metal ion removal. Heavy metals such as Cr(III), Ni(II), Zn(II), Cu(II), and Cd(II) have recently been removed from metal electroplating and acid mine wastewaters using zeolites. Carbon-based nanoparticles serve as sorbents in aqueous solutions since they have a large potential and selectivity for organic solutes. Fullerenes/Buckyballs (Carbon 60, Carbon 20, Carbon 70); carbon nanotubes; nanodiamonds; nanowires are a few instances of carbonaceous nano particles. Buckyballs, ellipsoids, tubes (nanotubes), 1nm wires (nanowires), and hexagonal structures are all examples (nanodiamonds). They are highly thermally and electrically conductive. Carbon-based NMs are robust, have low reactivity, are completely made of carbon, and are powerful antioxidants. U (VI) adsorption was effectively evaluated on acid-treated, surface-modified CNTs with increased colloidal stability.

Nanosized silver, gold, palladium, and other metal nanoparticles are examples. Colloidal silver, spun silver, nanosilver powder, and polymeric silver are all examples of nanosilver (engineered) types. They range in size from 10 to 200 nanometers. They have high surface reactivity and good antimicrobial properties since they are made up of several atoms of silver in the form of silver ions. Medicine, water purification, and antimicrobial applications are all possible. They're used to make a broad range of commercial goods. Gold nanorods have been used for colorimetric low-concentration identification of polynucleotides such as cysteine and glutathione using nanomaterials. Antimicrobial agents based on copper and silver compounds have been used to treat coliform bacteria present in wastewater.

Gold nanoparticles coated with palladium are 2,200 times more efficient than palladium alone at separating tri-chloroethane (TCE) from groundwater. Nanoscale zero-valent iron (nZVI) emulsified zero-valent iron (EZVI), and bimetallic nanoscale particles are both examples of zero-valent metals (engineered) nanoparticles (BNPs). BNPs are made up of iron and a chemical catalyst (such as gold, nickel, palladium, or platinum).

Cadmium selenide (CdSe), cadmium telluride (CdTe), and zinc selenide are used to make Quantum Dots (Engineered) (ZnSe). Their scale varies between 10 and 50 nanometers. They have a reactive center that regulates the optical properties of the material. Metal structures for the heart include CdSe, CdTe, CdSeTe, ZnSe, InAs, or PbSe, whereas metal structures for the shield include CdS or ZnS. Engineered composite nanomaterials are produced by combining two separate nanomaterials or nanomaterials with nanosized clay. Nanomaterials mixed with synthetic polymers or resins may also be used to create them. They include multifunctional components with unique electrical, magnetic, mechanical, thermal, imaging, and catalytic properties. The key causes of an increase in wastewater volume are industrialization and population. These are also the primary places where clean water is needed on a regular basis. To ensure a continuous supply of water for the necessary uses, many approaches are used. Nanotechnology is now being seen as a method of pollution remediation that is both cost-effective and environmentally safe. Nanoparticles of various sizes, metal oxides, zerovalent ions, and nanofiltration membranes have all been shown to be involved in the identification, removal, and/or destruction of pollutants. The word 'nano' is a prefix in science that means one billionth of a millionth of a millionth of a millionth of a millionth of a millionth of a (using billion in its American sense of a one followed by nine zeros). As a result, a 'nanometer' is one billionth of a meter and is very thin – only 10 atoms wide. Nanotechnology applies to innovations that operate at the nanometer scale which, as such, includes both a) manufacturing processes for items with nano-scale characteristics and b) nanomaterials generated in some way. In the field of modern electronics, both aspects are significant.

Transition metals, graphene, carbon (carbon nanotubes, fullerenes), and metal oxides make up the majority of nanoparticles currently in usage (zinc oxide and titanium dioxide). Engineered nanoparticles are often found as nanocrystals made up of a variety of substances such as silicon and metals (as is the case for quantum dots). While scientists are now researching a modern technique focused on self-assembly of atoms and molecules, the so-called "bottom up" approach, the current process used in the production of electronic devices is known as "top down" (i.e., manufacturing nanoscale parts and materials from larger starting materials). Quantum dots are semiconductor nanocrystals with unusual optical and electrical properties that range in size from 2 to 100 nm. Quantum dots are made up of a metalloid crystalline nucleus and a 'cap' or 'shell' that protects it. Metal conductors such as semiconductors, noble metals, and magnetic transition metals may be used to make quantum dot cores. The shells are made of a number of materials as well. As a result, quantum dots are not exactly the same, and they cannot be called a homogeneous set of substances.

CONCLUSION

In recent studies, nanomaterials and nanotechnologies have gotten a lot of coverage. With the advancement in nanoscience, new physical properties and developments in sample processing and product fabrication emerge. This study involves physicists, chemists, material scientists, and mechanical and electrical engineers from various disciplines. Various methods of processing nanomaterials, such as insulators, semiconductors, and metals, are addressed in this study. We describe the unusual physical properties of linear and nonlinear optical spectra, resistivity temperature dependency, spin resonance spectra, and magnetic susceptibility measurements. Quantum tunneling, quantum phase transformation, surface effect, quantum size-effect trapping, and nonlinear susceptibility improvements have also yielded a slew of interesting and provocative findings.

REFERENCES

Ali, N., Bahman, A. M., Aljuwayhel, N. F., Ebrahim, S. A., Mukherjee, S., & Alsayegh, A. (2021). Carbon-based nanofluids and their advances towards heat transfer applications—A review. *Nanomaterials (Basel, Switzerland)*, *11*(6), 1628. doi:10.3390/nano11061628 PMID:34205801

Chen, C. Y., Zhu, G., Hu, Y., Yu, J. W., Song, J., Cheng, K. Y., Peng, L.-H., Chou, L.-J., & Wang, Z. L. (2012). Gallium nitride nanowire based nanogenerators and light-emitting diodes. *ACS Nano*, *6*(6), 5687–5692. doi:10.1021/nn301814w PMID:22607154

Fresegna, A. M., Ursini, C. L., Ciervo, A., Maiello, R., Casciardi, S., Iavicoli, S., & Cavallo, D. (2021). Assessment of the influence of crystalline form on cyto-genotoxic and inflammatory effects induced by TiO2 nanoparticles on human bronchial and alveolar cells. *Nanomaterials (Basel, Switzerland)*, *11*(1), 253. doi:10.3390/nano11010253 PMID:33478013

Huang, L., Wan, K., Yan, J., Wang, L., Li, Q., Chen, H., Zhang, H., & Xiao, T. (2021). Nanomaterials in Water Applications: Adsorbing Materials for Fluoride Removal. *Nanomaterials (Basel, Switzerland)*, *11*(7), 1866. doi:10.3390/nano11071866 PMID:34361252

Jalali, N., Woolliams, P., Stewart, M., Weaver, P. M., Cain, M. G., Dunn, S., & Briscoe, J. (2014). Improved performance of p–n junction-based ZnO nanogenerators through CuSCN-passivation of ZnO nanorods. *Journal of Materials Chemistry. A, Materials for Energy and Sustainability*, *2*(28), 10945–10951. doi:10.1039/c4ta01714e

Meisak, D., Macutkevic, J., Selskis, A., Kuzhir, P., & Banys, J. (2021). Dielectric relaxation spectroscopy and synergy effects in epoxy/MWCNT/Ni@C composites. *Nanomaterials (Basel, Switzerland)*, *11*(2), 555. doi:10.3390/nano11020555 PMID:33672334

Pillai, V., Kumar, P., Hou, M. J., Ayyub, P., & Shah, D. O. (1995). Preparation of nanoparticles of silver halides, superconductors and magnetic materials using water-in-oil microemulsions as nano-reactors. *Advances in Colloid and Interface Science*, *55*, 241–269. doi:10.1016/0001-8686(94)00227-4

Polachan, K., Chatterjee, B., Weigand, S., & Sen, S. (2021). Human body–electrode interfaces for wide-frequency sensing and communication: A review. *Nanomaterials (Basel, Switzerland)*, *11*(8), 2152. doi:10.3390/nano11082152 PMID:34443980

Saravanan, P., Alam, S., & Mathur, G. N. (2003). Comparative study on the synthesis of γ-Fe2O3 and Fe3O4 nanocrystals using high-temperature solution-phase technique. *Journal of Materials Science Letters*, *22*(18), 1283–1285. doi:10.1023/A:1025470405000

Swekis, P., Sukhanov, A. S., Chen, Y. C., Gloskovskii, A., Fecher, G. H., Panagiotopoulos, I., Sichelschmidt, J., Ukleev, V., Devishvili, A., Vorobiev, A., Inosov, D. S., Goennenwein, S. T. B., Felser, C., & Markou, A. (2021). Magnetic and Electronic Properties of Weyl Semimetal Co2MnGa Thin Films. *Nanomaterials (Basel, Switzerland)*, *11*(1), 251. doi:10.3390/nano11010251 PMID:33477868

Thanner, C., & Eibelhuber, M. (2021). UV nanoimprint lithography: Geometrical impact on filling properties of nanoscale patterns. *Nanomaterials (Basel, Switzerland)*, *11*(3), 822. doi:10.3390/nano11030822 PMID:33806976

Wang, Q., Kuang, K., Gao, H., Chu, S., Yu, L., & Peng, W. (2021). Electromagnetically induced transparency-like effect by dark-dark mode coupling. *Nanomaterials (Basel, Switzerland)*, *11*(5), 1350. doi:10.3390/nano11051350 PMID:34065485

Zarinwall, A., Asadian-Birjand, M., Seleci, D. A., Maurer, V., Trautner, A., Garnweitner, G., & Fuchs, H. (2021). Magnetic Nanoparticle-Based Dianthin Targeting for Controlled Drug Release Using the Endosomal Escape Enhancer SO1861. *Nanomaterials (Basel, Switzerland)*, *11*(4), 1057. doi:10.3390/nano11041057 PMID:33924180

Zheng, Q., Luo, J., Luo, G., Ma, J., Xu, M., & Yao, H. (2010). Experimental study on adsorption of elemental mercury by liquid bromine-modified non-carbon-based adsorbent. [液溴改性非碳基吸附剂吸附元素汞的实验研究]. *Chinese Journal of Engineering Thermophysics*, (12), 2137–2140.

Zheng, Y., Jensen, A. D., Windelin, C., & Jensen, F. (2012). Review of technologies for mercury removal from flue gas from cement production processes. *Progress in Energy and Combustion Science*, *38*(5), 599–629. doi:10.1016/j.pecs.2012.05.001

Chapter 9
Recent Trends in Microstrip Patch Antenna Using Textile Applications

Kannadhasan S.
https://orcid.org/0000-0001-6443-9993
Study College of Engineering, Coimbatore, India

Nagarajan R.
https://orcid.org/0000-0002-4990-5869
Gnanamani College of Technology, India

Kanagaraj Venusamy
https://orcid.org/0000-0001-9479-8073
Rajalakshmi Engineering College, Chennai, India

ABSTRACT

Wireless body area networks (WBANs) have gotten a lot of interest as the need for wearable gadgets like smart watches, eyewear, and clothing grows. WBAN applications need the use of a conformal antenna. A low-profile IR-UWB antenna and an all-textile higher order mode circular patch antenna for omnidirectional radiation were used to meet this need. To achieve maximum power output, researchers need to maintain the antenna's efficiency as high as feasible while designing a lightweight antenna for wireless power transfer. The need for tiny textile antennas with high gain and broadband features has risen in response to the fast growth of wireless power transfer. Microstrip patch antennas provide a number of advantages, including a cheap cost, a low profile, a light weight, and a simple manufacturing method. Increases in substrate thickness, antenna efficiency, use of a low dielectric substrate, and different impedance matching and feeding techniques are all examples of ways to enhance antenna bandwidth.

DOI: 10.4018/978-1-6684-5058-1.ch009

INTRODUCTION

This document explains how to make a basic micro strip antenna (Balanis, 2015). Patch is used for the suggested antenna, and copper self-adhesive tape is used for the ground. The simulation results are shown, including the reflection coefficient, gain, and efficiency. Wearable computer system technology is rapidly evolving in order to improve the quality and efficiency of human existence by offering a flexible mobile system. A wearable system's use, functionality, durability, safety, and comfort have all become critical requirements. Health monitoring activities in the medical field, surveillance in military units, and sickness prevention and citizen medicine in the healthcare sector have all been established using the intelligent clothing, transmission of information, and communication system. Portable electronic gadgets have become an integral aspect of modern life. Modern mobile phones are often carried throughout the day, and they may be used for more than simply making phone conversations; they can also be used for internet access, multimedia, a personal digital assistant, and GPS navigation. This kind of "always on" and "always connected" state is a first step toward the ubiquitous computing paradigm. A person will likely carry a variety of gadgets and sensors in the future, including medical sensors, that are continually communicating with each other and the outside environment. It is critical to deliver this functionality in the least intrusive manner feasible. Wearable electronics and antennas are a critical technology for achieving this objective. The 2.45 GHz ISM unlicensed band is used for the development of wearable antennas because to its almost universal availability. Wearable antennas must be concealed and have a low profile for the user's comfort (DicCbshfsE et al., 2011; Kumar Singh et al., 2014).

This necessitates the antenna components' probable incorporation into daily apparel. Because it can be made conformal for incorporation into clothes, the microstrip patch is a good contender for any wearable application. In this publication, the authors report the design, development, and evaluation of flexible rectangle shaped microstrip wearable antennas for Bluetooth applications, which is similar to their prior research on circular disc antennas. In this study, four antennas are studied; antenna 1 uses wash cotton (textile material used in Bermuda manufacturing) fabric as its dielectric material, whereas antenna 2 uses curtain cotton fabric. The dielectric materials utilized in antennas 3 and 4 are polyester and polyester mixed cotton (65:35) fabric fabrics. Copper is used for the conducting portions in all four examples (Salonen and Rahmat-Samii, 2006; Kannadhasan and Nagarajan, 2022).

When these individual wearable antennas are held in the °at position, theoretical and experimental data on impedance characteristics are provided. For the purpose of studying radiation properties, antennas 1, 2, and 3 are evaluated. In an on-body setting, however, it is difficult to maintain the wearable antenna straight all of the time, as it bends often owing to body motions. As the antenna's resonant length changes, the bending may change its performance characteristics. As a result, an experimental research using at least one of the antennas (antenna 3) is carried out to explore the effects of antenna bending on performance attributes such as resonant frequency, return loss, impedance bandwidth, gain, and radiation patterns. Characteristics were investigated. The global positioning system (GPS) is a satellite-based navigation system that gives position and timing data at outdoor locations. GPS communication, on the other hand, is unable to offer service at an inside site. As a result, RFID communication must be employed to transmit GPS data in indoor locations. In this research, an all-textile antenna for GPS and RFID applications is incorporated into a military beret. Dual modes are used by the planned all-textile antenna, which has two ports (Hearle and Morton, 2008; Gupta, Sankaralingam, and Dhar, 2010). A ring patch with four shoring pins is meant for RFID applications with a monopole-like radiation characteristic at 915MHz, whereas a truncated patch is suited for GPS applications with a broadside radiation pattern with LHCP at 1.575GHz.

WEARBLE ANTENNA

Due to the fast advancement of wireless communication technology, wearable gadgets now have a significant influence in the area of communication. A wearable device's textile antenna is an essential component. Many wearable device researchers concentrate their efforts on the creation of textile antennas. Textiles are related with UWB technology, and a UWB antenna is constructed, simulated in HFSS, manufactured, and evaluated using a vector network analyzer. This wearable antenna connects to communication systems in smart clothing, which deliver real-time health information to patients. Wearable antennas that can be embedded into garments have gotten a lot of interest in recent years.

The performance and uses of the textile antenna for real-time applications have been documented by a number of writers. Varied feed lines, such as microstrip line, coplanar waveguide (CPW), and different forms, such as the crescent patch, have been explored and utilized in many kinds of UWB microstrip antennas. Wearable microchip technology must be lightweight, flexible, compact in size, economical, able to endure harm from impediments (robust), and easy to wear, according to the additional pointer. With the progress of communication technology, UWB antennas have attracted more and more attention since the Federal Communications Commission (FCC) permitted the commercial use of frequency bands from 3.1 to 10.6 GHz for Ultra-wideband (UWB) systems in 2002. The unique characteristics of UWB antennas, such as their low profile, cheap cost, and excellent radiation qualities, as well as their small size, increased the possibilities for shrinking the size of wearable devices and thereby simplifying the production process.

An insulating textile substrate is bonded with a conducting a thin copper plate as a ground and antenna patch to create a body wearing textile antenna. The patch antenna operating at a UWB frequency band is designed using four different substrate materials in this article. We present a Trident form planar microstrip antenna based on a mix of semicircular and triangular patches in this paper. The radiator radiates the incident energy throughout an ultra-wide frequency range as a result of the combination of these two. The proposed antenna's simulated and measured return loss is provided. When compared to a traditional structure, the return loss curve shows that this suggested construction achieves a high impedance and gain. The parametric substrate research is used to examine and display the features of the proposed antenna.

Because of the diverse uses of such devices in personal communication systems, research on body-centric wireless communication and wearable devices has exploded in recent years. Eldercare, medical crises, firefighting, military uses, and athlete tracking may all benefit from smart gear (Ouyang and Chappell, 2008). Printed circuit boards (PCBs) are used to make antennas in the past, but they are rigid, difficult to wear, and cannot be washed. Furthermore, the antennas on portable devices have a relatively restricted design area, resulting in performance limitations. Flectron, Shieldex, REMP, Shintron, and other metalized cloth products were commercially available. Textile antennas using metalized fabric are flexible, washable, and may be arranged in arrays to increase gain. The latest varieties of textile antennas were explored in, as well as the appropriate material selection, manufacturing processes, and analysis necessary for a wearable antenna design.

Permittivity and the loss tangent of a high-strength textile appropriate for military antenna applications were tested under varied temperature and humidity circumstances. A circular patch antenna for use in the WLAN band was constructed utilizing an indigo blue denim cotton fabric as the substrate. In addition, rectangular patch antennas made of taffeta and polyester have been created for use in the WLAN band. Under different bending circumstances, performance variances were assessed. Electrotextiles were used to make patchtype RF identification tag antennas for usage in the UHF band. A construction for a planar inverted-F antenna (PIFA)-type textile antenna that increases bandwidth while limiting frequency shift when it approaches a human body. Radiators were made from pure copper polyester taffeta and ShieldIt, and the substrate was prepared with a 6-mm fleece fabric. Under folding, heating, and wetting circumstances, a UWB wearable antenna was created employing liquid crystal polymer substrates with excellent performance in return loss and radiation pattern. Varactors were used to control nearby parasitic element antennas in a three-element antenna array controlled by a dipole (Nikhil, Singh, and Kumar, 2015). The horizontal sweeping angle of this antenna array was 95 degrees, with a peak gain of 6.9 dBi. A high-rigidity dual-band button antenna was built for usage at 2.4 and 5 GHz, and its radiation pattern was comparable to that of monopole antennas. Another dual-band textile antenna was presented. This antenna was made using a rectangular patch and a patch-etched slot dipole and was loaded with an artificial magnetic conductor (AMC) plane. The AMC was created with the goal of reducing substrate thickness and significantly reducing back radiation. Textile antennas with substrate-integrated waveguides (SIW) and other wearable circuitry made using copper tube eyelets have recently been created. SIW-on-textile integration yields an antenna with great bending resistance, little impact on the human body, and a high front-to-back ratio. The effects of human body posture on textile antenna coupling were investigated. With a pattern average difference of 24 percent, the chest had the most impact.

Since recent advancements in wearable computing have opened up various opportunities for integrating wireless functionalities into garments, flexible antennas are becoming more appealing (Ramadan et al., 2009). Wearable electronics and antennas are a critical technology for achieving this objective. One of the most exciting and cutting-edge study topics of the current period is textile antenna. Body-worn antennas should be inconspicuous and concealed. The topic of this research is a microstrip antenna built of textile material to maintain flexibility and comfort. This antenna features a flat, planar construction that makes it easy to wear. Because it is light and flexible, this antenna does not obstruct the wearer's mobility. A flat antenna surface is challenging to achieve with wearable antennas. As a result, the antenna should be built in such a way that it will function well even if it is bent often. Flexible antenna may be made from wearable substrates like cotton, denim, and leather. These antennas may be attached to the garment materials to make carrying them simpler (Malekpoor and Jam, 2013). Antennas made partially from conductive textile materials (also known as e-textiles) using traditional textile production processes. Antenna theorists and antenna producers are both paying greater attention to these strategies. Complete design flow and substrate material selection parameters will be included in the publication. The mathematical design for a standard Microstrip patch antenna should be followed when designing a wearable antenna.

An antenna is a radiating device that is used on both the sending and receiving ends of a communication system. The transmitting antenna takes electrical impulses from transmission lines and transforms them to radio waves, while the receiving antenna receives radio waves from space and converts them to corresponding electrical signals. Textile or cloth-based antennas have become standard in WLAN, Telemedicine, military, and navigation applications. In medical applications, the biggest disadvantage of antenna efficacy is its size, which makes the whole measurement apparatus larger and more difficult. A small microstrip antenna that can be stitched over dress material may be used to solve this issue. This microstrip antenna is used to monitor a patient in close proximity.

An antenna is a kind of transducer that transmits or receives electromagnetic waves. Microstrip antennas are being used in a broad range of industries and applications, and they are currently blooming in the commercial sector owing to the inexpensive cost of the substrate material and manufacturing. Microstrip antennas provide a number of benefits over traditional microwave antennas and are therefore frequently employed in a variety of applications. Microstrip patch antennas are well-known for their high performance, as well as their durable design, manufacture, and wide use. Microstrip antennas are intended to work with a variety of frequencies, including WLAN& Wi-Max, Bluetooth, Wi-Fi, WPAN, and X-band (Sun et al., 2012). Many Microstrip antennas are intended to function at X-band frequencies, according to the literature review. They have complicated structures from a fabrication standpoint. In this study, we present a Microstrip antenna with a basic construction that can function at X-band frequencies. This study proposes a square-shaped patch antenna with a resonance frequency of 9.6GHz for aeronautical radio navigation applications. The patch is made of Rogers RT Duroid 5880, which has a dielectric constant of 2.2 and a thickness of 0.8 mm. The total dimensions of the suggested antenna are 16mm*16mm*0.8mm. A lumped port is used to excite an antenna with a 50-ohm input characteristic impedance.

TEXTILE ANTENNA

Body-driven wireless communication has recently become a critical component of the fourth-generation mobile communication system (4G). The IEEE 802.15 institutionalization group was formed to institutionalize applications intended for on-body, off-body, or in-body communication in order to support the growing interest in antennas and to encourage research into body correspondence frameworks. Inside the circle of personal area networks (PANs) and body area networks, body-centric communication has an immovable place (BANs). One of the applications, on-body communications, depicts the connection between a body-worn device and a base unit or mobile device located in the surrounding environment, while off-body correspondence describes the radio connection between a body-worn device and a base unit or mobile device located in the surrounding environment. Finally, in-body communication is the exchange of information between distant medicinal inserts and on-body hubs.

Wearable, fabric-based Antennas are one of the most popular research topics in Antenna for body-driven interchanges. Wearable antenna requirements for all modern applications often include minimal weight, convenience, almost little support, and no setup. Paramedics, fire fighters, and military personnel are among the profession segments that use body-driven communication frameworks. Wearable Antenna may also be attached for youngsters, the elderly, and rivals for the purpose of watching. Outlining a textile antenna requires knowledge of electromagnetic characteristics as as permittivity and material misfortune digression. Conductive materials, such as Zelt, Flectron, and pure copper polyester fabric textiles, are often used as the emitting component, whereas non-conductive materials, such as silk, felt, and downy, are commonly used as substrates. These materials' magnetic characteristics are not immediately available. A transmission/reflection waveguide approach was used to measure the electromagnetic characteristics of various material substrates. The replication included essential permittivity and misfortune digression quality. In multi-functional wireless goods, the notion of combining dual- and multi-frequency antennas is popular because it efficiently decreases the needed number of components and the effectiveness of the hardware. Dual-frequency antennas, for example, may operate in a variety of operating bands and have distinct radiation characteristics to suit their applications. Meanwhile, circularly polarized (CP) antennas are useful in wireless communications because they enable signal reception regardless of the receiving antenna's orientation relative to the emitting antenna.

Multipath interference is therefore suppressed as a consequence of this. When linearly polarized antennas are in use, however, correct polarization alignment is required to enable effective signal transmission and reception. Meanwhile, designing dual- or multiband linearly polarized antennas is far easier than designing CP antennas that operate in several bands, making the former the preferable option for indoor localization. Circular polarization may be done in two ways: (1) by truncating the corners of the patch and (2) by creating a slit aligned with the patch's diagonal axis. A Green's function technique and the de-segmentation method were used in an examination of three distinct kinds of CP patch antennas. Circular polarization for conventional patch antennas has the maximum axial ratio bandwidth and may be accomplished using a square patch with a diagonal slit, whereas corner-truncated patches have the best axial ratio levels. To accomplish circular polarization, four asymmetric slits were added in the diagonal directions. A patch antenna with truncated corners and four slits was also built, with satisfactory matching and axial ratio at the operating frequency. Most notably, using such a strategy successfully reduced the antenna's size by 46%.

Many studies have been conducted in recent years to improve the operational safety and effectiveness of police, army, and rescue services. Wearable electronic devices, in particular, may considerably improve the utility of PRS clothes by allowing for sensing, localization, and wireless communication. Smart fabrics and interactive textiles (SFIT), which are unobtrusively integrated into garments, do not obstruct movement during interventions while continuously monitoring life signs, activities, and environmental conditions and wirelessly relaying this data to a remote location for supervision by the operations coordinator. Alarms and particular instructions may also be relayed back to each person in action in dangerous circumstances.

Because SFIT systems will be used in severe environments and during vital operations, the designers are concerned about their reliability and autonomy. The electronics must be very energy-efficient to allow adequate autonomy without the usage of hefty batteries. Textile antennas are crucial components in creating wireless communication networks since they use a lot of power, therefore they should ideally have a high gain and a high radiation efficiency.

Garments offer the area required to deploy antennas with these properties, and the use of a broad ground plane prevents antenna radiation from being absorbed by the human body. However, wearable antenna designers must take additional precautions to avoid antenna performance loss caused by the huge flexible textile antenna bending, wrinkling, and crumpling when the user moves about. Furthermore, to minimize high substrate losses owing to humidity trapped in the substrate fabric, a proper selection of materials is essential, and a TPU coating may be required to protect the antenna during washing.

Energy harvesters may be added to boost operational autonomy by scavenging energy from one or more energy sources present in the vicinity of the body, in addition to enhancing the SFIT system's power efficiency. We examine design solutions for integrating energy-efficient active wearable antennas with steady performance in professional clothes used during interventions in this contribution. We embed electronics on the planar textile antenna's feed plane, immediately below its ground plane, and install energy harvesters directly on the antenna plane to increase the active antenna modules' durability and autonomy. We describe the steps used to guarantee that the antenna's performance is not harmed as a result of the installation of these extra components.

Coal mines are one of the risky fields where different lethal elements threaten humans. Long-term harmful impacts on human health are caused by subsurface environmental conditions. Dust Density, Temperature, Gas Density, and Wind Speed are all critical characteristics. As a result, it's critical to keep an eye on the miners' health. Fitness trackers, smart watches, Biosensors, Brain sensing headbands, Bio scarves, Breathalyzers, Remote cardiac monitoring systems, and pain treatment gadgets are just a few of the health monitoring products on the market. Some of these devices may be worn directly on the body or attached to accessories like eyeglasses, belts, and shoes. Additional technological devices on employees' bodies may provide a distraction when working in fields. These employees' devices should be flexible and small enough to fit into any portion of their bodies. WBANs (Wireless Body Area Networks) are wearable, tiny devices that use computer technology to detect vital indicators in the human body. Health monitoring devices capture data from a person's body and send it to a Body Control Unit (BCU) using wireless communication networks including the Medical Implant Communication System (MICS), Wireless Medical Telemetry System (WMTS), and Ultra-Wide Band (UWB) 433MHz. BCU gathers data from a group of employees in a certain area and sends it to a distant monitoring station through wireless technologies like Bluetooth, ZigBee, and Wi-Fi. Textile antenna is one of the most complex advances in the realm of wearable technology.

Wearable antennas may be made of fabric or textile materials to give flexibility. The kind of substrate utilised affects the properties of the textile antenna, such as bandwidth, efficiency, and directivity. This work describes a flexible microstrip antenna for monitoring coal miners' health that operates at 2.45 GHz on a denim cotton substrate with a relative permittivity (r) of 1.67, a dissipation factor (tan) of 0.002, and a thickness of 3mm. Ansys HFSS 13.0 software was used to design and model the antenna, and the dimensions were computed using.

In recent study, wearable antennas have grown in popularity. Affluent body-centric communication mechanisms are prominent in culture, driving widespread use of wearable antennas. Wearable antennas are widely utilized because they are simple to install, light in weight, inexpensive, and need little maintenance. They are required in many occupational areas of real-time communication systems, such as health care, medical, time-critical systems, and mission-critical systems. They are also utilized in closed in-house systems for monitoring personalities, behavior growth, and so on. There are many prospective antenna types that might be used to create a wearable antenna. Preferably, PIFAs, micro strips, and planar monopoles outperform these categories, pre-fetching better compatibility for on-body wearable communication design and development.

Patch antennas are very useful for both on-body and off-body communication because of their modest profile. Antennas made of planar sheets are appropriate for fabrication utilizing traditional textile production methods. Furthermore, such an antenna's ground plane efficiently shelters the antenna from bodily tissues. This reduces both detuning and antenna efficiency loss. Circularly polarized patch antennas, on the other hand, are more susceptible to bending effects. For further investigation of circularly polarized textile antennas, a rectangular patch shape is used. This shape has been shown to be relatively resistant to bending effects.

Wireless communication technology is advancing research and playing an increasingly essential role in the development of new stereotypes and product prototypes, as well as the revision of Wireless Body Area Networks (WBANs). The living body is the WBAN's expanse, and it links the many electrical gadgets within with the human body. In the realms of medicine, national defense, and wearable computing, the need for WBAN applications is growing rapidly. WBANs use a variety of frequencies, including the Medical Implant Communication Systems (MICS: 400 MHz), the Industrial Scientifics

Medical (ISM: 2.4 GHz and 5.9 GHz), and the Ultra-Wideband (UWB: 3-10 GHz). WBAN applications that demand on military, omnipresent health care, sports, entertainment, and many others are grouped into two categories, according to IEEE 802.15.6: middle and non-medical.

Textiles provide a strong foundation for merging electronics and antennas to create smart textile systems. Because textile antennas are flexible and conformable to use in everyday life, they are an excellent choice. Smart textile antennas may be used to create a communication system that can be completely incorporated into many types of apparel. For example, one form of use for wearable antenna systems is to monitor activity and vital signs in order to protect and rescue personnel who are active in their area, with the electronics incorporated into protective textile antennas.

Creating a wireless communication connection between the user and the nearest base station off-body. Wearable intelligent smart textile systems are a rapidly expanding topic in the application-oriented sector. The creation of tiny, flexible, and intelligent smart antenna devices that may be placed on the human body or implanted within has been enabled by advancements in communication and electrical technologies. Hard dielectric substrate antennas with low profile and small area flexible antennas with felt or other textile substrates are two types of wearable smart textile antennas. The electrical performance and mechanical flexibility of these textile-based devices have been proven. However, the majority of electronic textiles that have been documented thus far are small metallic wires, metallic tapes embedded in clothing, or sputtered nanoparticles. The textile material utilized in this study is denim, which has a dielectric constant of 1.6 and a tangent loss of 0.0019, allowing the antenna to operate at 2.46 GHz with a return loss of -19.62 dB.

In ambulances, emergency rooms, operating theatres, postoperative recovery rooms, clinics, homes, and even on the move, wireless body area network (WBAN) technology has the potential to provide an unprecedented opportunity for ubiquitous real-time healthcare and fitness monitoring, such that many diseases could be prevented through early detection and doctors could give patients efficient advice on improving their health. In recent years, there has been growing worry regarding the safety of WBAN systems, especially wearable electronics, which may be used for medical, entertainment, or military purposes. The recent introduction of Body Area Networks (BAN) has piqued the attention of most academics in the area of wearable antennas. The majority of research has been done to increase the efficiency and flexibility of wearable antennas for in-body and on-body applications due to their broad appeal. Wearable antennas are antennas that operate close to the human body, absorbing part of the emitted energy and reducing the antenna's efficiency. Wearable antennas attached to the human body may communicate with one another or with an external antenna. Body Area Networks are the name for this form of network (BAN). On-body antennas are those that are mounted on the top of the human body and are usually used for medical purposes. In-body antennas are those that are implanted within the human body and are largely used for medical purposes.

Because the advent of BAN indicates that practically everyone will be a member of the network in the future, wearable antennas should be carefully built to accomplish all of the needed features when put near or within the human body. The availability of miniaturization of electronic equipment has boosted the need for wireless communication around the human body in the current day. Body Centric Communication is employed in a variety of applications, including telemedicine, battlegrounds, person tracking, and health monitoring for gamers. Textile antennas are utilized for Body Centric Communication. It facilitates both on- and off-body communication. The ground, patch, and substrate for microstrip antennas are constructed of conductive materials such as copper, while the substrate is built of dielectric materials such as FR4, RT/Duroid. Textile antennas, on the other hand, are composed of both conductive and non-conductive textiles. For ground, conductive clothing is utilised, as well as patches such as ShieldIt and Flectron. The substrate is made of non-conductive materials such as denim, felt, and Dacron. Textile antennas are employed for WBAN applications because, in comparison to traditional microstrip antennas, they are more comfortable and flexible to put on the human body. Wearable antennas are utilized extremely near to the human body in wearable applications. When the wearable antenna is near to the human body, it emits EM waves, which are more harmful to the human body's tissues. FCC guidelines require a SAR value of less than 1.6 Watts/kg (over 1g of tissue) while ICNIRP requires a value of less than 2 Watts/kg (over 10g of tissue). Previously, SAR could be reduced using a variety of strategies, including those suggested here. The multiband monopole antenna was created using a FR4 substrate and square form EBG cells, with a 1mm gap between the cells and a SAR value of less than 2W/kg. For SAR reduction, the PIFA antenna is built with Interdigitated and square form through EBG cells. To reduce SAR, the authors created a PIFA antenna with a strip-shaped Artificial Magnetic Conductor (AMC). Military applications aim to integrate these gadgets into military uniform to improve troop performance, awareness, and survival on the battlefield. Wearable textile antenna, especially when utilized in a sensor network, is critical for spotting wild animals in the forest. Bluetooth and WLAN are utilized for rescue and security communication.

The suggested wearable textile antenna for the ISM band has a resonance frequency of 2.45 GHz. The sole variation between the three antennas in terms of physical size and dimensions is the dielectric substrate material. For a resonance frequency of 2.45 GHz, the first suggested antenna patch is simulated using copper conducting material and leather dielectric substrate material. For a 2.45 GHz operating frequency, a second antenna patch with copper conducting material and silk dielectric substrate material is simulated. The third antenna patch is made of copper conductive material with nylon as the dielectric substrate, and it is modelled for a resonance frequency of 2.45 GHz. Fabric (or) textile material is used to make wearable textile antennas. The dielectric constant of these textile materials is relatively low, which lowers surface wave loss. Antenna impedance bandwidth may be increased by employing textiles. It was discovered that antennas may be created using common fabric materials at a minimal cost and readily integrated into fashion clothes. Cloth is integrated into the communication system through the wearable antenna. All wearable antennas are small, low-cost, and almost maintenance-free. The high dielectric constant of water causes a wearable antenna's performance to vary as it absorbs water. Textile antennas are designed for limited bandwidth applications and are not appropriate for ultra-wideband applications. A faulty ground construction is used to enhance bandwidth. The dielectric constant, moisture, temperature, loss tangents, thickness, conductivity, and deformation all affect the performance and features of the textile wearable antenna. The antenna should be stable and safe for the person's health when positioned near to the body for incorporation into the fabric. In this antenna, a denim textile with a dielectric constant of 1.6 is often utilized as the substrate. Textile antenna structures were tested in order to provide preliminary data on antenna performance. The antenna is constructed using a 1mm thick substrate. The return loss of the antenna is enhanced when DGS is used, as does the frequency selectivity. The fractal, dumbbell, circular, and L-shaped slots in the DGS design have a strong resonant nature, and the resonant frequency may be changed by altering the form of the slots. In compared to plane ground, DGS has the best fractional bandwidth and a substantial increase. One or more faults may be placed into the ground plane. To minimize harmonics and mutual interaction between components, flaws are added. presented a tiny strip filter with a small footprint. It features a low return loss, quick cut-off, and high insertion loss in the stop band, as well as a high return loss and low insertion loss in the pass band, which is the desirable attribute of an ideal micro strip low pass filter. The shield current distribution in the ground plane is disrupted by a flaw in the ground planar transmission line. The faulty ground is simple to set up, and the antenna area is lowered as well. When compared to a conventional antenna, the maximum antenna size was lowered by 59 percent with no reduction in antenna performance. Initially, DGS is used to construct filter antennas that are employed in a variety of applications.

The size of portable devices and wireless applications is shrinking as the number of devices and wireless apps grows. As a result, the space within a gadget becomes more important. Fundamental constraints define the requirements for successful antenna operation; hence it's understood that antenna shrinking reduces antenna performance. Taking the antenna out is sometimes a wise idea since even a downsized antenna is usually the biggest component of a portable device. Textile components are utilized to design wearable antennas for in- and on-Body Amount Networks (BAN), which are widely used and readily accessible. The antenna's layout is determined by the representation of their electric and electromagnetic properties. A wearable processor is constantly on, does not impose restrictions on the user's actions, and is aware of the user's surroundings. Fabric is assimilated into the communication system via the wearable antenna. Because of the rapid advancement of wireless communication technology, a growing number of experts are focusing their efforts on the research of wireless body area networks (WBANs). Several electronic policies in and on the social body are linked through WBAN. Integration of communication equipment into user apparel is generally acknowledged as a viable strategy for improving overall system performance. A high-performance circularly polarized antenna, for example, is likely too big to fit in a mobile phone but may be readily disguised within the sleeve of a jacket using current material combinations. Patch antennas are very useful for both on-body and off-body communication because of their modest profile. Antennas made of planar sheets are suited for use in the textile industry's traditional production methods. Furthermore, the antenna's ground plane efficiently protects the antenna from bodily tissues. This reduces detuning as well as antenna efficiency loss. Circularly polarized patch antennas, on the other hand, are more susceptible to bending effects. For a more in-depth look into circularly polarized textile antennas, a rectangular patch shape is used. This shape has been demonstrated to be quite resistant to bending effects.

WBANs are increasingly being used in medical services, national defense, and wearable computing, among other areas. The Medical Implant Communication System (MICS: 400 MHz) band, the Industrial Scientific Medical (ISM: 2.4 and 5.8 GHz) band, and the Ultrawideband (UWB: 3–10 GHz) band have all been allocated to WBAN systems. The IEEE 802.15.6 standard categorizes the large range of WBAN applications, including military, ubiquitous health care, sport, entertainment, and many more, into two key domains.

Natural and artificial fibers are the two kinds of textile materials utilized as antenna substrates. Because of their molecular structure, man-made fibers are classified as synthetic fibers. Many characteristics of wearable antennas contribute to the antennas' overall design qualities. The following are some features of textile materials: Moisture Absorption When a fabric antenna absorbs water, its performance characteristics vary substantially because water has a considerably higher dielectric constant than the fabric. The fibers are continually exchanging water molecules with the air, and their dynamic balance is affected by the temperature and humidity of the environment. The sensitivity of the fabric to moisture is measured by the ratio of the mass of absorbed water in the specimen to the mass of the dry specimen, represented as a percentage. The increased dielectric constant of water reduces the resonant frequency and bandwidth. Because fabric antennas are utilized so close to the skin, the issue of fabric dampness caused by human perspiration becomes increasingly critical. Wearable systems may also be put on top of jackets or suits if moisture issues have arisen as a result of rain or washing the textile materials. In addition to these effects, as textile fibers absorb water, they expand transversely and axially, causing textiles to tighten.

Because it can be constructed from textile substrate materials, the micro strip antenna is a better contender for wearable applications. Because textiles have a low dielectric constant (1 to 2), they may minimize surface wave losses and increase antenna bandwidth. The antenna may bend while moving or undertaking strenuous labor. The physical parameter of the antenna may vary if it is bent, and the antenna radiation parameter may also change if the physical parameter changes. The antenna in this study was developed and produced at a large scale. The textile antenna bends less the smaller it is. Copper antennas may be miniaturized using a variety of techniques. Work on the shrinking of textile antennas might be a future project. The tiny cloth antenna is less prone to bending, resulting in a steadier output from the antenna. One of the primary problems for the antenna built of textile material is to improve the radiation efficiency.

CONCLUSION

As a result, additional research may be done on this subject. Also, if performance degradation under wet circumstances is to be avoided, future wearable communication solutions should look at water-resistant materials. For any antenna design, the specific absorption rate (SAR) is a critical metric to monitor. Due to their near closeness to the body, SAR is potentially relevant for any wearable antenna. Wearable gadgets are not covered by any particular law; yet minimizing SAR is a logical design aim. As a result, future work might include calculating SAR properties of wearable antennas developed in research. Because self-adhesive copper tape is utilized for the radiating and conducting parts of this study, such as the ground and patch, it is referred to as a partly wearable antenna. Nowadays, conductive parts are made of electro-textile material. As a result, we can create a totally wearable or textile material employing electrical textile material. Different sorts of textile materials are available on the market, and these materials may be used to create various types of antennas. If textile material is utilized as the substrate and E- textile material is used as the ground and radiating element, the wearable antenna may be washed. This work can be done in the future.

REFERENCES

Balanis, C. A. (2015). *Antenna theory: analysis and design*. John wiley & sons.

Gupta, B., Sankaralingam, S., & Dhar, S. (2010, August). Development of wearable and implantable antennas in the last decade: A review. In *10th Mediterranean Microwave Symposium,* (pp. 251-267). IEEE.

Hearle, J. W., & Morton, W. E. (2008). *Physical properties of textile fibres*. Elsevier.

Kannadhasan, S., & Nagarajan, R. (2021). Development of an H-shaped antenna with FR4 for 1–10 GHz wireless communications. *Textile Research Journal, 91*(15-16), 1687–1697.

Kannadhasan, S., & Nagarajan, R. (2022). Performance improvement of H-shaped antenna with zener diode for textile applications. *Journal of the Textile Institute, 113*(8), 1707–1714.

Kumar Singh, V., Ali, Z., Ayub, S., & Kumar Singh, A. (2014). A wide band Compact Microstrip Antenna forGPS/DCS/PCS/WLAN Applications. *Intelligent Computing, Networking, and Informatics, 243*, 1107–1113.

Malekpoor, H., & Jam, S. (2013). Miniaturised asymmetric E-shaped microstrip patch antenna with folded-patch feed. *IET Microwaves, Antennas & Propagation, 7*(2), 85–91.

Nikhil, S., Singh, A. K., & Kumar, S. V. (2015). Design and performance of wearable ultra wide band textile antenna for medical application. *Microwave and Optical Technology Letters, 57*(7).

Osman, M. A. R., Abd Rahim, M. K., Azfar Abdullah, M., Samsuri, N. A., Zubir, F., & Kamardin, K. (2011). Design, implementation and performance of ultra-wideband textile antenna. *Progress in Electromagnetics Research B. Pier B, 27*, 307–325. doi:10.2528/PIERB10102005

Ouyang, Y., & Chappell, W. J. (2008). High frequency properties of electro-textiles for wearable antenna applications. *IEEE Transactions on Antennas and Propagation, 56*(2), 381–389. doi:10.1109/TAP.2007.915435

Ramadan, A. H., Mervat, M., El-Hajj, A., Khoury, S., & Al-Husseini, M. (2009). A reconfigurable U-Koch microstrip antenna for wireless applications. *Progress in Electromagnetics Research, 93*, 355–367.

Salonen, P., & Rahmat-Samii, Y. (2006, November). Textile antennas: Effects of antenna bending on input matching and impedance bandwidth. In *2006 First European Conference on Antennas and Propagation* (pp. 1-5). IEEE.

Singh, D. K., Kanaujia, B., Dwari, S., Pandey, G. P., & Kumar, S. (2015). Multiband circularly polarized stacked microstrip antenna. *Progress in Electromagnetics Research C, 56*, 55–64. doi:10.2528/PIERC14121101

Sun, X. B., Cao, M. Y., Hao, J. J., & Guo, Y. J. (2012). A rectangular slot antenna with improved bandwidth. *AEÜ. International Journal of Electronics and Communications, 66*(6), 465–466.

Zhu, S., & Langley, R. (2007). Dual-band wearable antennas over EBG substrate. *Electronics Letters, 43*(3), 1.

Chapter 10
Cloud-Based Detection of Forged Passport and Extraction of True Identity:
Surf Match Algorithm for Fraudulence Reduction

Kanthavel R.
King Khalid University, India

ABSTRACT

The forgery of primary documents has become a cause of great concern in recent times. Forged passports have been used in significant numbers, and the number continues to rise year after year. As a result, there is a need for a quick, inexpensive technique that can recognize false passports. This is the same cause why researchers adapted our basic tasks to recognize persons effectively even at a stretch using the SURF matching technique for use in counterfeit passport detection applications. The use of the SURF matching algorithm to identify and so discover the targeting individual has been expanded to the detecting of false passports. This has broadened the area of the paper's application in both detection and tracking and the identification of duplicated passports. The outcome and applicability of our technology can be changed depending on the photographs associated with the input. In the case of a phony passport, the authors' article likewise tries to remove the patient's genuine identity.

DOI: 10.4018/978-1-6684-5058-1.ch010

INTRODUCTION

The fundamental history of stereo imaging is covered in this overview, as well as how depth knowledge may be extracted from images using this technique. Two-dimensional camera's image does not carry any detailed information. Nevertheless, depth data is necessitated by many applications, such as automatic map-making, robots sensing, and target acquisition. Figure 1 a, b represents the stereo image design (Lo and Chalmers, 2003). There are numerous methods for extracting detailed information, including:

- **Active Measurement:** A variety of pulse-echo modalities, such as radar, ultrasonic, laser pulses, or laser line scan, can be used to calculate the distance to a spot. The most popular of these techniques is the laser line scan, which rotates solid, three-dimensional objects while scanning it with a laser beam.
- **Stereo imaging:** Create images from various perspectives by combining images from two or more geographically distant cameras. The depth data is then derived from the variations
- **Holography** is an optical transmission device that captures accurate tri image data. It's very challenging to gather the data and as a depth purpose - designed, it's not particularly beneficial.

Figure 1. (a) Basic parallel stereo image design (b) Two stereo images for a cube

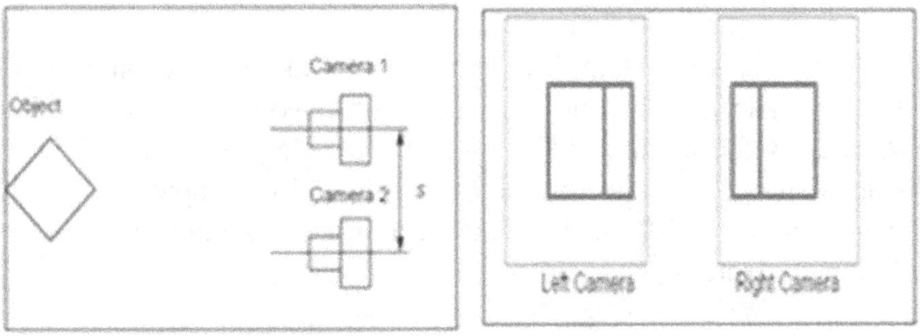

We receive two separate views of the same item from the two cameras, with the usual perspective of a cube depicted in figure 2. As a result, we only notice shifts in the vertical lines, something we may use to measure the depth. This technology is comparable to the human visual system, which has two eyes spaced roughly 60–70 mm apart, resulting in two somewhat distinct views of a tri objects.

Figure 2. Usual perspective of a cube

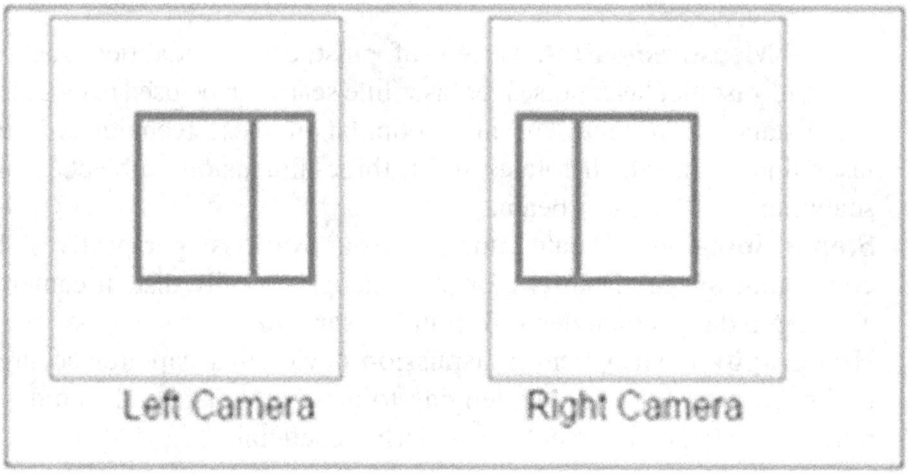

Error in Depth Measure

While deploying this system, it is important to take into account the faults that may be made and how they may impact the workflow. We will only be able to identify the picture of P with a specific degree of precision in any image acquisition, which is normally determined by the spatial sampling of the image (Liu et al., 2013). Hence, if we assume a dx inaccuracy in the Dx calculation, we obtain

$$\Delta x = \Delta x_0 \pm \delta x$$

Therefore, if we define as the ideal distance between the lens and object position P provided by

$$v_0 = \frac{uS}{\Delta x0}$$

The depth measurement we will then acquire is $v = v0\}$ dv. Since the error in Dx, will cause an error in the depth measure of dv. Using Taylor expansion, we can then determine that dv is terms of dx, to be

$$\delta v = \frac{uS}{\Delta x_0^2} \delta x$$

So substituting for Dx0, we get that

$$\delta v = \frac{v_0^2}{uS} \delta x$$

This demonstrates that the error in the depth measurement increases with the square of the distance from the camera for a fixed S and dx. Therefore, a large S and thus a large camera separation are required to obtain strong depth resolution, but we should also anticipate low depth resolution for distant objects (Fröhlich et al., 1995).

Typical System: Consider a typical, real-world example of stereo imaging utilising two CCD cameras with standard video quality. The size of the one CCD sensor, which is normally around 20 mm for a respectable camera, determines the error dx for a CCD camera. The other parameters are typical. 20 m Sensor Size (dx) 25mm focal length (typical) separation If we plug in the figures for various approximations of distances, we arrive at 100mm (Boher et al., 2014). Figure 3 explains the Stereo photography from a moving aircraft.

v0 » 1m Þ dv » 8mm
v0 » 10m Þ dv » 800mm

For entities that are very close to us, up to a length of approximately 100c m, we are capable of attaining a depth resolution that is better than 1%, but as the distance goes to 1000 cm, the error extends to over 10%, which is rather inadequate. Stereo vision works well up to around 1000 cm, much like the human visual system; after that, we utilise size and perspective to gauge distance.

Figure 3. Stereo photography from a moving aircraft

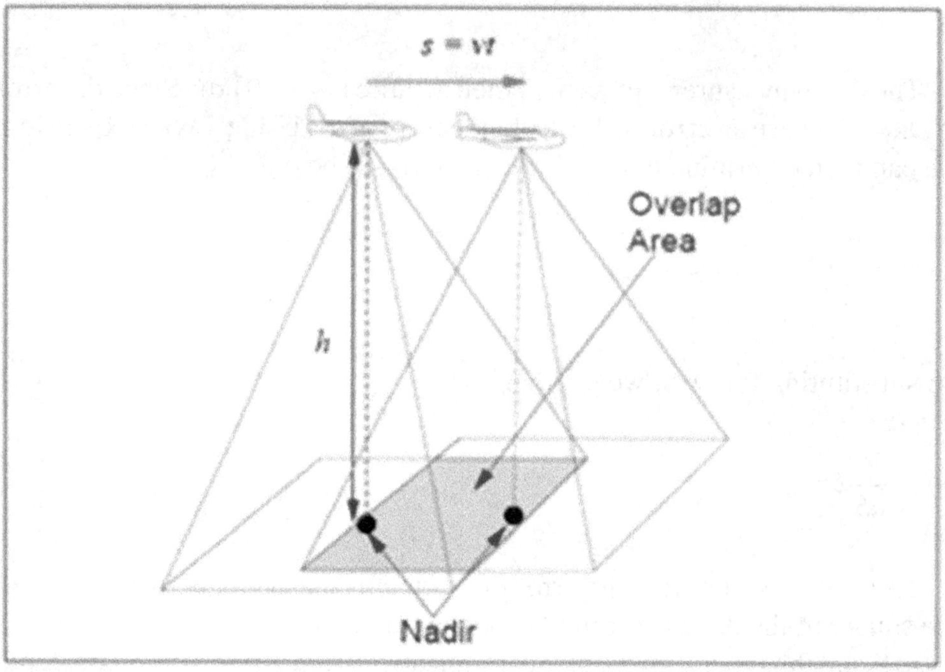

Aerial Photography

Among the most typical uses for stereo photography is aerial photography taken from a survey plane flying level. The nadir, or position where the camera's optic axis touches the ground, serves as the field's centre when it is pointed straight down (Bolas et al., 1994). We then take two photographs separated by time t, thus if the plane's speed relative to the ground is v, the camera separation will be equal to s=vt as illustrated in figure 4. Here, the same camera was used to capture the two photos, and the distance between them could be as great as needed to get accurate depth data. Knowing camera separation allows us to determine the height variation in the overlap area, which is crucial for automatic mapping. The aircraft's orientation might shift dramatically between exposures, making this method much more challenging than it appears. As a result, the optical axis of the cameras changes direction, affecting the geometry of the imaging system as a whole. Using pricey self-levelling camera mounts and precise tracking of the aircraft speed and angles, which greatly complicates the system, can make up for this.

Satellite Stereo

Stereo imaging from a remote sensing satellite is a very useful system in which the two images are acquired from various orbits at various times, as shown in figure 4. Since a satellite's orbits are relatively stable and there are no atmospheric disturbances, the majority of issues with aircraft stereo are avoided, making high-quality stereo particularly useful. The imaging sensor on some satellite systems can be aimed to maximise the area of overlap. The SPOT technology yields particularly good stereo images (Benton, 1993).

Figure 4. Stereo photography from a remote satellite

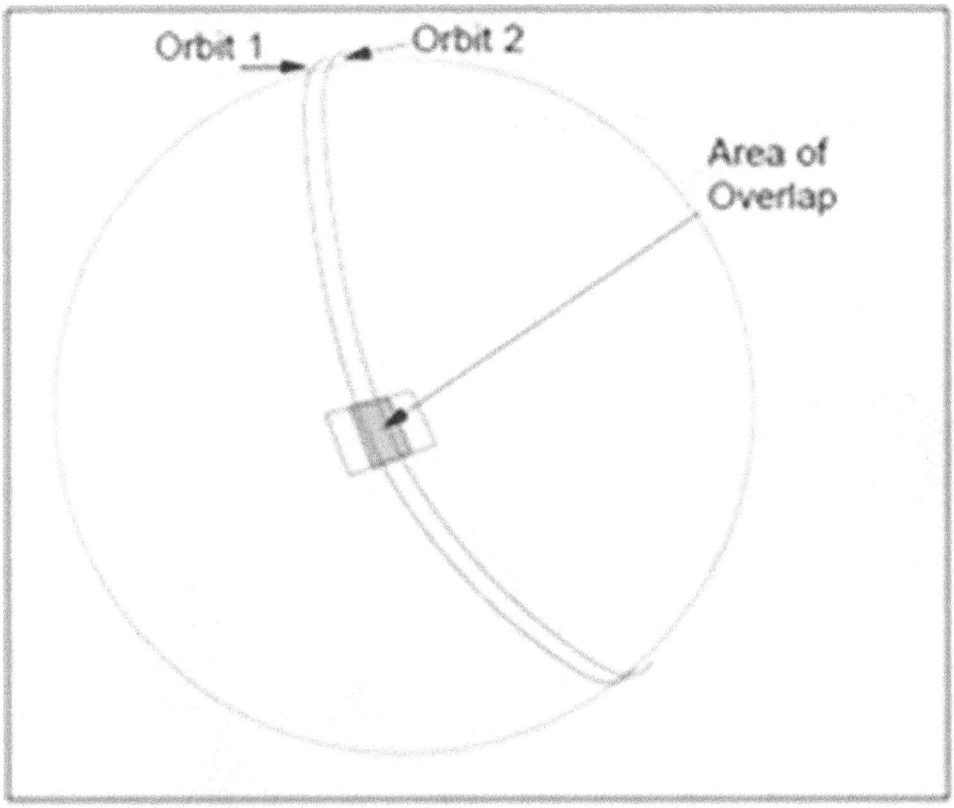

Converging Systems

As illustrated in figure 5, in a real system, the cameras are not orthogonal but instead converge to a common point in the plane at a distance of z0. Out from coordinates x0 and x1 in the two photos, we can calculate for Dz. Statements have the same form and issues as the parallel case, but they are far more challenging (Dhaya, Kanthavel, and Venusamy, 2021a).

Information Extraction from Depth

Using a manual override and an optics monitoring equipment, the manual technique. Used to trace outlines in the majority of commercial mapmaking tools.

Figure 5. Geometry for converging stereo system

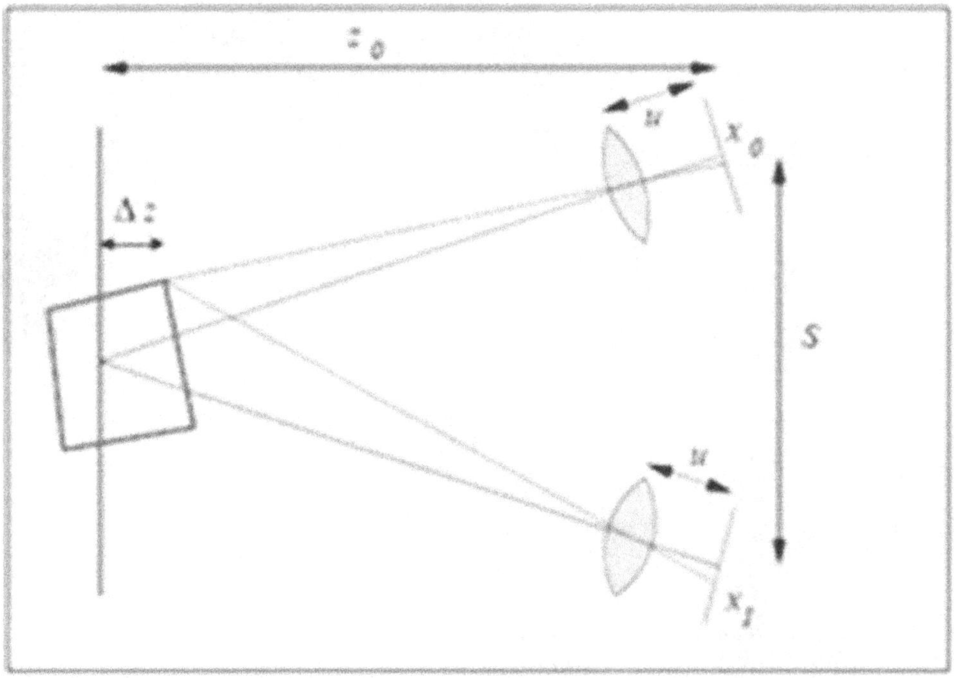

Extraction of Information in a Plane

A Real-World Computer Vision Problem We worked on the Esprit report. A system for in-vehicle use that can recognise traffic signs is required. With as little backdrop distraction as practicable, we would really like to create an image of the approaching road sign that is a recognised size to help with recognition. Figure 6 explains the Road scene with two road signs and binary threshold of edge image (Trayner and Orr, 1996).

Figure 6. Road scene with two road signs and binary threshold of edge image.

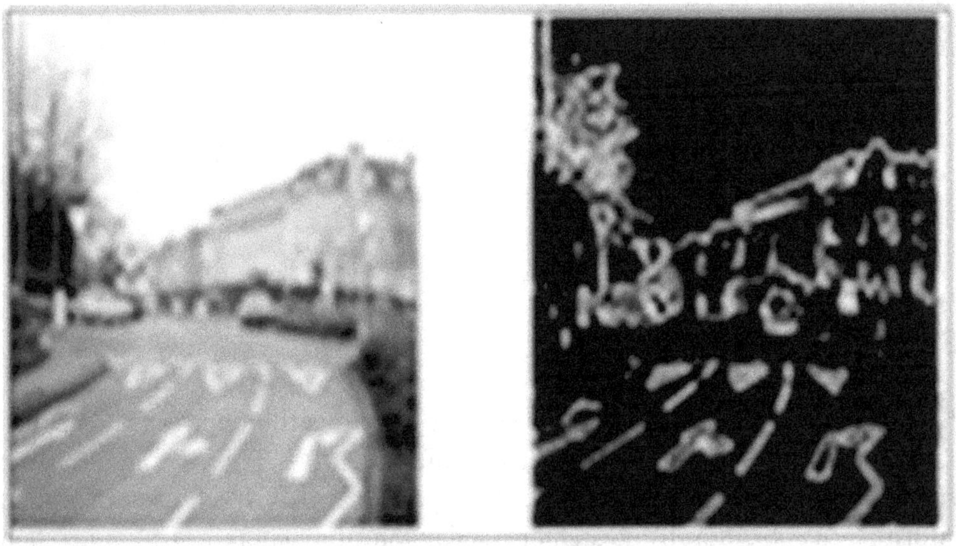

There are three standard sizes for all traffic signs; ((ECE regulation, assume single size at the moment). attempting to extract the sign with this. We want to identify edges from a specific plane as the car approached the road, so if the sign is in that plane, we will detect the sign of the appropriate size and disregard all other edge points in the image. Figure 7 defines the geometry of an imaging system for read sign recognition (Hodges and McAllister, 1993).

Two cameras will be mounted in the car and will be spaced apart by a distance S according to the system architecture. Images from both cameras are detected, real-time (basic) edge detection is performed, each image is threshold to create a binary edge image, and all edge points are rejected unless they appear in both images with the same displacement Dx. Following that, we extract region(s) from the input image using the chosen edge points. In fact, all operations are straightforward and may be carried out using analogue hardware. Although the early outcomes of laboratory tests appeared promising, it was never applied to real people (Toda, Takahashi, and Iwata, 1995).

Figure 7. Geometry of an imaging system for read sign recognition

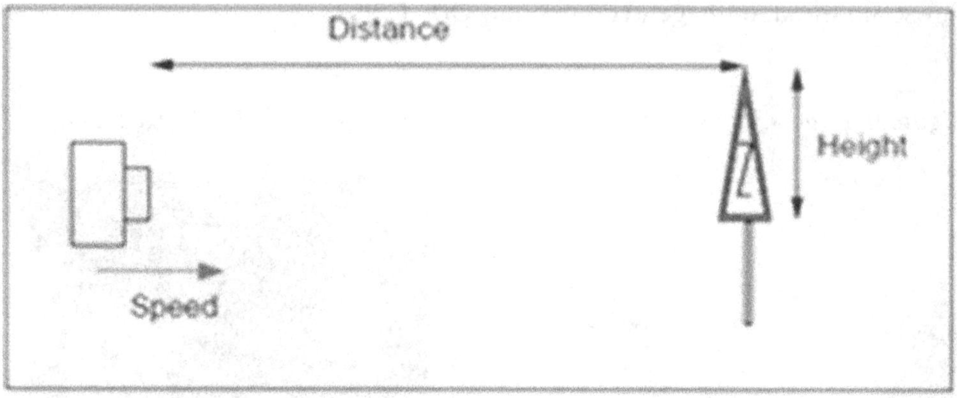

STEREOSCOPY

The ability of the human visual system to perceive the depth of the scenes being observed is one of its most astounding features. This is made feasible via the stereoscopy procedure. The cyclopean picture, which has embedded information about depth and an increased resolution of detail, is created when the two images viewed by the eyes (the stereo image pair) are combined by our brain. The world appears to us normally as seen from an imaginary eye that is positioned halfway between the left and right eye positions (Schulze, 1995). This straightforward geometric arrangement has a significant result. No sensory array ever directly records the image we see of the world because it appears differently from each of these views; instead, our cerebral machinery does this. However, we may artificially excite our sense of stereo vision by taking two images of the same subject and showing the left image to the left eye and the right image to the right eye. The two images will then be combined by the brain to give the impression of three dimensionality (3D). The process of acquiring, storing, modifying, transmitting, and presenting such "stationary" and "moving" images is known as stereo imaging. The first application of stereo imagery was in photography. Sales of stereoscopes and stereo images significantly increased Following the computer graphics industry's explosive growth in the 1990s, a general understanding that the two-dimensional paper ions of three-dimensional scenes, traditionally referred to as "three-dimensional computer graphics," are inadequate for inspection, navigation, and comprehension of some types of multivariate data emerged. Human depth signals, which are sometimes neglected, are essential for an image's understanding of such data. These cues include stereopsis, motion parallax, and to a lesser extent, ocular accommodation. The growing demand for consumer goods has led to the identification of numerous new application fields where such additional information might be put to use (McCormick, 1995). The development of stereo picture technologies has historically been significantly influenced by the entertainment sector, and this trend has not changed. However, the markets for three-dimensional video games, virtual reality simulations, three-dimensional graphical user interfaces, infrastructure development projects for specifying data structures for transferring 3D objects (VRML), and 3D video conferencing (RACE and ACTS) all work to advance the technology.

Stereoscopic Image / Sequence Capture

Stereovision may be mimicked by taking two views of a 3D scene and presenting them to the left and right eyes independently. For the first stage of this process, stereo capture equipment is crucial. The actual designs of capture equipment differ greatly in both technological and operational aspects. The reader is introduced to the fundamental concepts behind a few capture methods that have primarily been patented in the US, Europe, and Japan in the sections that follow (Dhaya, Kanthavel, and Venusamy, 2021b).

Using two horizontally separated points to take two pictures of the same scene with the same camera is an obvious technique to capture a stereo image pair. Recently, this fundamental technique has been used in robotics and stereo photogrammetric thanks to the deployment of accurate optical, electro-optic, mechanical, and electronic technologies to increase camera calibration. Multiple components of a single sensor camera have also been used to analyse the frequency, polarisation, and spatial statistics of one or more light beams that have been focused on an object in order to determine its position. As an alternative, two photos may be captured with the same camera, polarised differently, completely overlapped, and then separated. Mechanical and electro-optical technologies that separate the camera lens into left and right halves have been utilised for close-up stereo imaging, such as stereo endoscopy (Börner, 1993). An approach that has been utilised more commonly is to insert an optical adapter in front of the current lens in order to capture the two views separately. Using camera-lens combinations that cyclically change their refractive index to capture the scene at various depths is a distinctly different method from the ones listed above. In the most recent single camera stereo image capture methods, depth information is extracted from a single point of view together with other scene data.

Display Technology

A three-dimensional human perception is the ultimate goal of a stereoscopic image system. The ways in which the left and right views can be directed to the matching eye, however, differ widely. Off-head displays (OHDs), head mounted displays (HMDs), and auto-stereoscopic displays are the three categories into which we divide stereoscopic display systems. In contrast to auto-stereoscopic displays, which have eye-addressing mechanisms fully integrated into the display itself, OHDs and HMDs require optical components to be placed close to the observer's eyes (Seera et al., 2021).

Off-Head Displays

The OHDs currently in use often need that the observer wear the devices for the image separation. By utilising three different multiplexing techniques, these devices are employed to guide the left and right optical impulses to the proper eye.

Color Multiplexing

Sometimes known as anaglyph, this is one of the more basic methods of perceiving stereoscopic images. The observer wears appropriate color-filter glasses for separation, and the left and right eye views are re-filtered with almost complimentary colours (for example, red / green). However, the employment of this approach is constrained by colour rivalry effects and visually unpleasant temporary shifts in chromatic adaptation (Ramakrishnan and Ramakrishnan, 2022).

Polarization Glasses

Polarization glasses (linear or circular), along with orthogonally polarised pictures displayed on two monitors, offer a remedy for the anaglyph technique's colour rivalry effects. However, more than 60% of the light would be lost through the filters, and the necessary beam combiners would reduce the remaining light flow by almost 50%. However, seeing stereoscopic video paperion displays still makes extensive use of polarisation methods. Overhead panels and LCD-based direct-view monitors have recently been commercially available.

Time Multiplexed Displays

These displays take advantage of the visual system's ability to combine stereo pair components over a time-lag of up to 50 ms. The left and right eye images are displayed in quick succession and synchronised with an LC shutter that covers one eye while opening the other eye in turns. An IR link is used to control the shutter system. Geometrical and colour disparities are avoided because both constituent images are reproduced at full spatial resolution by a single display (Ezra et al., 1995).

Time Sequentially Controlled Polarisation

This technique basically combines time and polarization multiplex methods. The concept is to adjust an LC panel's polarisation on the monitor in time with the shift in left- and right-eye perspectives. In comparison to systems using active shutter-glasses, this method uses cheap, lightweight polarising glasses and offers two useful advantages. Each eye will only be exposed to the required visual contents thanks to the LC panel's ability to be built from multiple segments that work independently on the active areas of the screen, reducing cross talk. It is possible to run several display arrays without using any additional synchronising equipment (Kang, Choi, and Hwang, 2022).

Head-Mounted Displays

Location multiplexing is a technique used by HMDs, which are frequently seen in virtual reality and 3D visualisation. In this technique, the two views are formed at separate locations and transmitted to the appropriate eye over separate channels. Either at a constant accommodation distance or at a variable, gaze-controlled position, the image plane is visible. The natural surroundings are typically optionally obscured by sight, creating the impression that the viewer is completely immersed in the scenario being portrayed. In order to prevent lost of view due to head motions, head tracking sensors are utilised to provide eye-point dependent changes in perspective when the user moves. Thus, musculoskeletal issues are prevented. Contrarily, latencies and tracking errors frequently result in strange, unsettling sensations due to conflicting visual stimulus and postural feedback. In this instance, the viewer approaches the stereo pictures as though via a pair of binoculars (Dhaya and Kanthavel, 2021). The "3-D display with accommodative correction" (3DDAC) [ATR Labs] is a recent innovation in HMD technology. Here, an infrared gaze-tracker senses the convergence distance and a set of moveable relay lenses' positions are continuously adjusted such that the screen surface (picture plane) appears at the same distance as the gaze-lines' convergence point. HMDs often provide wider fields but are burdened by issues with weight, resolution, computing power needs, and user discomfort (headaches and nausea). Many free-viewing 3-D displays (auto-stereoscopic) have recently been developed with the goal of resolving the majority of these issues.

Automatic Stereo Displays

The three main categories of these displays are electro-holographic displays, volumetric displays, and direction-multiplexed displays. The following explains them:

Holographic Displays

These can recreate and store the characteristics of light waves. Because of the great degree of realism that can be achieved, this method is perfect for creating 3-D displays that may be viewed for free. A moving hologram constructed of acousto-optic material has been attempted to be created using sonic waves. Furthermore, optically addressed spatial light modulators have been used to make moving holograms. However, while recording and reproduction, coherent light is required to illuminate the scene and the recorded interface pattern. This technique's main flaw restricts its applicability to situations where the stereo scene can only be seen under specific viewing circumstances. A number of research organisations are working to apply the holographic principle to an LCD setting (Hamagishi, 1995). The handling of vast amounts of data contained in a hologram and the extremely high spatial resolution needs of the LC panels that could be utilised in this regard, however, remain unresolved issues.

Volumetric Displays

Depending on where the picture points representing a 3D scene appear to be seen, these can be classified into two basic groupings. A self-luminous or light-reflecting media (screens with disc, spiral, or helix shapes) is utilised in the first type of device, and it either permanently occupies the volume or periodically sweeps it out. The multi-planar display type of volumetric displays, which produces aerial pictures in empty space, is the second kind. The observer views the screen through a spherical mirror with a range of focus lengths while the images denoting different depth levels are written time-sequentially to a stationary CRT (Isono, Yasuda, and Sasazawa, 1993). Since the light energy sent to points in space cannot be absorbed by the things being displayed in volumetric displays, the items look transparent.

Direction-Multiplexed Displays

Depending on the optical technique employed to focus the rays emitted by the pixels of the two viewpoint views, these can be generally divided into four types. We go over these strategies' guiding ideas in the parts that follow.

- The Diffractive Optical Elements (DOE) method groups together what are referred to as "partial pixels" the matching elements of nearby perspective views. Each of these arrays has a diffractive grating in front of it that directs incident light into the appropriate perspective image and viewing region. These kinds of sophisticated displays combine the aforementioned two phases into a single, highly detailed spatial light modulator.
- Holographic methods are utilised to model the optical properties of traditional optical components in the Holographic Optical Elements (HOE) approach. In a recent design, a holographic pattern recorded on a plate fixed to the back of an LCD directs light from an ordinary light source contained in a backlighting unit towards each eye. The device makes sure that light travelling through rows with even numbers

is directed toward the left eye and vice versa. As a result, if the viewer's eyes are in the proper place, they will perceive distinct images (Eichenlaub, 1994).

- Integral imaging using refraction-based directional multiplexing: A collection of tiny convex micro lenses is used to capture the scene. The same scene is captured by each micro lens from a slightly varied angle, resulting in a variety of tiny 2D photos of the same scene. The display uses a number of the same type of micro lenses. By aligning the image plane with the focal plane of the micro lens array, the light from each image point is released into the viewing area as a beam of parallel rays in a particular direction. As a result, the viewer sees various picture point compositions from various points of view. Since each pixel is spread to the lens diameter at playback, the micro lenses must be as small as possible to ensure that the image created behind each one is as comprehensive and detailed as possible. Lenticular imaging: A group of convex lenses that are vertically oriented and are arranged next to one another in a vertical plane record the scene (Dhaya, R et al, 2021). Each picture point in the horizontal plane emits light in a certain direction. They are non-selectively emitted in the vertical plane, making it impossible to use optical techniques to shift perspective in response to vertical head motions. To lessen these effects, however, head tracking and computational picture processing are applied.
- This type of stereo picture displays has been the subject of a large amount of research. Direct-view lenticular imaging and rear paperion lenticular imaging are the two basic categories into which these displays can be classified. To create a left and right image pair that is papered to the lenticular screen in the first type, a cathode ray tube (CRT) or an LC panel is utilised behind each lens. By moving the lenticular screen, itself or by inserting a movable plane with vertical slits between the screen and the CRT, head tracking can be accomplished. In the second form, a stereo paperor is used in place of the LC panel (Eichenlaub, Hollands, and Hutchins, 1995). The papered pictures are focused onto vertically oriented left-right image pairs that are generated on a translucent diffuser plate, which is positioned between the two lenticular screens. The front lenticular screen's lenses organise the images into the proper viewing areas. Either the front lenticular frame or the paperion unit can be moved to track the head. Various paperion units must be utilised for viewing by multiple users.

Field Lens Displays

The fundamental concept is to employ one or two field lenses to focus the scene's light rays to the left and right eyes, keeping the left view dark to the right and vice versa. Different research groups have suggested various implementations. In one such technique, the images are initially created on two LCD panels that are positioned at an angle to one another. These panels are illuminated by two light sources through close-set lenses. A half mirror (beam combiner) is positioned at the bisection of the angle between the LCD panels, superimposing the generated light rays and directing them to the right and left eyes, respectively. A different suggestion is to utilise two separate lenses. The prism mask is constructed in such a way as to alternately deflect columns of light into the left and right viewing zones. A stereo paperor is used to paper the left and right images on to a field lens that is situated between the observer and the stereo paperor in a third type of field lens-based display. The stereo images thus appear as floating aerial images in front of or behind the field lens rather than being papered onto a solid media. By altering the focussing properties of the stereo paperion optics, the position of the floating picture plane can be adjusted. The brief point of fixation of the viewer is detected by a gaze tracker. Reflection-based directional multiplexing: Retro-reflective screens, a unique type of screen that only reflects light in its original direction, are used to perform directional multiplexing. This screen receives light from a stereo image paperor with lateral movement flexibility and separates and prints the two pictures to the spectator through a half mirror. The system has the capacity to determine the observer's current head position, and to modify the paperor and half-mirror angle as needed. The main idea behind occlusion-based directional multiplexing is to use parallax effects to hide certain portions of the image from one eye while making them visible to the other (Han et al., 2013).

Two Barrier Grids Make Up the Most Recent Version of this Type of Display

Between the LCD display's backlight casing and one. On the observer's side, the second is positioned in front of the LCD display. The left and right perspectives are directed to the two eyes by the placement and movement of the two barrier grids. Barrier grids are created utilising LCD screens in some systems, enabling software-based control and gaze tracking (Choi, Pantofaru, Savarese. 2012).

Parallax-illumination Displays

A lattice of extremely thin vertical lines of light is positioned at a distance behind an LCD panel to provide the parallax effect. Because of the parallax, each eye only sees light moving across different image columns. A sheet of lenticular lens is used to create the lattice. The translucent diffuser's lit lines are illuminated by a large number of fluorescent light sources that are concentrated into a small number of light sources. A broad field lens is incorporated into the display, and many sets of light sources are used to accomplish head tracking. By alternating between groups of laterally displaced lights, the position of the light sources can be altered. A number of light source sets are simultaneously used for multiple viewing., for a single observer, they are each producing the image pair. In a more contemporary version, two sets of blinking LEDs are used to provide two laterally dispersed blinking lines behind each LCD column (Dan et al., 2012). This gives both photos their complete spatial resolution. Multiple sets of intersecting light lines form a stationary multi-view display with look-around functionality in an even more complex sort of design.

Moving-Slit Displays

By positioning a rapid switching LCD screen in front of a CRT, a single slit is created that can be moved to scan the screen at a frequency of roughly 60 Hz. It directs various viewpoints to neighbouring zones. On the premise mentioned above, several designs have been put forth. One of these methods allows 16 users to see content (Han et al., 2012). To deliver comprehensive photos to these places, it makes use of three significant spherical lenses. However, this design needs a CRT that operates at 960 Hz frame rate. An alternate system creates the moving slit effect using independent electron cannons with magnetic beam control.

STEREOSCOPIC COMPRESSION TECHNIQUES

The transfer of two perspective views between the capture and display equipment is necessary for the majority of the stereo image capture and display systems mentioned above. The data gathered by a stereo camera pair may further need to be stored for some purposes. The redundancies between the two perspective photos allow for compression, which reduces the amount of transmission bandwidth and storage space needed. This section provides an introduction to several stereo image and sequence compression methods that have been put forth by researchers from around the world (Enzweiler et al., 2010).

Compression of Stereo Images

The sum and difference of the two images were coded in the first stereo image compression technique that was put forth. However, when the discrepancy values rise, this approach performs worse. This approach can be changed by horizontally shifting one of the images until the cross correlation between the stereo pair of images reaches its highest value. The companion image of the shifted image is then subtracted, and the difference is encoded. This method is not very effective because it presupposes that all of the items in the scene have comparable disparity values. Instead of translating the entire image, another strategy is to translate the row blocks.

It has also been suggested to use asymmetrical methods that subsample one of the two images to take use of the suppression theory (Ess et al., 2009). Although these techniques are appealing, they are not suitable for applications requiring the perception of small details.

Another illustration of asymmetrical coding is disparity compensation. The concept of disparity-compensated prediction was first introduced. Estimating the differences between the objects in a stereo pair is the goal of disparity correction, which uses these estimations to eliminate stereo redundancy. The discrepancy is often determined using a block-based model. First, an independent coding is applied to the left image. The right image is then split into separate, non-overlapping chunks. Blocks can be either fixed or variable in size. These bricks are all horizontally shifted and compared to their equivalent blocks in the coded left image using a metric (MSE, SAD, etc.) to ascertain how similar the two blocks are to one another. The disparity compensated prediction and the corresponding translation have the block's disparity as their common denominator. A disparity vector field and the correct image to be encoded allow for the employment of a number of different coding schemes. For instance, the disparity adjusted prediction residual could be encoded and sent. Disparity Compensated Residual Coding is the name given to this technique by Yamaguchi et al. An alternate method entails either separately coding each block using an adaptive Discrete Cosine Transform (DCT) or encoding each block using disparity compensated prediction. The precision of the disparity corrected prediction dictates the approach taken for a given block. An alternate method uses a linear function of the type y=Ax + B to estimate the transform of each right image block from the transform (DCT) of the corresponding left image block. It is possible to implement disparity correction using both fixed and variable block sizes. The distinctive benefit of avoiding the overhead need to define block locations is one of fixed block size methods. These approaches, however, are unable to properly take advantage of the stereo redundancy if there are many objects or an obscured item present in a block. Reduce the block size as one solution. The disparity field's overall bit rate will go up as a result, though. A segmentation approach is an additional strategy. Due to the large number of bits needed to indicate the size and location of each section, not all segmentation techniques are suitable. Quadtree decomposition offers a reasonably cost-efficient and successful solution to this issue. When the forecast is incorrect, the plan is to adaptively reduce the block size. Block matching cannot handle non-linear deformations like perspective distortion; hence a generalised block matching technique has been presented that approximates object deformations by deforming the relevant blocks in the image.

Also suggested by Ramakrishnan and Ramakrishnan (2022) is an algorithm for extracting regions from images, labelling line segments (border, join, or isolated), and then utilising the method for stereo matching. An alternate strategy divides regions into three categories: occlusion, edge, and smooth regions. Due to the limited viewing area, the portion of the right image that is obscured is independently coded. Disparities are evaluated using a block-based methodology after the non-occluded region is divided into edge and smooth portions. The impacts of photometric changes are then eliminated using a Subspace Paperion Technique (SPT) as a post-processing method.

Stereo Sequence Compression

Numerous redundancy sources, such as intra-image structure, motion, and stereoscopy, are simultaneously present in the case of stereoscopic sequences. To take advantage of stereoscopic redundancy, a number of techniques have been put forth that were influenced by the MPEG compression standard. The following is a simple MPEG-2-based design. DCT is used to code the left channel while compensating for motion. The right channel is coded using one of three methods: direct block encoding using a DCT, disparity compensation, or motion compensation, with each block being encoded using the estimate with the smallest reconstruction error. It is also possible to treat the image information in terms of two-dimensional objects to prevent the artefacts connected with block-based techniques when high compression rates are used. Segmenting the images into consistent sections that correspond to objects is one such method., using available stereoscopic and motion information. Moving objects are then transmitted with a set of parameters describing their colour, form, motion, and disparity.

In a common and condensed representation of the scene that consists of a 3-D structure and 3-D motion characteristics, stereoscopic and dynamic information can also be combined. Instead, object modelling has been utilised to make motion and disparity estimates easier by, for example, accounting for the difference between the present image and the projected 3D model. The transmitted data can also be seen as three-dimensional (three-dimensional) objects made of planar surfaces, with rotation and translation acting as the motion components. As an alternative, depth data at zero crossings that have been gathered by a contour detector can also be used to represent three-dimensional surfaces.

To make it easier to estimate motion and disparity vectors at various resolutions, a multi-resolution framework has been modified. In addition, a plan that preserves disparity discontinuities while maintaining smoother and more precise disparity fields than fixed block size-based plans has been put forth. By applying quad-tree decomposition and using the disparity adjusted error as the splitting criterion, segmentation is accomplished. Another plan put forth by the same authors segments each frame in one of the streams based on disparity. The disparity map obtained during segmentation is reversed to encode the relevant segments in the other stream. A disparity map-based predictive error concealment method is used to fill in areas in this stream that lack correspondence due to binocular occlusions and disparity estimate mistakes. Additionally, a compression method for interlaced stereoscopic sequences has been put forth. This method distinguishes between a zone of fixation and a peripheral area and subsequently compresses the stereoscopic information into the spectral space of a monocular video channel. By delivering high frequency information selectively within and close to the area with the greatest observer acuity, rather than over the full image, spectral compression is made possible.

Absolute 3D surface coordinates from a single stereo pair are produced using a stereo disparity estimate procedure using calibrated cameras. The genuine 3D motion parameters of moving objects may be precisely determined when paired with monocular motion cues. Further analysis allows for the segmentation of body parts based on motion, and although the 3D surface feature structure is already present, it can be merged. An object-based stereo image coding approach has also been proposed that depends on modelling the object structure using 3D wireframe models and motion prediction using globally rigid and locally deformable motion models. Additionally, the authors proposed modelling the local interaction to jointly estimate motion and disparity vector fields from stereoscopic image sequences. processes using Markov Random Fields(MRF). Several schemes based on motion modelling has also been proposed.

A 3D motion model with a translation and a rotation is used to simulate the 2D motion of each object seen in one of the two viewpoints. A motion-based split and merge technique is used to identify the areas where the 3D model is applied. It has also been suggested to expand on the 3D motion estimate technique by using a single 3D motion model to describe the apparent 2D motion in both channels. Then, a stereoscopic inter-frame coding scheme is merged with these 3D motion estimation techniques. It has also been suggested to use a hybrid coder that falls back to block-based coding when 3D-motion estimation is unsuccessful and an object-based coding technique that is very similar to the above method. Initialization is done using a multi-resolution block-based motion estimation technique, while disparity estimation is done using a pixel-based hierarchical dynamic programming algorithm. The regions with similar motion and depth parameters are then identified using a split and merge segmentation approach based on both 3D motion and disparity. These two things work together to provide complete depth information at the decoder location through an effective depth modelling technique. The segmentation data is then provided to the decoder together with the quantized motion and depth model parameters. After that, the segmentation approach's produced objects are used to recreate the original image using an object-based motion compensation system.

Human Factors in Stereo Imaging

When a technology is developing into a mature state, human factors concerns are crucial. Here, we give a brief overview of the problems that must be solved in order to create and develop stereo imaging technologies (NHK, ATR-HIP, CCETT, HHI). Previous studies have demonstrated that even among the vast majority of those with high stereovision abilities, there are significant differences in depth perception. Therefore, these effects must be taken into account while designing and evaluating stereo imaging solutions. It has been demonstrated that over time and with use, a person's stereovision ability may advance, facilitating quick and comfortable binocular fusion and making the subjective evaluation of stereo imaging technology nearly impossible. The overall viewing comfort of a stereo scene will be determined by the viewing distance, screen size, horizontal and vertical parallax, binocular asymmetries, and nonstop depth cues. For instance, the size distortion of stereo pictures can be seen when the exhibited object's apparent distance and its angular size do not coincide as they would in real-world settings. As a result, unwanted miniaturisation effects could be seen on smaller displays. According to research, there are no distortion effects for television-like motion picture presentation on displays between 34" and 50". Large binocular parallaxes (disparities), on the other hand, frequently cause eye strain. According to research, deviations up to 35 minarc do not manifest any observable pain. In addition, ghosting, or double contours created by cross talk between the left and right pictures, would cause headaches. Additionally, it has been demonstrated that cross talk grows when contrast and binocular parallax rise. Practically speaking, cross talk cannot be entirely eliminated. Cross talk might be advantageous for multi-view displays with a constrained number of views, though. This is because it reduces image flipping, which is basically the visual transition from one point of view to another that is obvious. Flipping and cross talk would both need to be undetectable; therefore, a very large number of perspective views would be necessary. The visual comfort that a stereo imaging system design offers the viewer for the prolonged viewing of high-quality stereo pictures will be a key factor in determining whether it is successful or unsuccessful. Therefore, considering human characteristics will continue to be crucial when designing current and future stereo imaging technology.

METHODOLIES AND THE PROCESS MECHANISMS

Existing System

- Automatic detection and tracking of target human is done.
- RANSAC matching algorithm is used.
- New PEI representation is used to demonstrate detection and tracking in 3D space.
- Classifiers such as HOHD and JHCH are used.

Objectives

- In this paper, we are going to detect and track the forged passport using surf matching point algorithm.
- A methodology for objectively assessing stereoscopic graphics performance is also suggested.
- This technique evaluates the passport image, does SURF matching, rates the degree of quality, and finds fake passports.

Motivations

- Our motive is to develop a system to detect and track the passport fraud in a real time airport environment.
- Several metrics have been put forth in the literature to rate the quality of 2D photographs, but there aren't many metrics specifically designed to analyze the quality of stereoscopic images.
- So, along with detecting and tracking the forged passport we also check the quality level of the matching performed.

Existing Problems

- The result of the existing paper shows that the detection accuracy is higher for more near people. But for more far people it is comparatively less.
- They have used video images obtained from a high cost RGB-D camera for processing.

- There is no quality check employed for the detected images.
- Kalman filter method is used.
- The processing goes slow.

Proposed Solutions

- Real time stereo image acquisition can be performed.
- Here, the stereo image quality is calibrated.
- The 3 D stereo disparity(1/depth) algorithm can be used.
- Surf matching point algorithm can be used for matching the images.
- The processing is done in high speed.
- The existing system uses PEI representation algorithm to detect and track people and there is no quality check.
- We work on modified algorithms to check the quality of the images, to detect and track the target human.

Parameters/Constraints

- Miss rate-The miss rate of the base system in an office environment is 0.06.
- False positive per image-The FPPI produced by the base version of our system in an office environment is 27.The figure illustrates the stereo image formation

Software Used

- Matlab 13a
- Image data acquisition
- Image processing tool box

Figure 9 illustrates the flowchart and Figure 10 explains the Block diagram of the system which comprise the following:

- The candidate who is entering the security check is photographed.
- The camera image obtained at security is sent for SURF matching along with the scanned passport image.
- SURF matching algorithm is used for matching the two images since it is found to be more efficient than the base algorithm.

- If the passport is forged, then the amount of matching obtained is less with more false positives per image.
- On the hand if the passport is authentic then the number of false positives per image will be less and the matching output will be
- If the passport is found to be fake, then the camera image is matched with the scanned a national-card image.
- By doing so we obtain the true identity of the fraudulent.

Figure 8. Illustration for stereo image formation

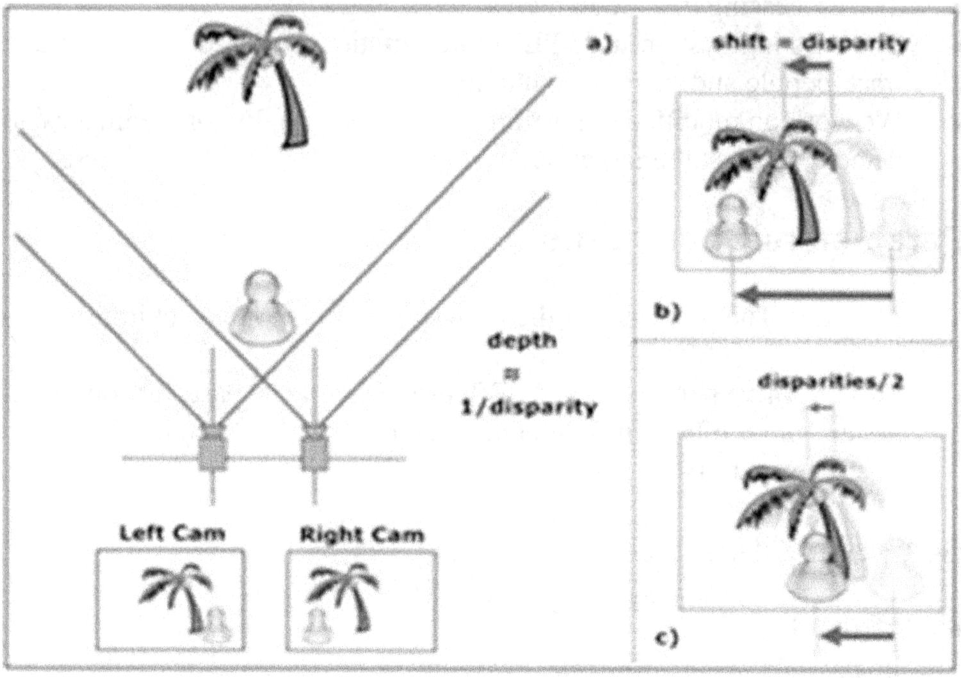

Figure 9. Flow chart stereo image formation

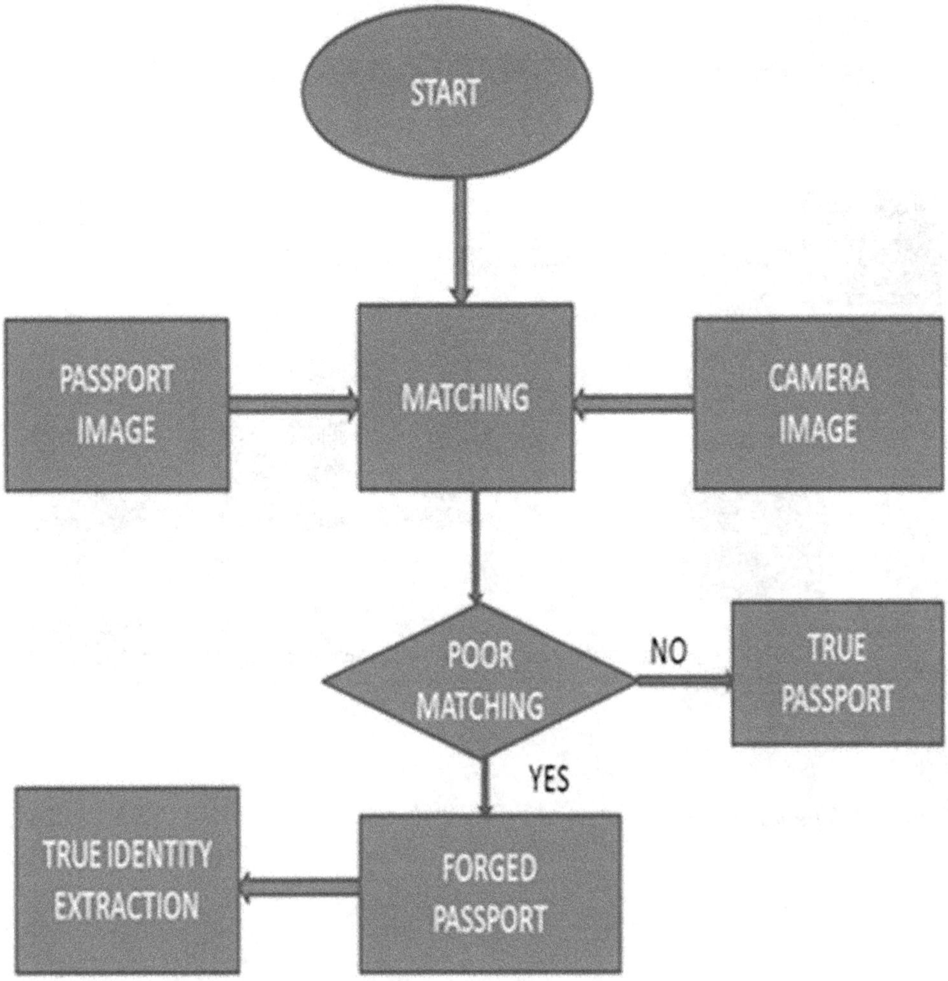

OBSERVATIONS AND OUTPUT

Observations

It is seen in the graph that our proposed system has miss rates and fppi lesser than that of other systems and proposed system's efficiency has improved which shows in the table also.

Figure 10. Block diagram of the system

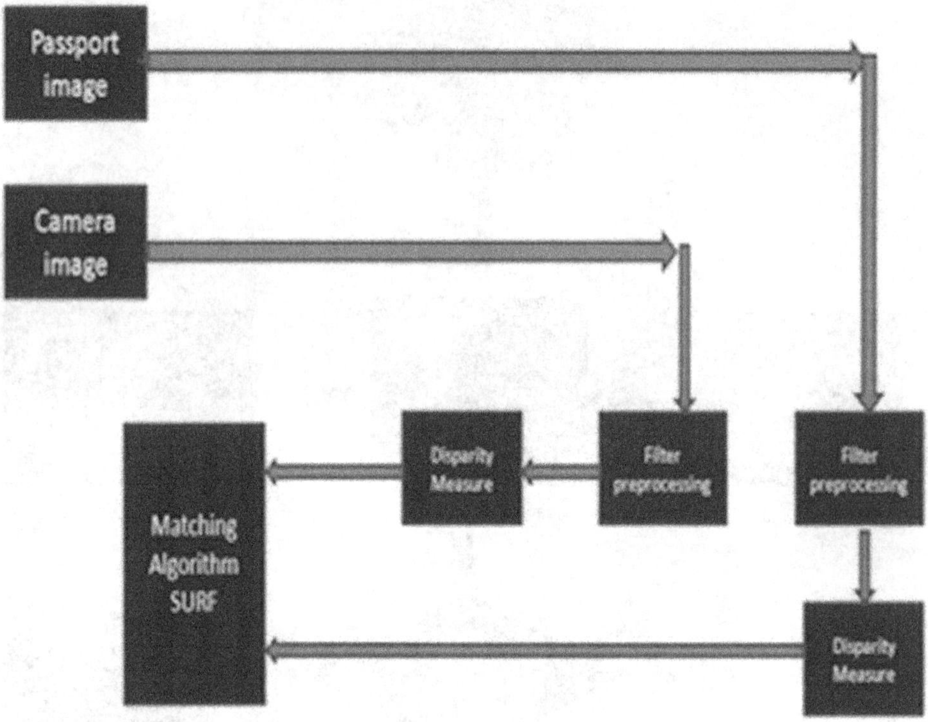

Figure 11. The tables graph

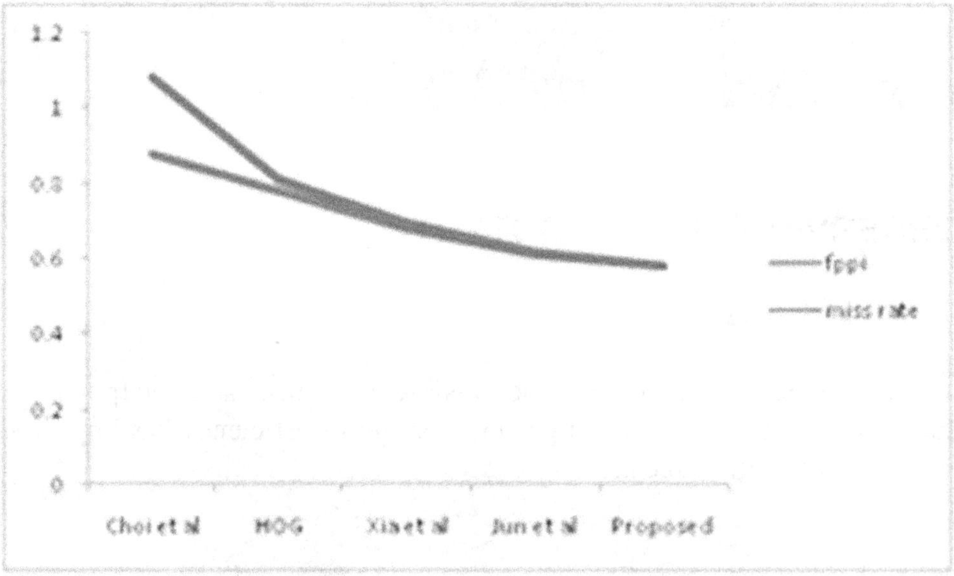

Table 1. Comparison of the performance of the proposed system with that of the previous systems.

Systems	Miss Rate	Fppi
Choi et al	0.88	0.2
HOG	0.78	0.03
Xia et al	0.68	0.016
Liu et al., 2013	0.61	0.01
Proposed	0.58	0.003

CORRELATION GRAPH FOR MORPHED AND CAMERA IMAGE MATCHING

Correlation Graphs For Anational And Camera Image Matching

When a SURF matching is performed between a morphed image and a camera image, the correlation between the two images decreases and the number of miss rates and fppi gets increased. As these two parameters increases, the graph gets denser as shown in figure 12 to figure 13.

Figure 12. Plot for Correlation 1

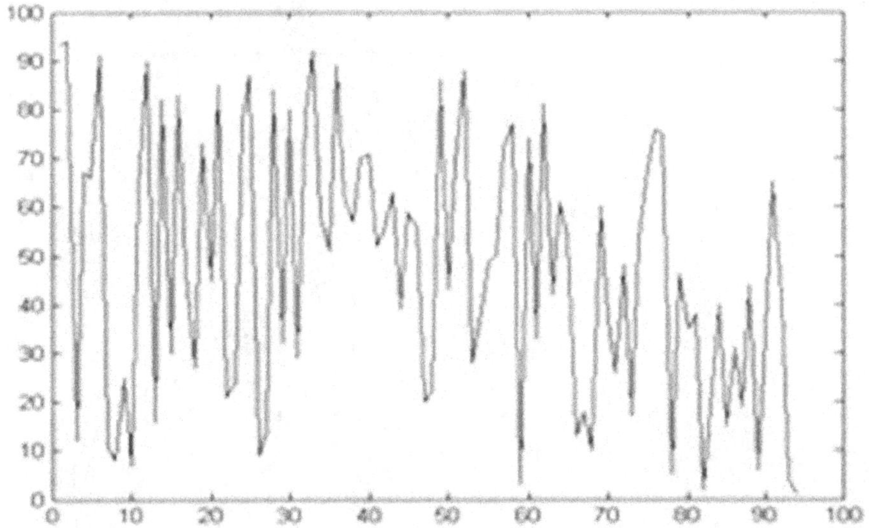

Figure 13. Plot for Correlation 2

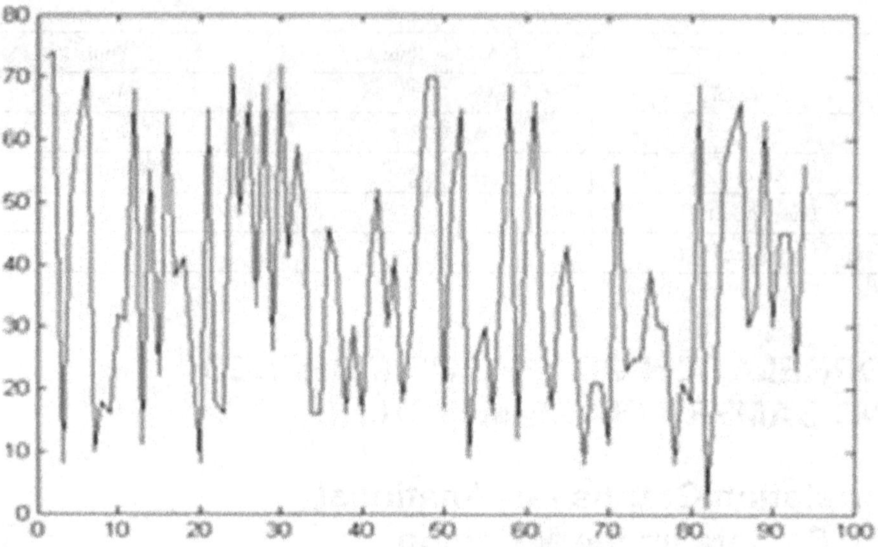

When SURF matching is performed between a national image and a camera image, the correlation between the two images increases and the number of miss rates and fppi gets decreased. As these two parameters decreases, the graph looks sparse as shown in figure 14 and figure 15

Figure 14. Plot for Correlation 1

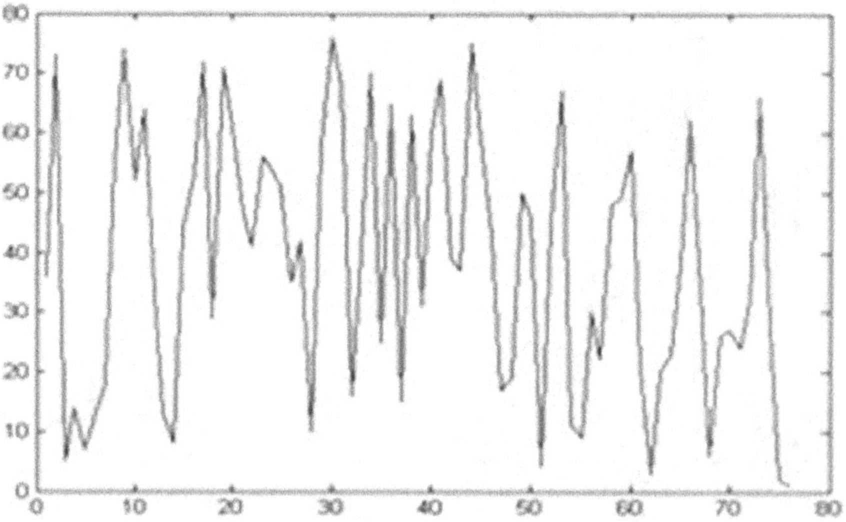

Figure 15. Plot for Correlation 2

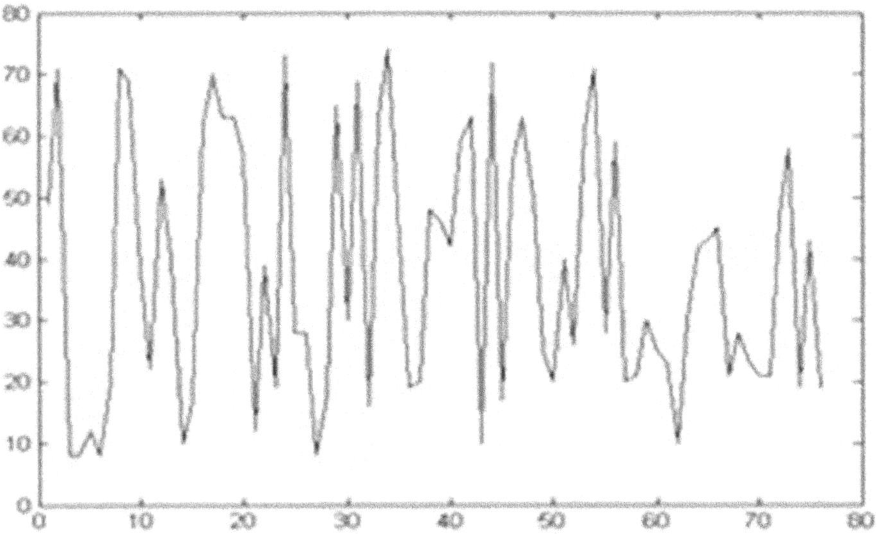

ERROR PLOTS

When a SURF matching is performed between a morphed image and a camera image, the error plot increases exponentially as shown in the below figure 16.

When a SURF matching is performed between a morphed image and a camera image, the error plot increases linearly as shown in the below figure 17.

Forged Passport Detection

When the passport is forged the matching result obtained is of poor quality. Only a few points are perfectly matched, whereas majority of the matching obtained are mismatched points. Thus the false positive for this matching result will be high, is shown in figure 18.

Figure 16. Error Plot for Morphed Image Matching

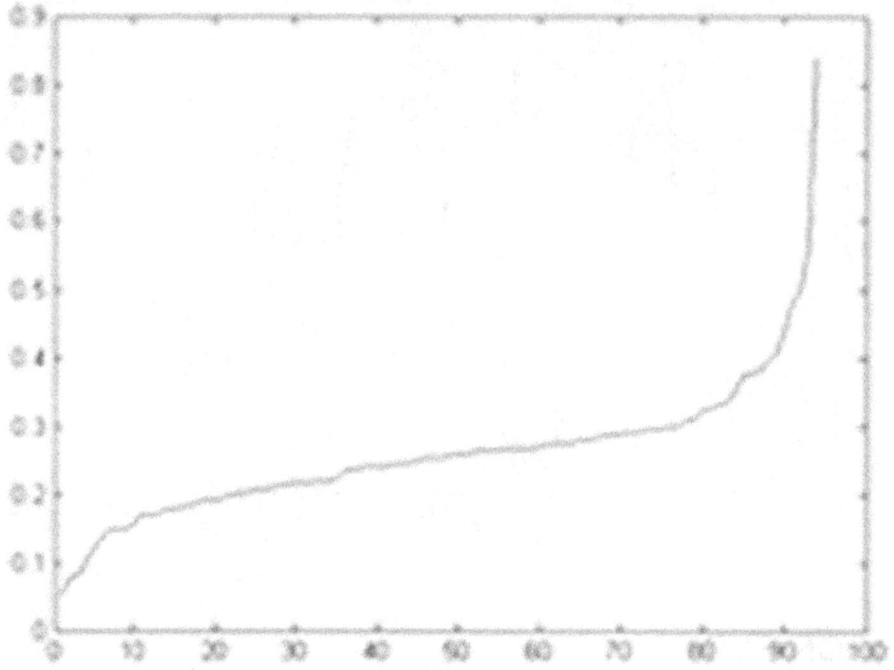

ORIGINAL PASSPORT HOLDER

If we consider this image the two images are perfectly matched indicating that the forged passport originally belongs to that person. The morphed image has been obtained by placing the image of the fraudulent over the original image, hence we obtain accurate matching result., in figure 19.

TRUE IDENTITY EXTRACTION

The matching result obtained between the imaged supposed to be considered as the image of the person in a national card is well matched with the camera image. This helps us to reveal the true identity of the person. The false positive per image for this output is less compared to that obtained for the morphed photo in figure 20.

Figure 17. Error Plot for Anational Image Matching

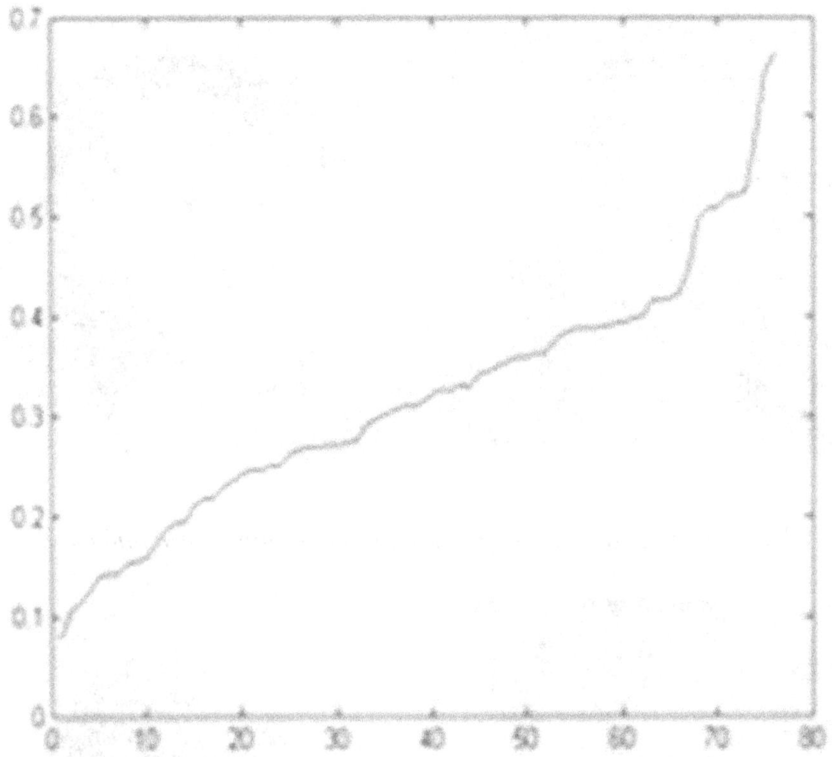

Figure 18. SURF matching output for forged passport and camera image

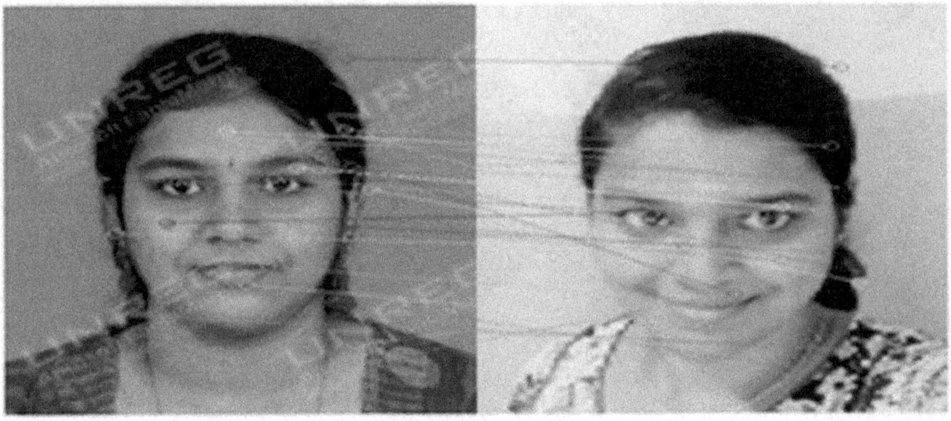

Figure 19. SURF matching output to show that the passport originally belongs to someone else

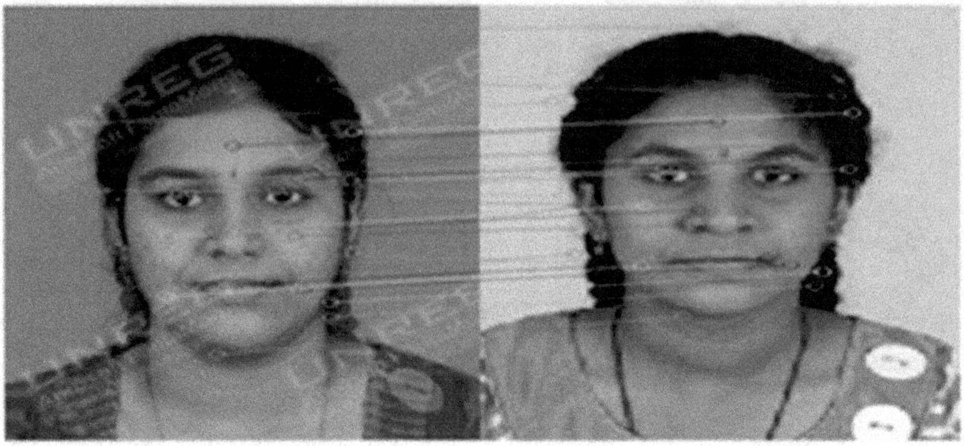

Figure 20. SURF matching output for supposed a national card and camera image

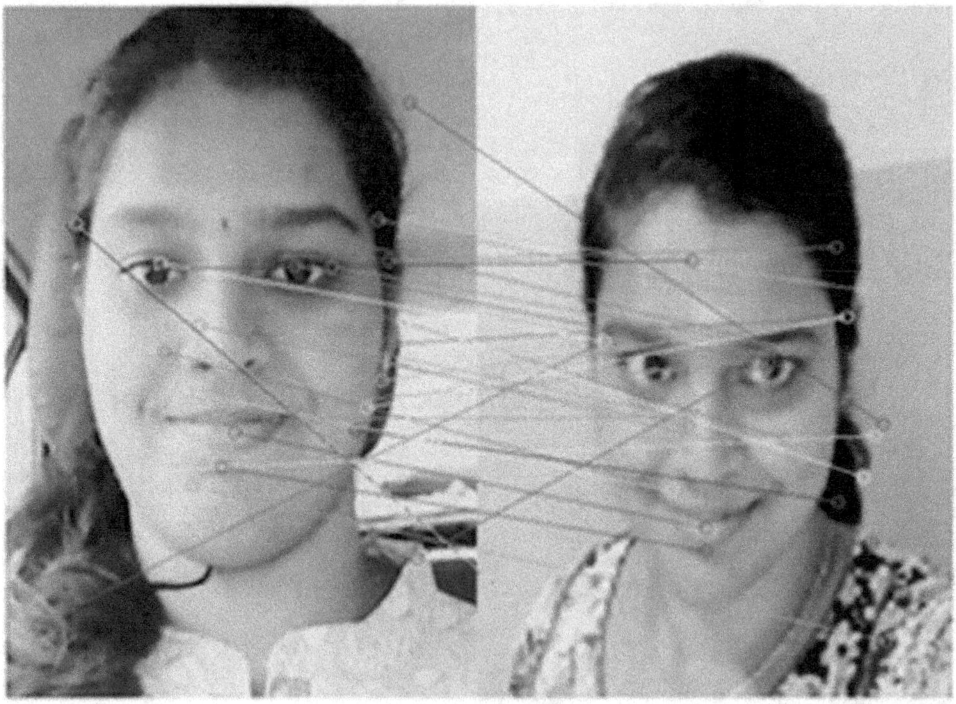

CONCLUSION

Every next transformation in digitalization and entertainment industries is expected to come from the quickly developing field of stereoscopic imagery. As stereoscopic scanning technology and the supporting techniques progress, more everyday tasks in science, economics, and other fields will be solved and presented utilising this approach. We have presented a thorough overview of stereoscopic imaging technologies, their history, uses, and promise in the future in this study. The suggested technique efficiently detects and tracks individuals in a variety of stances and demeanors. Thus, we identify and follow the target human using the wavelet filtering and surf matching algorithms. We also performed the quality check that helps in calibrating the quality of the stereoscopic images. Finally, we successfully applied this method to detect the forged passport.

Advantages

- Forged passports are found in an efficient way.
- By wavelet filtering and SURF matching using an algorithms, we find and follow the suspect.
- The quality of stereoscopic image can be found.
- SURF matching point algorithm is more effective than the SIFT and other matching algorithms.

Limitations

- This system is limited only to a national card holders as of now.
- A bank of legally authorised data needs to be accessed for extraction of true identity.

Future Work

SURF matching point algorithm being an effective matching algorithm can be used in various image processing applications. In our paper, we have simply applied this technique to detect the forged passport by matching the person's image in the passport with that of the corresponding person's image in his/her A national card. This can be extended to find and follow the intended person in the real time 3D environment using video cameras instead of the costly RGB-D camera that is used in our base work. And can be further extended to many of the surveillance applications.

REFERENCES

Benton, S. A. (1993). The second generation of the MIT holographic video system. In *Proc. of TAO First International Symposium on Three Dimensional Image Communication Technology,* (pp. S-3).

Boher, P., Leroux, T., Bignon, T., & Collomb-Patton, V. (2014, February). Optical characterization of auto-stereoscopic 3D displays: interest of the resolution and comparison to human eye properties. In *Advances in Display Technologies IV* (Vol. 9005, pp. 11–22). SPIE.

Bolas, M. T., Lorimer, E. R., McDowall, I. E., & Mead, R. X. (1994, April). Proliferation of counterbalanced, CRT-based stereoscopic displays for virtual environment viewing and control. In *Stereoscopic Displays and Virtual Reality Systems* (Vol. 2177, pp. 325–334). SPIE.

Börner, R. (1993). Autostereoscopic 3D-imaging by front and rear paperion and on flat panel displays. *Displays*, *14*(1), 39–46.

Choi, W., Pantofaru, C., & Savarese, S. (2012). A general framework for tracking multiple people from a moving camera. *IEEE Transactions on Pattern Analysis and Machine Intelligence*, *35*(7), 1577–1591.

Dan, B. K., Kim, Y. S., Jung, J. Y., & Ko, S. J. (2012). Robust people counting system based on sensor fusion. *IEEE Transactions on Consumer Electronics*, *58*(3), 1013–1021.

Dhaya, R., & Kanthavel, R. (2021). Cloud—based multiple importance sampling algorithm with AI based CNN classifier for secure infrastructure. *Automated Software Engineering*, *28*(2), 1–28.

Dhaya, R., Kanthavel, R., & Venusamy, K. (2021a). Cloud computing security protocol analysis with parity- based distributed file system. *Annals of Operations Research*, 1–20.

Dhaya, R., Kanthavel, R., & Venusamy, K. (2021b). Dynamic secure and automated infrastructure for private cloud data center. *Annals of Operations Research*, 1–21.

Eichenlaub, J. B. (1994, April). Autostereoscopic display with high brightness and power efficiency. In *Stereoscopic Displays and Virtual Reality Systems* (Vol. 2177, pp. 4–15). SPIE.

Eichenlaub, J. B., Hollands, D., & Hutchins, J. M. (1995, March). Prototype flat panel hologram-like display that produces multiple perspective views at full resolution. In *Stereoscopic Displays and Virtual Reality Systems II* (Vol. 2409, pp. 102–112). SPIE.

Enzweiler, M., Eigenstetter, A., Schiele, B., & Gavrila, D. M. (2010, June). Multi-cue pedestrian classification with partial occlusion handling. In IEEE computer society conference on computer vision and pattern recognition. IEEE.

Ess, A., Leibe, B., Schindler, K., & Van Gool, L. (2009). Robust multiperson tracking from a mobile platform. *IEEE Transactions on Pattern Analysis and Machine Intelligence*, *31*(10), 1831–1846.

Ezra, D., Woodgate, G. J., Omar, B. A., Holliman, N. S., Harrold, J., & Shapiro, L. S. (1995, March). New autostereoscopic display system. In *Stereoscopic Displays and Virtual Reality Systems II* (Vol. 2409, pp. 31–40). SPIE.

Fröhlich, B., Kirsch, B., Krüger, W., & Wesche, G. (1995). Further development of the responsive workbench. In *Virtual Environments' 95* (pp. 237–246). Springer. doi:10.1007/978-3-7091-9433-1_20

Hamagishi, G. (1995). New stereoscopic LC displays without special glasses. *Asia Display*, *95*, 791–794.

Han, J., Pauwels, E. J., de Zeeuw, P. M., & de With, P. H. (2012). Employing a RGB-D sensor for real-time tracking of humans across multiple re-entries in a smart environment. *IEEE Transactions on Consumer Electronics*, *58*(2), 255–263.

Han, J., Shao, L., Xu, D., & Shotton, J. (2013). Enhanced computer vision with microsoft kinect sensor: A review. *IEEE Transactions on Cybernetics*, *43*(5), 1318–1334.

Hodges, L., & McAllister, D. F. (1993). Stereo Computer Graphics and other True 3D Technologies. *Chapter*, *5*, 71–89.

Isono, H., Yasuda, M., & Sasazawa, H. (1993). Autostereoscopic 3-D display using LCD-generated parallax barrier. *Electronics and Communications in Japan (Part II Electronics)*, *76*(7), 77–84.

Kang, D., Choi, J. H., & Hwang, H. (2022). Autostereoscopic 3D Display System for 3D Medical Images. *Applied Sciences*, *12*(9), 4288.

Liu, X., Chen, S. C., Ma, J., & Yang, L. T. (2013). 3D video representation and design for ubiquitous environments. *Multimedia Tools and Applications*, *67*(1), 1–6. doi:10.100711042-013-1540-7

Lo, C. H., & Chalmers, A. (2003, April). Stereo vision for computer graphics: the effect that stereo vision has on human judgments of visual realism. In *Proceedings of the 19th spring conference on Computer graphics,* (pp. 109-117). 10.1145/984952.984971

McCormick, M. (1995). Integral 3D image for broadcast. In *Proc. 2nd International Display Workshop*, 1995.

Ramakrishnan, D., & Radhakrishnan, K. (2022). Applying deep convolutional neural network (DCNN) algorithm in the cloud autonomous vehicles traffic model. *The International Arab Journal of Information Technology*, *19*(2), 186–194.

Schulze, E. (1995, April). Synthesis of moving holographic stereograms with high-resolution spatial light modulators. In *Practical Holography IX* (Vol. 2406, pp. 124–131). SPIE.

Seera, M., Lim, C. P., Kumar, A., Dhamotharan, L., & Tan, K. H. (2021). An intelligent payment card fraud detection system. *Annals of Operations Research*, 1–23.

Toda, T., Takahashi, S., & Iwata, F. (1995, April). Three-dimensional (3D) video system using grating image. In Practical Holography IX (2406), pp. 191-198). SPIE.

Trayner, D. J., & Orr, E. (1996, April). Autostereoscopic display using holographic optical elements. In *Stereoscopic Displays and Virtual Reality Systems III* (Vol. 2653, pp. 65–74). SPIE.

ADDITIONAL READING

YamadaH.AkiyamaK.MuraokaK.YamaguchiY. (1993). The comparison of three kinds of screens for a volume scanning type 3D display. In Proc. 1st Int. Symp. Three Dimensional Image Communication Technologies (pp. S-5).

Dhaya, R., & Kanthavel, R. (2022). Dynamic automated infrastructure for efficient cloud data centre. *CMC-Computers Materials & Continua*, *71*(1), 1625–1639. doi:10.32604/cmc.2022.022213

Dhaya, R., Kanthavel, R., & Mahalakshmi, M. (2021c). Enriched recognition and monitoring algorithm for private cloud data centre. *Soft Computing*, 1-11.

Chapter 11
IoT-Based Solar Charged Wireless Vehicle Parking Network

Dhaya R.
https://orcid.org/0000-0002-3599-7272
King Khalid University, Saudi Arabia

ABSTRACT

Vehicle parking and vehicle parking place have become inevitable things for the present situation and it contributes to traffic congestion in an indirect manner. The proposed work aims to solve the problem of effectively utilizing the available parking space through an IoT-based parking network during peak hours as well as to charge the system with solar energy as a renewable to ensure reliability in terms of saving time, space, and energy. Because IoT can convey information via the network without encompassing human contacts in the cloud and also permits a user to use affordable wireless technology. the innovative idea of this proposed vehicle parking network is of using solar as renewable energy to charge the sensors in the network. Hence, it is proposed to use the Infrared sensor to be positioned alongside the parking space ESP module. IR sensors will update the current state of available parking spaces for ESP uses light energy observed by the sensors will be used to charge the network. The outcome will benefit the users to manage the parking space effectively and efficiently.

DOI: 10.4018/978-1-6684-5058-1.ch011

INTRODUCTION

With the rise in the usage of vehicles in cities and urban areas, traffic congestion is the main challenge to be addressed. Through designing an IoT-based solar vehicle parking network that comprises a complete wireless sensor network could provide the solution for a vehicle-park organization using sensor nodes. Remote computers connected to the Internet may be used to monitor, control, or manage people (Yuvaraju and Monika, 2017). The development of an IoT-based solar-charged wireless vehicle parking network task entails the creation of an internet-based system that sends data about available and occupied parking spaces through a web page. Each parking space will have an IoT unit, which will include sensors and microcontrollers. The availability of all parking spaces is updated in real-time on the website. The key concept is to build a solar- powered IoT-based wireless vehicle parking network using the Internet of Things and IR sensors, with accessible parking spaces displayed on a web page and solar energy used to charge the wireless network.

Task Motivations

After reviewing the previous tasks, we concluded that there is a possibility to improve in terms of integrating wireless sensors with modern technologies like IoT and Cloud environment effectively and efficiently. The main goal of the IoT-based solar-powered wireless vehicle parking network task is to assist drivers in locating open parking spots in this parking area. Leading up to the scheduled release, drivers can search for a parking place on the internet and look for empty slots using a working Internet connection (Ramakrishnan and Radhakrishnan, 2022).

Problem Definition / Statement

Although the majority of suggested responses focus on the challenge of finding an unoccupied parking space, they ignore other serious problems such as facts about nearby vehicle parking and traffic congestion on the highways (Biswas and Morris, 2004). On the other hand, the Internet of Things (IoT) has recently become a hot topic in smart vehicle parking. A modern urban city can have over a million vehicles on its highways, but it lacks adequate parking space. Furthermore, almost all current researchers advocate data storage in the cloud. However, since raw data is sent on time from distributed sensors to the parking area via the cloud and then received back after processing, this method may be considered a problem. In terms of data transmission, as well as energy expense and utilization, this is a costly strategy. As a result, a proposal is urgently required to design a smart vehicle parking system that will assist users in resolving the problem of monitoring a parking space and reducing the time spent looking for the nearest accessible vehicle park using IoT, ESP, and solar as an energy charger (Kansal et al., 2007). The three key issues concerning managing the parking infrastructure effectively and smartly, as a result of the rising volume of vehicles and the decreasing quality of modern busy parking, are:

- Time spent in parking lots that are inconvenient and inefficient.
- Additional fuel is burned when idling or driving through parking garages, resulting in increased pollution.
- Possibility of fatal accidents caused by vehicles in disordered.

Task Objectives

The use of low-cost sensors, real-time data, and applications in an IoT- based solar-powered wireless vehicle parking network allows users to monitor empty and inaccessible parking spaces (Kanthavel et al., 2022). The objective is to simplify the process and reduce the amount of time spent manually looking for the perfect parking spot. Both the customer and the space provider will benefit greatly from a parking solution using the combination of technology like the internet, sensors, and solar charging. By the end of this task, we will be able to:

- Attain reduced time for parking the Vehicle.
- Ensuring the authentication to enter the parking through IoT-based context.

Background and Relevant Work

As traffic is becoming heavier every day detecting suitable parking slots has been a challenging task. Each parking space may have an IoT system, such as sensors and microcontrollers. The user will get a real-time update on the availability of all available parking spaces. (Tanaka et al., 2006) proposed an image processing technique-based parking system tool. In this case, a video camera is used to invent the car and keep the server updated, and an infrared sensor is connected to the parking area to detect the vehicle (Barriga et al., 2019) reviewed several works related to the implementation of smart parking results in 2019. They also came up with a list of corresponding features based on the types of components that should be calculated while using a smart parking system. With the introduction of the smart parking system, (Idris et al., 2020) was able to quickly discover and secure a vacant parking space at any vehicle park considered appropriate to them. As a result, the different sensor systems used to install the systems have been investigated, as vehicle detection plays an important role in the smart parking system. In an outdoor vehicle park, (Lee, Tan, and Han, 2011) introduced and implemented a battery storage wireless sensor network to provide parking guidance to automobiles. Hence, there is a need of designing an IoT-based solar charge vehicle parking network that should have the capability of solving the problem of vehicle parking smartly (Kanthavel and Dhaya, 2022a).

Significance

IoT offers wireless connectivity to the device, allowing customers to keep a record of the parking area's accessibility. Using IoT to send parking status to users to be displayed. A web will be used with the ability to assess the availability of parking slots and also to enable the service of reserve parking for a limited time. Besides, the light that is observed by the solar panel, embedded in the vehicle parking system will be used to charge the sensor system (Kanthavel and Dhaya, 2022a).

SYSTEM DESIGN ALTERNATIVES

Design Alternatives

Selecting the right design is essential for the task. In this task, an IoT-based solar-charged wireless vehicle parking network is aimed at providing embedded, modern, and secure parking systems, to help users for knowing the free space for parking based on ESP and IoT. This section is a very important phase of this task which allows us to choose the correct design to achieve our task objectives. Hence, the following two different design alternatives are considered to make the right design decision (Rupani and Doshi, 2019).

Design Alternative 1

Figure 1 depicts the planned concept alternative 1's overall block diagram. The device is made up of an Arduino microcontroller unit that has been interfaced with an infrared sensor and a power supply to monitor the operation. The LCD is used to display the parking status. An infrared sensor is used to detect the parking slot and determine if it is occupied or not (Dhaya and Kanthavel, 2021).

The Arduino board is connected to the infrared sensor, which is connected to a 5V supply. This data has been modified to include Liquid Crystal Display (LCD). LCD aims to provide information about available parking spaces (Kanthavel and Dhaya, 2022a).

Figure 1. Design Alternatives 1

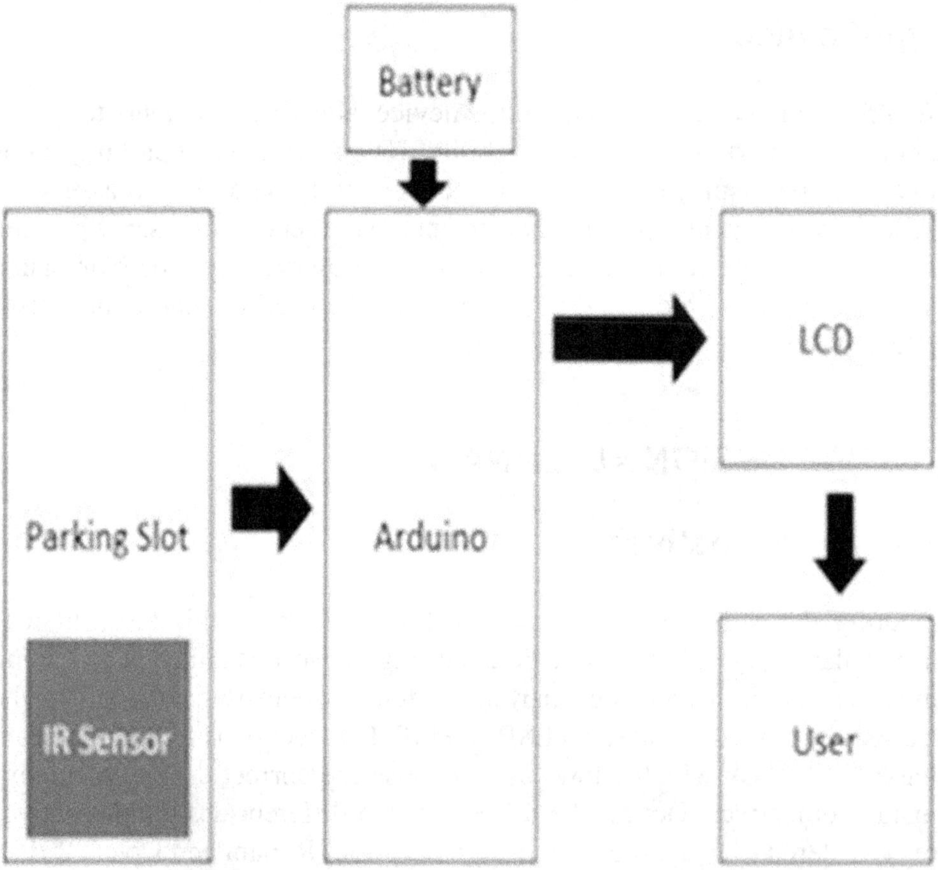

Design Alternative 2

Figure 2 depicts the proposed system's block diagram as a Design option 2. The device consists of an Arduino microcontroller with an infrared sensor, a power supply, an ESP8266, and a solar slot that can provide the system with the required power (Vigorito, C. M et al,2007).

In the design alternative, an innovative idea of replacing existing battery by solar slot to the sensor of the system by which it is assured of continuous renewable source of energy in all times. This Infrared sensor linked with the Arduino board can be provided the necessary power by a solar slot embedded in the system. Like the design alternative 1, the updated information to the server using ESP and by IoT to offer data about the unoccupied parking space can be effectively accomplished (Ess et al., 2009).

Figure 2. Design Alternative 2

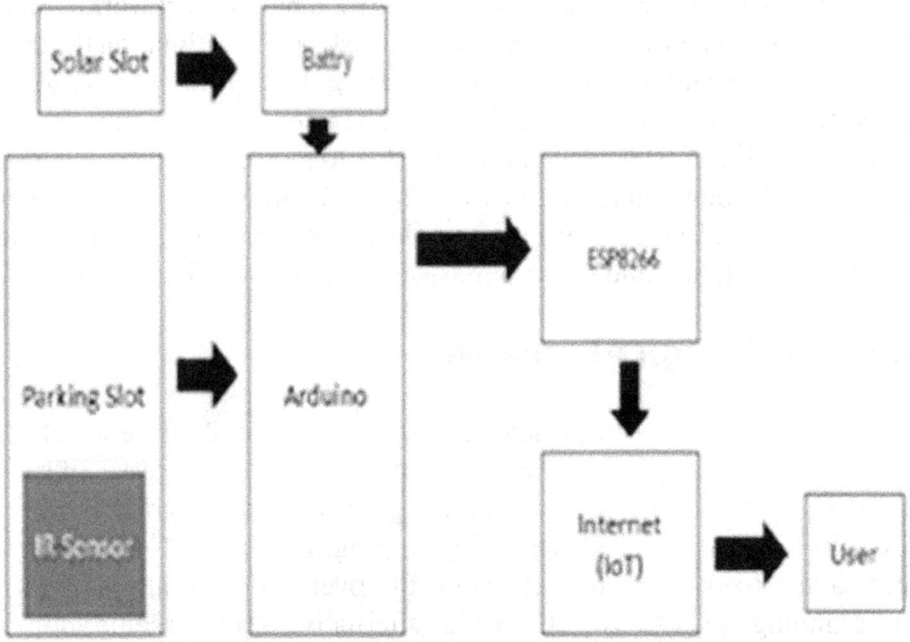

Design Alternatives Evaluation Criteria

In design 1, a sensor is connected to a 5V supply and an infrared sensor is connected to the Arduino board. This data has been modified to include Liquid Crystal Display (LCD). LCD aims to provide information about available parking spaces. In design 2, this Infrared sensor linked with the Arduino board can be provided the necessary power by a solar slot embedded in the system (Kanthavel et al., 2022). In this section, we define the evaluation criteria to compare it between two different designs as follows:

- **Cost:** It is the total amount of money required to complete the task or work, which includes both direct and indirect costs.
- **Real-time:** It means the system updates the data of IoT.

Programming

The total program code is written on the microcontroller to function. The cost is a very important phase that should be clarified before start working on the task. Because when we start working on the task before estimating the overall task cost, may result in a cost excise exceeding the capacity of task workers that will not be easy to complete the task. The internet connection on design alternatives1 is a very critical phase. We should take on our consideration in terms of evaluation criteria because any failing on internet connection due to any reason beyond our control. For example, internet connection failing caused by "ISP" issue that could cause our system to fail also (Zhang et al., 2021).

Selected Design Alternative

Based on what we describe in table 3, design alternatives 2 can be selected due to its design advantages over that of design alternatives-1 in terms of grades. The design alternatives-2 has 21 points grades when design alternatives-2 has only 17 points grades. According to programming in C++ the design alternatives 1 got 2 out of 2, because the overall design alternatives-1 is programming by C++, while the design alternatives-2 needs some additional programming by Hypertext Markup Language HTML to program the web page for the system. According to display the important information to the user in real-time, the design alternatives-2 send the information to the user through the "ESP" module while the design alternatives-1 send the information to the user through LCD, which means the design alternatives-2 is based on the "ESP" network while the design alternatives-1 is based on the wire connection, therefore the design alternatives-2 will be more exposed(Ullah, Z et al,2020). According to the overall cost, the design alternatives-2 is lower than design alternatives-1 in terms of cost. According to the real-time term, the design alternatives-2 based on ESP will be more reliable than design alternatives-1. Finally in terms of system programming; the design alternatives-2 will be easier than the design alternatives-1 (Chen and Chang, 2011).

System Requirements

In this task, our requirements are divided into two main sections. First the software requirements and second the hardware requirements. This requirement depends on our needs. We decided to use an open-source OS and cheap Hardware. This will make it easy to implement by anyone interested in the task. The following figure 3 shows the System Requirements of the Task (Dhaya and Kanthavel, 2022b).

To build a successful 'IoT based solar-charged wireless vehicle parking network' three main part that should be present on the system. First of all, we need to build a system that can track the vehicle when it is stolen. Secondly, the proposed system should be able to partially show from a remote location state (Dhaya and Kanthavel, 2021). Thirdly the system must provide the latest information to the users about the status of the unoccupied parking space in a real-time manner. ESP in the proposed system will allow the communication between user and vehicle parking network from parking to show real-time parking state (Sharma et al., 2011).

FUNCTIONAL REQUIREMENTS

Sensitivity

Readings are obtained from sensors such as the light sensor and the motion sensor. The ESP is to do the main function by sending the available space information of the parking area. Here, an IR sensor is utilized to find the parking space and assess if it is occupied or not (Dhaya and Kanthavel, 2021).

Figure 3. System Requirements

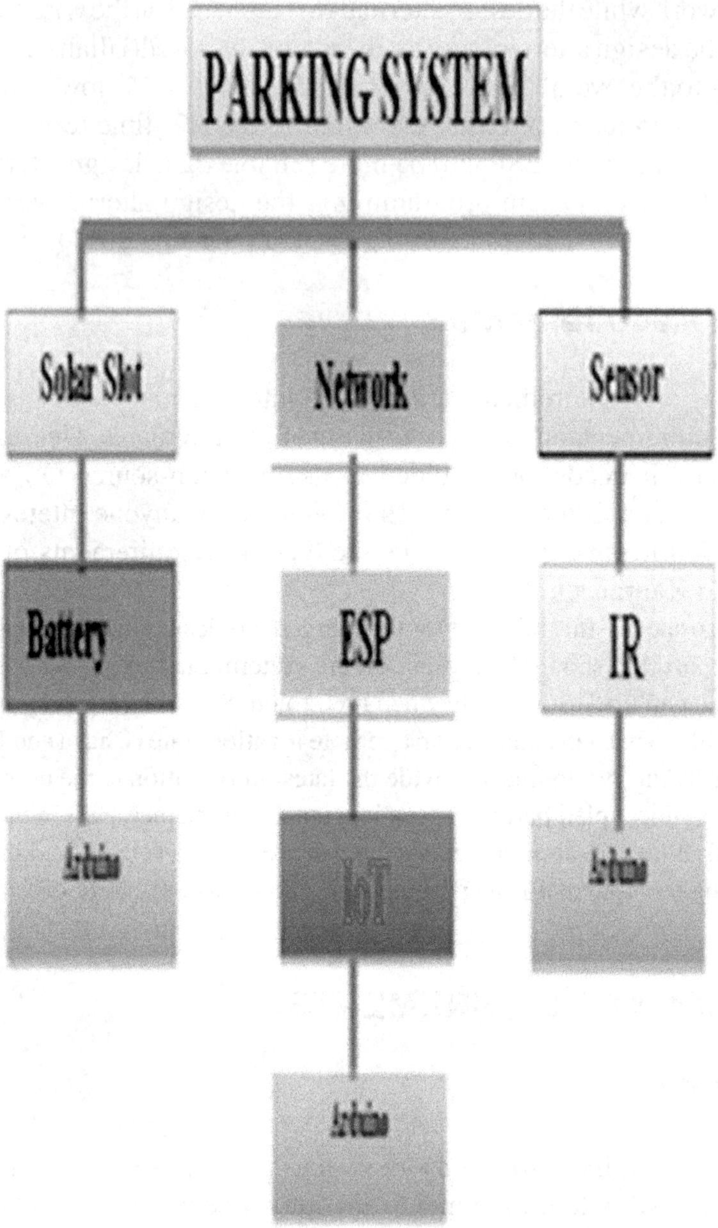

Processing

The data from the sensors is processed by Ardunio Processor to perform operations such as operation, on or off, and sending information. The Arduino Uno will be programming all of the system design module requirements (Dhaya and Kanthavel, 2022a).

Actions

Depending on the operations performed by the Ardunio Processor, the devices connected to it as outputs take actions, either by on or off or sending information. The Solar slot will be providing the necessary power to the system.

Storage

Some data are stored according to consumer demand, either as local storage or IoT/Cloud storage.

Hardware Requirements

The task needs the following hardware components:

- Arduino UNO processor with 6 analog inputs,16 MHz Quartz Crystal, a USB Connection,
- ESP8266 – Node MCU, VCC +3.3 V; can handle up to 3.6 V.
- Solar Slot
- IR Sensor –power supply 3 V-5V, Current Consumption 23 mA - 43 mA
- Battery 5V Supply
- Laptop

Software Requirements

The task needs the following software tools:

- Arduino IDE with including library
- ESP8266 Wi-Fi Library.
- SERVO Library

- Wi-Fi UDP Library
- NTP Client Library
- Solar library
- Operating System Linux

Realistic Constraints

The user of the product should abide by the following constraints enacted during the product development:

- The components should be out of reach of children below 12 years
- The system must work with efficiency between 1° C to 50 ° C
- Movement of the device between places must be vehicle under the supervision of the trained technician
- In an anti-static location, only Sensors should be positioned to get accurate readings.

Sustainability Analysis

Sustainability analysis includes economic, environmental, and social impacts of the proposed 'IoT based solar-charged wireless sensor system' are given as follows:

- **Economics (cost) impact:** The proposed vehicle parking system is cost-effective in terms of design and implements the novel product.
- **Environmental impact:** The emissions of the proposed vehicle parking task will not produce that will affect the environment since solar slot be used as renewable energy (Chinrungrueng, Sununtachaikul, and Triamlumlerd, 2006).
- **Social impact of the product:** Social awareness will be created to utilize the unoccupied places for effective vehicle parking during office or busy hours

SYSTEM DESIGN AND IMPLEMENTATION

This is the stage of hardware and software creation that is focused on the needs of the users. The system design aims to come up with a technological solution that meets the functional needs of IoT based solar wireless vehicle parking network. This network is designed using a microcontroller, IR sensor, and Solar panel. The network is designed such a way to accept input information from the IR sensors about the updated unoccupied space in the vehicle parking slot and is processed by the Arduino processor. The information is then sent to the user's communication device through the ESP (Dhaya, Kanthavel, and Ahilan, 2021).

Detailed Design Description

This section illustrates to dive down into details of our design description. The main components of the IoT based wireless solar vehicle parking network are as follows:

- Microcontroller (ArduinoUNO)
- IR sensor
- ESP8266 model
- Solar Slots
- ESP8266 Wi-Fi library
- Arduino libraries

The functions of all parts have been explained as follows:

Microcontroller (Arduino UNO)

The Arduino Uno which is shown in figure 4, is a micro- controller board that uses the ATmega328 microcontroller (datasheet). Arduino library is a piece of software Serial contact can be done on any of Uno's digital pins using the serial library. The Arduino software is used to program the Arduino Uno (download).

IR Sensor

Infrared detectors are small microchips with a photocell that are set to detect infrared light. Infrared detectors are sorted exclusively for infrared light (Dhaya, Kanthavel, and Mahalakshmil, 2020).

Solar Slots

A photovoltaic module is referred to as a solar panel informally. A PV module is a photovoltaic cell assembly built into a system for installation.

ESP8266 model

Although the ESP8266 is often used as a Serial-to-Wi-Fi bridge, it is also a very versatile microcontroller. Digital input/output pins (I/O or GPIO, General Purpose Input/ Output pins) are available on the ESP8266.

Servo Motor

A servo motor is a rotary or linear actuator that can control angular or linear orientation, velocity, and acceleration precisely.

ESP 8266 Wi-Fi library

The ESP8266WiFi library contains a large number of C++ methods (functions) and properties for configuring and operating an ESP8266 module as a station and/or soft open network.

SERVO Library

This library is capable of controlling a large number of servos. It makes full use of timers in the vehicle: the library can power 12 servos with only one-timer.

Wi-Fi UDP Library

The Wi-Fi UDP class creates a named instance that can send and receive UDP messages.

NTP Client Library

To bind to a time server, use an NTP client. Obtain time from an NTP server and maintain it.

SIMULATION

This section explains the modeling and simulation of the proposed IoT-based solar wireless vehicle parking network. Procedural Steps for Compilation: The steps of compilation is as follows:

- Step 1: Hardwiring the devices on the Breadboard, which include the sensor, Arduino Board, and Solar Battery.
- Step 2: Configure the sensors and Arduino controller to act as desired, and then assign values to the Arduino and sensor outlets, such as Vcc, field, trigger, echo, and so on.
- Step 3: Data Service Provider uses HTML as the language, CSS for design, and PHP for logic to link this data to the webpage.
- Step 4: The Arduino interface links the Arduino to the PC's USB port, allowing data to be streamed.
- Step 5: The design's final assembly is needed for it to work. Step 6: Test and put the plan into action.

Simulation / Prototype / Mathematical model (Feasibility Study)

This task proposed the prototype of IoT-based wireless vehicle parking powered by a solar power network. The key goals of this concept are to build a parking sensor circuit that can detect any obstacles while parking and to develop a successful vehicle parking prototype. The main components of a smart vehicle parking system are distance sensors, LEDs, an Arduino UNO potentiometer, and a solar panel. Where even the Arduino UNO serves as a microcontroller, receiving signals from sensors and transmitting them to LEDs to show vehicle range (Dhaya and Kanthavel, 2022c). The IR sensor is being used to determine the distance between sensor positions and a vehicle. The red or green LED will light up when another vehicle approaches the sensor inside the designated range, and the situation will be sent to the web page for updating. The framework will show the current condition, and the solar cell with a built-in battery pack can provide sufficient power to the smart vehicle parking.

Hardware Implementation

In order to meet out the objectives of the proposed task, the hardware part that involves detailed circuit design, component selection and packaging have been explained in this section.

Implementation Steps

The implementation steps are given as follows:

- **Step 1:** The proposal's key part is an Arduino Uno microcontroller, to which a servo motor, ESP8266, and an IR sensor are linked. When the IR sensor senses the presence of a car, the servo motor functions as a gate at the entry, opening, and closing. The web page shows the parking spaces that are available for vehicle drivers. The Arduino Uno uses the feedback to sense its surroundings. The input is a variety of sensors, which can influence its environment by regulating motors, lights, and other actuators, among other things. The Arduino board's ATmega328 microcontroller is programmed using the Arduino programming language and IDE (Integrated Development Environment).
- **Step 2:** Programming with Arduino: Connect the Arduino board to the device using the USB cable once the Arduino IDE tool is mounted on the PC. Select the right board by going to Tools–>Board..>Arduino Uno in the Arduino IDE, and the right port by going to Tools–>Port in the Arduino IDE. This board is designed using the Arduino programming language, which is based on Wiring.
- **Step 3:** Dump the software code with Files–> Examples.>Basics.> to unlock the Arduino board and flash the LED on the board.
- **Step 4:** It happens in a flash. When the programming codes have been loaded into the IDE, go to the top bar and press the 'upload' button. Check the LED flash on the board until this phase is complete.
- **Step 5:** Connections to Hardware: Connect the Vcc stick to your breadboard's positive rail. Connect the Gnd stick to the breadboard's negative rail. Connect the Arduino's Trig stick to some advanced stick. Connect the Echo stick to any Arduino computerized stick. • Finally, connect the breadboard's positive rail to the Arduino's 5V stick and the breadboard's negative rail to the Arduino's GND stick.

Figure 4. ESP 8266 processor

Demonstration of Implementation

This segment contains a demonstration of the implementation. Figure 8 depicts the three stages of the applied scheme at work.

Figure 5. Infrared sensors connected in the board

SYSTEM TESTING AND EVALUATION

This section elaborates on the verification test description, analysis, and results.

Verification Test Description

To get the desired results, a programming language and interface were needed, as well as logic that would allow the Arduino board to learn the desired requirements. Arduino continues to use its code editor, which supports the

C and C++ programming languages. Over and above, the use of modules to build a virtual runtime environment to run the hardware has also aided Java. Besides, the IR sensor must be configured to work. The Arduino Web Editor, which includes features such as interrupts, bursts, time-outs, and signals, was used to code it. A temporary webpage may be used to view a database of parking space availability. As a result, HTML with a little CSS is used, followed by PHP logic for viewing the parking sensor.

Figure 6. Servo system to open the parking area gate

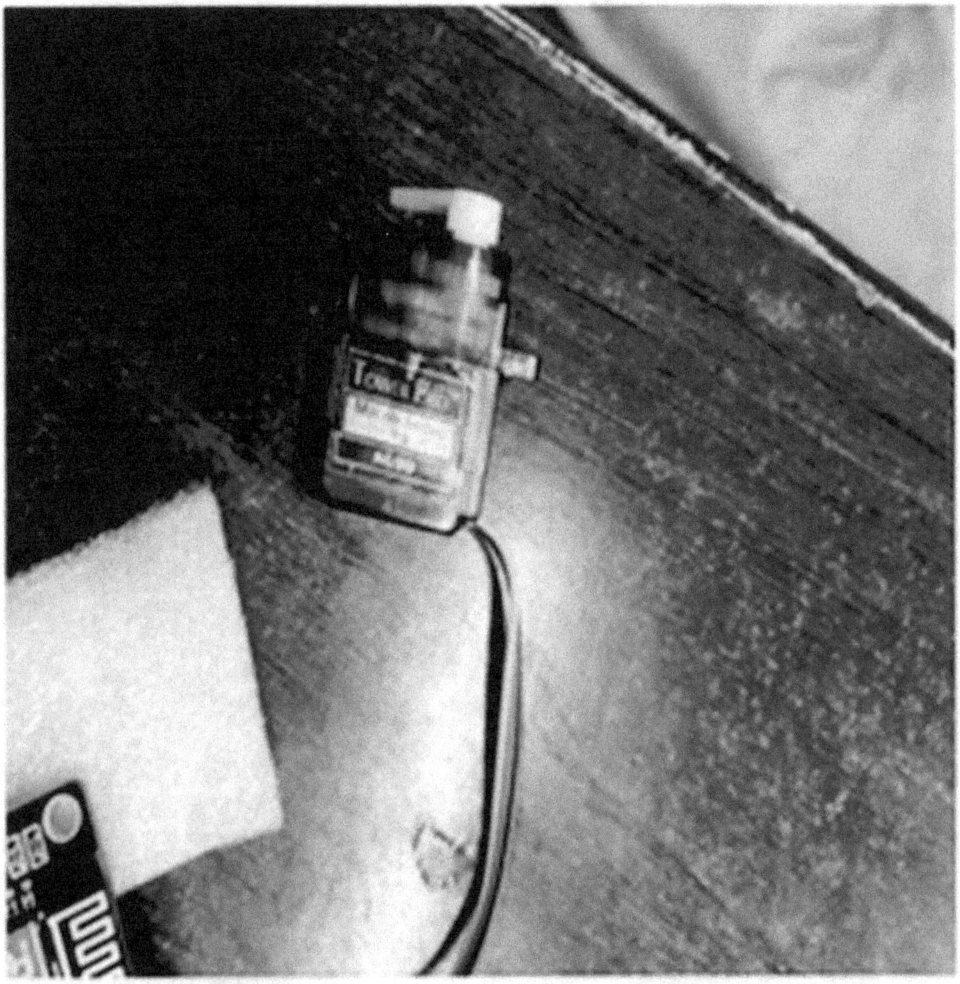

Figure 7. LEDs connected in the Board

Figure 8. Arduino IDE for the controller of the parking network

Figure 9. Parking slots with controller node

Figure 10. Solar panel connected with the battery for the sensor network to Charge

Figure 11. Overall building of proposed wireless vehicle parking network

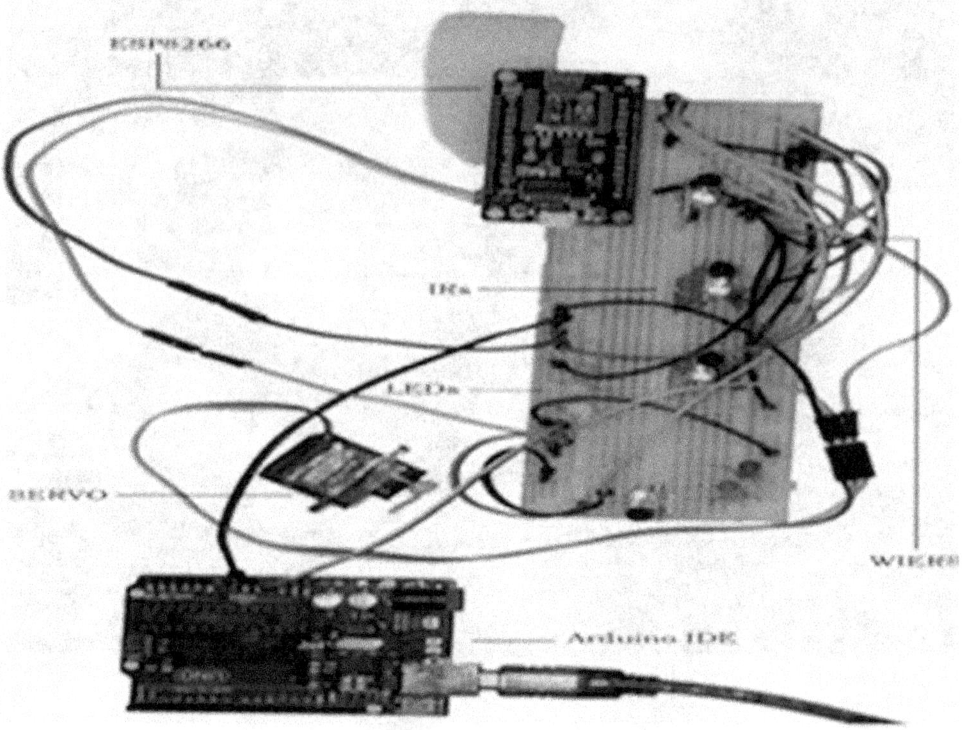

ANALYSIS AND RESULTS

Analysis

The proposed Smart Since it employs a vehicle parking system, it is simpler, more effective, and less time-consuming as it utilizes an IoT-based network that is being connected with the users who wish to park their vehicles to the nearest parking slot. The system also provides high performance in tracking the parking area well in advance before entering into the area of the parking slot. Analysis Steps:

- Step 1: Entry gate sensor detects vehicle.
- Step 2: Servo motor, open the gate
- Step 3: Vehicle looking for parking

- Step 4: Parking sensor detect vehicle (change status in website to green). Save the entry time.
- Step 5: Vehicle going out from parking (change status in website to red).

REFERENCES

Barriga, J. J., Sulca, J., León, J. L., Ulloa, A., Portero, D., Andrade, R., & Yoo, S. G. (2019). Smart parking: A literature review from the technological perspective. *Applied Sciences (Basel, Switzerland)*, *9*(21), 4569. doi:10.3390/app9214569

Biswas, S., & Morris, R. (2004). Opportunistic routing in multi-hop wireless networks. *Computer Communication Review*, *34*(1), 69–74. doi:10.1145/972374.972387

Chen, M., & Chang, T. (2011, June). A parking guidance and information system based on wireless sensor network. In *2011 IEEE International Conference on Information and Automation,* (pp. 601-605). IEEE.

Chinrungrueng, J., Sununtachaikul, U., & Triamlumlerd, S. (2006, June). A vehicular monitoring system with power-efficient wireless sensor networks. In *6th International Conference on ITS Telecommunications,* (pp. 951-954). IEEE.

Dhaya, R., & Kanthavel, R. (2021). Cloud—based multiple importance sampling algorithm with AI based CNN classifier for secure infrastructure. *Automated Software Engineering*, *28*(2), 1–28.

Dhaya, R., & Kanthavel, R. (2022a). Dynamic automated infrastructure for efficient cloud data centre. *CMC-COMPUTERS MATERIALS & CONTINUA*, *71*(1), 1625–1639.

Dhaya, R., & Kanthavel, R. (2022b). IoE based private multi-data center cloud architecture framework. *Computers & Electrical Engineering*, *100*, 107933.

Dhaya, R., & Kanthavel, R. (2022c). Energy Efficient Resource Allocation Algorithm for Agriculture IoT. *Wireless Personal Communications*, 1–23.

Dhaya, R., Kanthavel, R., & Ahilan, A. (2021). Developing an energy-efficient ubiquitous agriculture mobile sensor network-based threshold built-in MAC routing protocol (TBMP). *Soft Computing*, *25*(18), 12333–12342.

Dhaya, R., Kanthavel, R., & Mahalaskhmil, M. (2020). Smart Human Object Identification and Tracking on Soc Through Adaptive TRI-Class Thresholding in Real Time Environment. *Solid State Technology*, *63*(5), 87–101.

Ess, A., Leibe, B., Schindler, K., & Van Gool, L. (2009). Robust multiperson tracking from a mobile platform. *IEEE Transactions on Pattern Analysis and Machine Intelligence*, *31*(10), 1831–1846. doi:10.1109/TPAMI.2009.109 PMID:19696453

Idris, M. I., Leng, Y. Y., Tamil, E. M., Noor, N. M., & Razak, Z. (2009). Car park system: A review of smart parking system and its technology. *Information Technology Journal*, *8*(2), 101–113. doi:10.3923/itj.2009.101.113

Kansal, A., Hsu, J., Zahedi, S., & Srivastava, M. B. (2007). Power management in energy harvesting sensor networks. *ACM Transactions on Embedded Computing Systems*, *6*(4), 32. doi:10.1145/1274858.1274870

Kanthavel, R., & Dhaya, R. (2022a). Wireless underground sensor networks channel using energy efficient clustered communication. *Intelligent Automation and Soft Computing*, *31*(1), 649–659.

Kanthavel, R., Dhaya, R., & Venusamy, K. (2022). Detection of Osteoarthritis Based on EHO Thresholding. *CMC-COMPUTERS MATERIALS & CONTINUA*, *71*(3), 5783–5798.

Kanthavel, R., Priyadharshini, S. I., Sudha, D., Velrani, K. S., & Dhaya, R. (2022). Multi-hoped cooperative communication-based wireless underground sensor network design. *International Journal of Communication Systems*, *35*(10), e5174.

Lee, P., Tan, H. P., & Han, M. (2011, November). A solar-powered wireless parking guidance system for outdoor car parks. In *Proceedings of the 9th ACM Conference on Embedded Networked Sensor Systems,* (pp. 423-424). 10.1145/2070942.2071020

Ramakrishnan, D., & Radhakrishnan, K. (2022). Applying deep convolutional neural network (DCNN) algorithm in the cloud autonomous vehicles traffic model. *The International Arab Journal of Information Technology*, *19*(2), 186–194. doi:10.34028/iajit/19/2/5

Rupani, S., & Doshi, N. (2019). A review of smart parking using internet of things (IoT). *Procedia Computer Science*, *160*, 706–711. doi:10.1016/j.procs.2019.11.023

Shaheen, S. (2005). Smart parking management field test: A bay area rapid transit (bart) district parking demonstration.

Sharma, A., Chaki, R., & Bhattacharya, U. (2011, April). Applications of wireless sensor network in Intelligent Traffic System: A review. In *3rd International Conference on Electronics Computer Technology, 5*, (pp. 53-57). IEEE.

Tanaka, Y., Saiki, M., Katoh, M., & Endo, T. (2006). Development of image recognition for a parking assist system. *Proc. 13th World Congr. Intell. Transp. Syst. Services*, 1-7.

Ullah, Z., Al-Turjman, F., Mostarda, L., & Gagliardi, R. (2020). Applications of artificial intelligence and machine learning in smart cities. *Computer Communications*, *154*, 313–323. doi:10.1016/j.comcom.2020.02.069

Vigorito, C. M., Ganesan, D., & Barto, A. G. (2007, June). Adaptive control of duty cycling in energy-harvesting wireless sensor networks. In *4th Annual IEEE communications society conference on sensor, mesh and ad hoc communications and networks,* (pp. 21-30). IEEE. 10.1109/SAHCN.2007.4292814

Yuvaraju, M., & Monika, M. (2017). IoT based vehicle parking place detection using arduino. *International Journal of Engineering Sciences & Research Technology*, 536–542.

Zhang, C., Zhou, R., Lei, L., & Yang, X. (2021). Research on Automatic Parking System Strategy. *World Electric Vehicle Journal*, *12*(4), 200. doi:10.3390/wevj12040200

ADDITIONAL READING

Dhaya, R., & Kanthavel, R. (2022b). Video surveillance-based urban flood monitoring system using a convolutional neural network. *INTELLIGENT AUTOMATION AND SOFT COMPUTING*, *32*(1), 183–192. doi:10.32604/iasc.2022.021538

Dhaya, R., & Kanthavel, R. (2022c). Energy Efficient Resource Allocation Algorithm for Agriculture IoT. *Wireless Personal Communications*, *125*(2), 1–23. doi:10.100711277-022-09607-z

Dhaya, R., Kanthavel, R., & Mahalakshmi, M. (2021). Enriched recognition and monitoring algorithm for private cloud data centre. *Soft Computing*, 1–11. doi:10.100700500-021-05967-z

Dhaya, R., Kanthavel, R., & Venusamy, K. (2021a). Dynamic secure and automated infrastructure for private cloud data center. *Annals of Operations Research*, 1–21. doi:10.100710479-021-04442-0

Dhaya, R., Kanthavel, R., & Venusamy, K. (2021b). Cloud computing security protocol analysis with parity-based distributed file system. *Annals of Operations Research*, 1–20. doi:10.100710479-021-04413-5

Kanthavel, R., & Dhaya, R. (2022b). Prediction Model Using Reinforcement Deep Learning Technique for Osteoarthritis Disease Diagnosis. *Computer Systems Science and Engineering*, *42*(1), 257–269. doi:10.32604/csse.2022.021606

Compilation of References

Ali, N., Bahman, A. M., Aljuwayhel, N. F., Ebrahim, S. A., Mukherjee, S., & Alsayegh, A. (2021). Carbon-based nanofluids and their advances towards heat transfer applications—A review. *Nanomaterials (Basel, Switzerland)*, *11*(6), 1628. doi:10.3390/nano11061628 PMID:34205801

Anderson, J. A. (1995). *An introduction to neural networks*. MIT press.

Andrieu, C., De Freitas, N., Doucet, A., & Jordan, M. I. (2003). An introduction to MCMC for machine learning. *Machine Learning*, *50*(1), 5–43. doi:10.1023/A:1020281327116

Arsham, H. (1994 February 25). Computer-assisted Learning Concepts & Techniques. UBalt. http://home.ubalt.edu/ntsbarsh/business-stat/opre/partX.htm#rLPSotGuide

Atzori, L., Iera, A., & Morabito, G. (2010). The internet of things: A survey. *Computer Networks*, *54*(15), 2787–2805. doi:10.1016/j.comnet.2010.05.010

Balanis, C. A. (2015). *Antenna theory: analysis and design*. John wiley & sons.

Banumathi, J., Sangeetha, S. K. B., & Dhaya, R. (2022). Robust Cooperative Spectrum Sensing Techniques for a Practical Framework Employing Cognitive Radios in 5G Networks. *Artificial Intelligent Techniques for Wireless Communication and Networking*, 121-138.

Banupriya, D., Pandi, S. P., & Prathisha, R. R. (2018). A study on use of artificial intelligence in wireless communications. *Asian Journal of Applied Science and Technology*, *2*(1), 354–360.

Barriga, J. J., Sulca, J., León, J. L., Ulloa, A., Portero, D., Andrade, R., & Yoo, S. G. (2019). Smart parking: A literature review from the technological perspective. *Applied Sciences (Basel, Switzerland)*, *9*(21), 4569. doi:10.3390/app9214569

Bayam, Y., Unal, H., & Ekiz, H. (2003). Distance education application on logic circuits [Mantıksal devreler üzerinde uzaktan eğitim uygulaması.]. *The Turkish Online Journal of Educational Technology*, *2*, 92–94.

Beatty, K. (2013). *Teaching & researching: Computer-assisted language learning*. Routledge. doi:10.4324/9781315833774

Benson, P. (2001). *Teaching and researching autonomy in language learning. Harlow.* Pearson Education.

Benton, S. A. (1993). The second generation of the MIT holographic video system. In *Proc. of TAO First International Symposium on Three Dimensional Image Communication Technology,* (pp. S-3).

Biswas, S., & Morris, R. (2004). Opportunistic routing in multi-hop wireless networks. *Computer Communication Review, 34*(1), 69–74. doi:10.1145/972374.972387

Bobrow, D. G. (1964). Natural language input for a computer problem solving system.

Boher, P., Leroux, T., Bignon, T., & Collomb-Patton, V. (2014, February). Optical characterization of auto-stereoscopic 3D displays: interest of the resolution and comparison to human eye properties. In *Advances in Display Technologies IV* (Vol. 9005, pp. 11–22). SPIE.

Bohlouli, M., Schulz, F., Angelis, L., Pahor, D., Brandic, I., Atlan, D., & Tate, R. (2013). Towards an integrated platform for big data analysis. In *Integration of practice-oriented knowledge technology: Trends and prospectives* (pp. 47–56). Springer. doi:10.1007/978-3-642-34471-8_4

Bolas, M. T., Lorimer, E. R., McDowall, I. E., & Mead, R. X. (1994, April). Proliferation of counterbalanced, CRT-based stereoscopic displays for virtual environment viewing and control. In *Stereoscopic Displays and Virtual Reality Systems* (Vol. 2177, pp. 325–334). SPIE.

Bolton, W. (2015). *Programmable logic controllers.* Newnes.

Börner, R. (1993). Autostereoscopic 3D-imaging by front and rear paperion and on flat panel displays. *Displays, 14*(1), 39–46.

Boussada, R., Hamdane, B., Elhdhili, M. E., & Saidane, L. A. (2019, April). PP-NDNoT: On preserving privacy in IoT-based E-health systems over NDN. In IEEE Wireless Communications and Networking Conference (WCNC,) (pp. 1-6). IEEE.

Bryan, G. L. (1969). Computers and education. *Computers and Automation, 18*(3), 1–4.

Businesswire. (2018, June 18). *IDC forecasts worldwide technology spending on the internet of things to reach $1.2 trillion in 2022.* **Error! Hyperlink reference not valid.**

Büyükbayraktar, M. (2006). *The effect of computer-aided application of logic circuit design on student success. [Lojik devre tasarımının bilgisayar destekli olarak uygulanmasının öğrenci başarısına etkisi]* [Doctoral dissertation]. Sakarya Universitesi, Turkey.

Byrne, J. R., O'Sullivan, K., & Sullivan, K. (2016). An IoT and wearable technology hackathon for promoting careers in computer science. *IEEE Transactions on Education, 60*(1), 50–58.

Calabrese, F. D., Wang, L., Ghadimi, E., Peters, G., Hanzo, L., & Soldati, P. (2018). Learning radio resource management in RANs: Framework, opportunities, and challenges. *IEEE Communications Magazine, 56*(9), 138–145. doi:10.1109/MCOM.2018.1701031

Câmara, D., & Nikaein, N. (Eds.). (2016). *Wireless public safety networks 2: a systematic approach*. Elsevier.

Carbonell, J. R. (1969, September). Interactive non-deterministic computer-assisted instruction. In *Proc. Internat. Symp. on Man-Machine Syst*

Cattell, R. (2011). Scalable SQL and NoSQL data stores. *SIGMOD Record, 39*(4), 12–27. doi:10.1145/1978915.1978919

Chapelle, C. A. (2001). *Computer applications in second language acquisition*. Cambridge University Press. doi:10.1017/CBO9781139524681

Chapelle, C. A., & Hegelheimer, V. (2013). The language teacher in the 21st century. In *New perspectives on CALL for second language classrooms,* (pp. 311–328). Routledge.

Charpentier, E., & Laurin, J. J. (1999). An implementation of a direction-finding antenna for mobile communications using a neural network. *IEEE Transactions on Antennas and Propagation, 47*(7), 1152–1159.

Chen, M., Challita, U., Saad, W., Yin, C., & Debbah, M. (2017). Machine learning for wireless networks with artificial intelligence: A tutorial on neural networks. arXiv preprint arXiv:1710.02913, 9.

Chen, C. Y., Zhu, G., Hu, Y., Yu, J. W., Song, J., Cheng, K. Y., Peng, L.-H., Chou, L.-J., & Wang, Z. L. (2012). Gallium nitride nanowire based nanogenerators and light-emitting diodes. *ACS Nano, 6*(6), 5687–5692. doi:10.1021/nn301814w PMID:22607154

Chen, M., & Chang, T. (2011, June). A parking guidance and information system based on wireless sensor network. In *2011 IEEE International Conference on Information and Automation,* (pp. 601-605). IEEE.

Chen, S. L. (2015). Research on fuzzy comprehensive evaluation in practice teaching assessment of computer majors. *International Journal of Modern Education & Computer Science, 7*(11), 12–19. doi:10.5815/ijmecs.2015.11.02

Cheon, H. (2003). The viability of computer mediated communication in the Korean secondary EFL classroom. *Asian EFL Journal, 5*(1), 1–61.

Chinrungrueng, J., Sununtachaikul, U., & Triamlumlerd, S. (2006, June). A vehicular monitoring system with power-efficient wireless sensor networks. In *6th International Conference on ITS Telecommunications,* (pp. 951-954). IEEE.

Choi, W., Pantofaru, C., & Savarese, S. (2012). A general framework for tracking multiple people from a moving camera. *IEEE Transactions on Pattern Analysis and Machine Intelligence, 35*(7), 1577–1591.

Cisco. (2022, August 18). *Internet of things (IOT) products & solutions*. Cisco. https://www.cisco.com/c/en/us/solutions/internet-of-things/overview.html#~industries

Clarke, D. (1989). Design consideration in writing CALL software with particular reference to extended materials. In Computer assisted language learning: Program structure and principles, (pp. 28-37).

Collins, A., & Quillian, M. (1969). Retrieval time from semantic memory. journal of. *Verbal Learning and Verbal Behavior, 8*,240, 247.

Collobert, R., & Weston, J. (2008, July). A unified architecture for natural language processing: Deep neural networks with multitask learning. In *Proceedings of the 25th international conference on Machine learning*, (pp. 160-167). doi:10.1145/1390156.1390177

Coniam, D., & Wong, R. (2004). Internet Relay Chat as a tool in the autonomous development of ESL learners' English language ability: An exploratory study. *System*, *32*(3), 321–335. doi:10.1016/j.system.2004.03.001

Dan, B. K., Kim, Y. S., Jung, J. Y., & Ko, S. J. (2012). Robust people counting system based on sensor fusion. *IEEE Transactions on Consumer Electronics*, *58*(3), 1013–1021.

David, K., & Berndt, H. (2018). 6G vision and requirements: Is there any need for beyond 5G? *IEEE Vehicular Technology Magazine*, *13*(3), 72–80.

Davies, G. (1997). Lessons from the past, lessons for the future: 20 years of CALL. *New technologies in language learning and teaching, Strasbourg: Council of Europe.[Electronic resource]*.: http://www. camsoftpartners. co. uk/coegdd1. Htm/

Davies, G. (2005, June). Computer Assisted Language Learning: Where are we now and where are we going. In Keynote speech at the University of Ulster Centre for Research in Applied Languages UCALL conference:"Developing a pedagogy for CALL (pp. 13-15).

Davies, G., Bangs, P., Frisby, R., & Walton, E. (2005). languages ICT. *Setting up effective digital language laboratories and multimedia ICT suites for MFL.* CILT.

Davies, G. (1982). *Computer, Language and Language Learning*. Centre for Information on Language Teaching and Research.

De Szendeffy, J. (2005). *A practical guide to using computers in language teaching*. University of Michigan Press. doi:10.3998/mpub.97662

Devi, M., Dhaya, R., Kanthavel, R., Algarni, F., & Dixikha, P. (2019, May). Data Science for Internet of Things (IoT). In *International Conference on Computer Networks and Inventive Communication Technologies,* (pp. 60-70). Springer, Cham.

Dhaya, R., & Kanthavel, R. (2022). IoE based private multi-data center cloud architecture framework. Computers & Electrical Engineering, 100, 107933.

Dhaya, R., & Kanthavel, R. (2021). Cloud—based multiple importance sampling algorithm with AI based CNN classifier for secure infrastructure. *Automated Software Engineering*, *28*(2), 1–28.

Dhaya, R., & Kanthavel, R. (2021). Cloud—Based multiple importance sampling algorithm with AI based CNN classifier for secure infrastructure. *Automated Software Engineering*, *28*(2), 1–28. doi:10.100710515-021-00293-y

Dhaya, R., & Kanthavel, R. (2022). Energy Efficient Resource Allocation Algorithm for Agriculture IoT. *Wireless Personal Communications*, 1–23.

Dhaya, R., & Kanthavel, R. (2022a). Dynamic automated infrastructure for efficient cloud data centre. *CMC-COMPUTERS MATERIALS & CONTINUA*, *71*(1), 1625–1639.

Dhaya, R., & Kanthavel, R. (2022b). IoE based private multi-data center cloud architecture framework. *Computers & Electrical Engineering*, *100*, 107933.

Dhaya, R., Kanthavel, R., & Ahilan, A. (2021). Developing an energy-efficient ubiquitous agriculture mobile sensor network-based threshold built-in MAC routing protocol (TBMP). *Soft Computing*, *25*(18), 12333–12342. doi:10.100700500-021-05927-7

Dhaya, R., Kanthavel, R., Algarni, F., Jayarajan, P., & Mahor, A. (2020). Reinforcement Learning Concepts Ministering Smart City Applications Using IoT. In *Internet of Things in Smart Technologies for Sustainable Urban Development,* (pp. 19–41). Springer.

Dhaya, R., Kanthavel, R., & Mahalakshmi, M. (2021). Enriched recognition and monitoring algorithm for private cloud data centre. *Soft Computing*, 1–11. doi:10.100700500-021-05967-z

Dhaya, R., Kanthavel, R., & Mahalaskhmil, M. (2020). Smart Human Object Identification and Tracking on Soc Through Adaptive TRI-Class Thresholding in Real Time Environment. *Solid State Technology*, *63*(5), 87–101.

Dhaya, R., Kanthavel, R., & Venusamy, K. (2021a). Cloud computing security protocol analysis with parity- based distributed file system. *Annals of Operations Research*, 1–20.

Dhaya, R., Kanthavel, R., & Venusamy, K. (2021b). Dynamic secure and automated infrastructure for private cloud data center. *Annals of Operations Research*, 1–21.

Diana, L. (1993). Rethinking University Teaching: A framework for the effective use of educational technology. Routledge, London/New York, 93, 94.

Dobrilovic, D., & Zeljko, S. (2016, May). Design of open-source platform for introducing Internet of Things in university curricula. In *IEEE 11th International Symposium on Applied Computational Intelligence and Informatics (SACI),* (pp. 273-276). IEEE.

Egbert, J., & Hanson-Smith, E. (1999). CALL environments: Research, practice, and critical issues. Teachers of English to Speakers of Other Languages.

Egbert, J. L., & Petrie, G. M. (Eds.). (2006). *CALL research perspectives*. Routledge. doi:10.4324/9781410613578

Eichenlaub, J. B. (1994, April). Autostereoscopic display with high brightness and power efficiency. In *Stereoscopic Displays and Virtual Reality Systems* (Vol. 2177, pp. 4–15). SPIE.

Eichenlaub, J. B., Hollands, D., & Hutchins, J. M. (1995, March). Prototype flat panel hologram-like display that produces multiple perspective views at full resolution. In *Stereoscopic Displays and Virtual Reality Systems II* (Vol. 2409, pp. 102–112). SPIE.

El Zooghby, A. H., Christodoulou, C. G., & Georgiopoulos, M. (2000). A neural network-based smart antenna for multiple source tracking. *IEEE Transactions on Antennas and Propagation*, *48*(5), 768–776.

Enzweiler, M., Eigenstetter, A., Schiele, B., & Gavrila, D. M. (2010, June). Multi-cue pedestrian classification with partial occlusion handling. In IEEE computer society conference on computer vision and pattern recognition. IEEE.

Erman, M., Mohammed, A., & Rakus-Andersson, E. (2009, July). Fuzzy Logic Applications in Wireless Communications. In *IFSA/EUSFLAT Conf,* (pp. 763-767).

Ess, A., Leibe, B., Schindler, K., & Van Gool, L. (2009). Robust multiperson tracking from a mobile platform. *IEEE Transactions on Pattern Analysis and Machine Intelligence*, *31*(10), 1831–1846.

Ezra, D., Woodgate, G. J., Omar, B. A., Holliman, N. S., Harrold, J., & Shapiro, L. S. (1995, March). New autostereoscopic display system. In *Stereoscopic Displays and Virtual Reality Systems II* (Vol. 2409, pp. 31–40). SPIE.

Felix, U. (2001). Beyond Babel: Language Learning Online. Publications and Clearinghouse Manager, Language Australia.

Felix, U. (2002). The web as a vehicle for constructivist approaches in language teaching. *ReCALL*, *14*(1), 2–15. doi:10.1017/S0958344002000216

Feurzeig, W., Papert, S., Bloom, M., Grant, R., & Solomon, C. (1970). Programming-languages as a conceptual framework for teaching mathematics. *ACM SIGCUE Outlook*, *4*(2), 13–17. doi:10.1145/965754.965757

Fitzpatrick, A. (2004). Information and communication technology in foreign language teaching and learning–An Overview. *Analytical Survey*, 10.

Fotos, S. (2013). Writing as talking: E-mail exchange for promoting proficiency and motivation in the foreign language classroom. In *New perspectives on CALL for second language classrooms,* (pp. 121–142). Routledge. doi:10.4324/9781410610775

Freeman, W. T., Pasztor, E. C., & Carmichael, O. T. (2000). Learning low-level vision. *International Journal of Computer Vision*, *40*(1), 25–47. doi:10.1023/A:1026501619075

Fresegna, A. M., Ursini, C. L., Ciervo, A., Maiello, R., Casciardi, S., Iavicoli, S., & Cavallo, D. (2021). Assessment of the influence of crystalline form on cyto-genotoxic and inflammatory effects induced by TiO2 nanoparticles on human bronchial and alveolar cells. *Nanomaterials (Basel, Switzerland)*, *11*(1), 253. doi:10.3390/nano11010253 PMID:33478013

Fröhlich, B., Kirsch, B., Krüger, W., & Wesche, G. (1995). Further development of the responsive workbench. In *Virtual Environments' 95* (pp. 237–246). Springer. doi:10.1007/978-3-7091-9433-1_20

Gani, A., Siddiqa, A., Shamshirband, S., & Hanum, F. (2016). A survey on indexing techniques for big data: Taxonomy and performance evaluation. *Knowledge and Information Systems, 46*(2), 241–284. doi:10.100710115-015-0830-y

Garofalo, F., Mota-Moya, P., Munday, A., & Romy, S. (2017). Total extraperitoneal hernia repair: Residency teaching program and outcome evaluation. *World Journal of Surgery, 41*(1), 100–105. doi:10.100700268-016-3710-z PMID:27637604

Ghosh, A., Chakraborty, D., & Law, A. (2018). Artificial intelligence in Internet of things. *CAAI Transactions on Intelligence Technology, 3*(4), 208–218.

Gong, G., & Liu, S. (2016). Consideration of evaluation of teaching at colleges. *Open Journal of Social Sciences, 4*(07), 82–84. doi:10.4236/jss.2016.47013

Gorelik, E. (2013). *Cloud computing models*. [Doctoral dissertation]. Massachusetts Institute of Technology, Massachusetts.

Gubbi, J., Buyya, R., Marusic, S., & Palaniswami, M. (2013). Internet of Things (IoT): A vision, architectural elements, and future directions. *Future Generation Computer Systems, 29*(7), 1645–1660. doi:10.1016/j.future.2013.01.010

Gunawardhana, L. P. D. (2020). Introduction to Computer-Aided Learning. *Global Journal of Computer Science and Technology*.

Gunawardhana, L. P. D. (2020). *Introduction to Computer-Aided Learning*. Global Journal of Computer Science and Technology.

Gupta, B., Sankaralingam, S., & Dhar, S. (2010, August). Development of wearable and implantable antennas in the last decade: A review. In *10th Mediterranean Microwave Symposium,* (pp. 251-267). IEEE.

Hamagishi, G. (1995). New stereoscopic LC displays without special glasses. *Asia Display, 95*, 791–794.

Han, J., Pauwels, E. J., de Zeeuw, P. M., & de With, P. H. (2012). Employing a RGB-D sensor for real-time tracking of humans across multiple re-entries in a smart environment. *IEEE Transactions on Consumer Electronics, 58*(2), 255–263.

Han, J., Shao, L., Xu, D., & Shotton, J. (2013). Enhanced computer vision with microsoft kinect sensor: A review. *IEEE Transactions on Cybernetics, 43*(5), 1318–1334.

Haykin, S., & Network, N. (2004). A comprehensive foundation. *Neural Networks, 2*, 41.

Hearle, J. W., & Morton, W. E. (2008). *Physical properties of textile fibres*. Elsevier.

He, H., Wen, C. K., Jin, S., & Li, G. Y. (2018). Deep learning-based channel estimation for beamspace mmWave massive MIMO systems. *IEEE Wireless Communications Letters*, *7*(5), 852–855. doi:10.1109/LWC.2018.2832128

Hendrick, S. (2015 September 9). Why Gateways and Controllers Are Critical for IoT Architecture. RTInsights. https://www.rtinsights.com/why-gateways-and-controllers-are-critical-for-iot-architecture/

Hilker, S. (2012). Survey Distributed Databases—Toad for Cloud.

Hoang, D. T., Nguyen, D. N., Alsheikh, M. A., Gong, S., Dutkiewicz, E., Niyato, D., & Han, Z. (2020). Borrowing Arrows with Thatched Boats": The Art of Defeating Reactive Jammers in IoT Networks. *IEEE Wireless Communications*, *27*(3), 79–87.

Hodges, L., & McAllister, D. F. (1993). Stereo Computer Graphics and other True 3D Technologies. *Chapter*, *5*, 71–89.

Hodges, S., Taylor, S., Villar, N., Scott, J., Bial, D., & Fischer, P. T. (2012). Prototyping connected devices for the internet of things. *Computer*, *46*(2), 26–34. doi:10.1109/MC.2012.394

Huang, L., Wan, K., Yan, J., Wang, L., Li, Q., Chen, H., Zhang, H., & Xiao, T. (2021). Nanomaterials in Water Applications: Adsorbing Materials for Fluoride Removal. *Nanomaterials (Basel, Switzerland)*, *11*(7), 1866. doi:10.3390/nano11071866 PMID:34361252

Hubbard, P. (2006). A Review of Subject and Treatment Characteristics in CMC Research, PacSLRF Conference. Brisbane, Australia. www.stanford.edu/~efs/pacslrf06

Hubbard, P. (2003). A survey of unanswered questions in CALL. *Computer Assisted Language Learning*, *16*(2-3), 141–154. doi:10.1076/call.16.2.141.15882

Hubbard, P. (2005). A review of subject characteristics in CALL research. *Computer Assisted Language Learning*, *18*(5), 351–368. doi:10.1080/09588220500442632

Idris, M. I., Leng, Y. Y., Tamil, E. M., Noor, N. M., & Razak, Z. (2009). Car park system: A review of smart parking system and its technology. *Information Technology Journal*, *8*(2), 101–113. doi:10.3923/itj.2009.101.113

Isono, H., Yasuda, M., & Sasazawa, H. (1993). Autostereoscopic 3-D display using LCD-generated parallax barrier. *Electronics and Communications in Japan (Part II Electronics)*, *76*(7), 77–84.

Jalali, N., Woolliams, P., Stewart, M., Weaver, P. M., Cain, M. G., Dunn, S., & Briscoe, J. (2014). Improved performance of p–n junction-based ZnO nanogenerators through CuSCN-passivation of ZnO nanorods. *Journal of Materials Chemistry. A, Materials for Energy and Sustainability*, *2*(28), 10945–10951. doi:10.1039/c4ta01714e

Jarvis, H. (2005). Technology and change in English language teaching (ELT). *The Asian EFL Journal*, *7*(4), 213–227.

Johnson, L., Adams Becker, S., Cummins, M., Estrada, V., Freeman, A., & Hall, C. (2012). The NMC horizon report: 2012 higher education ed. Austin, TX: The New Media Consortium.

Kang, D., Choi, J. H., & Hwang, H. (2022). Autostereoscopic 3D Display System for 3D Medical Images. *Applied Sciences*, *12*(9), 4288.

Kannadhasan, S., & Nagarajan, R. (2021). Development of an H-shaped antenna with FR4 for 1–10 GHz wireless communications. *Textile Research Journal*, *91*(15-16), 1687–1697.

Kannadhasan, S., & Nagarajan, R. (2022). Performance improvement of H-shaped antenna with zener diode for textile applications. *Journal of the Textile Institute*, *113*(8), 1707–1714.

Kansal, A., Hsu, J., Zahedi, S., & Srivastava, M. B. (2007). Power management in energy harvesting sensor networks. *ACM Transactions on Embedded Computing Systems*, *6*(4), 32. doi:10.1145/1274858.1274870

Kanthavel, R., & Dhaya, R. (2022a). Wireless underground sensor networks channel using energy efficient clustered communication. *Intelligent Automation and Soft Computing*, *31*(1), 649–659.

Kanthavel, R., Dhaya, R., & Venusamy, K. (2022). Detection of Osteoarthritis Based on EHO Thresholding. *CMC-COMPUTERS MATERIALS & CONTINUA*, *71*(3), 5783–5798.

Kanthavel, R., Indra Priyadharshini, S., Sudha, D., Sundara Velrani, K., & Dhaya, R. (2022). Multi-hoped cooperative communication-based wireless underground sensor network design. *International Journal of Communication Systems*, *35*(10), e5174.

Karthik Ganesh, R., Kanthavel, R., & Dhaya, R. (2020). Development of video compression using EWNS linear transformation and un-repetition simulated contrary based resurgence procedure. *Multimedia Tools and Applications*, *79*(5), 3519–3541.

Kellogg, C. H. (1968, December). A natural language compiler for on-line data management. In *Proceedings of fall joint computer conference, part I* (pp. 473-492).

Kelly, J. (2014). Big data: Hadoop, business analytics and beyond. *Wikibon, 5*(2).

Kessler, G. (2006). Assessing CALL Teacher Training: What are We Doing and What Could We Do Better? In P. Hubbard & M. Levy (Eds.), *Teacher education in CALL*. John Benjamins. doi:10.1075/lllt.14.05kes

Kessler, G. (2007). *Formal and Informal CALL Preparation and Teacher Attitude toward Technology. CALL Journal*. Taylor & Francis.

Kumar Singh, V., Ali, Z., Ayub, S., & Kumar Singh, A. (2014). A wide band Compact Microstrip Antenna forGPS/DCS/PCS/WLAN Applications. *Intelligent Computing, Networking, and Informatics*, *243*, 1107–1113.

Lee, P., Tan, H. P., & Han, M. (2011, November). A solar-powered wireless parking guidance system for outdoor car parks. In *Proceedings of the 9th ACM Conference on Embedded Networked Sensor Systems,* (pp. 423-424). 10.1145/2070942.2071020

Levy, M. (1997). *CALL: context and conceptualisation.* Oxford University Press.

Levy, M. (1997). *Computer-assisted language learning: Context and conceptualization.* Oxford University Press.

Levy, M., & Hubbard, P. (2005). Why call call "CALL"? *Computer Assisted Language Learning*, *18*(3), 143–149. doi:10.1080/09588220500208884

Levy, M., & Stockwell, G. (2013). *CALL dimensions: Options and issues in computer-assisted language learning*. Routledge. doi:10.4324/9780203708200

Liang, Z., & Li, L. (2011, July). Self-assessment in autonomous Computer-Assisted Language Learning. In *2011 International Symposium on Computer Science and Society* (pp. 396-399). IEEE.

Li, L. C., Grimshaw, J. M., Nielsen, C., Judd, M., Coyte, P. C., & Graham, I. D. (2009). Evolution of Wenger's concept of community of practice. *Implementation Science; IS*, *4*(1), 1–8. doi:10.1186/1748-5908-4-11 PMID:19250556

Lily, D., Chan, B., & Wang, T. G. (2013). A Simple Explanation of Neural Network in Artificial Intelligence. *IEEE. Trans on Control System*, *247*, 1529–5651.

Li, R., Zhao, Z., Zhou, X., Ding, G., Chen, Y., Wang, Z., & Zhang, H. (2017). Intelligent 5G: When cellular networks meet artificial intelligence. *IEEE Wireless Communications*, *24*(5), 175–183.

Liu, G. Z., & Chen, A. S. W. (2007). A taxonomy of Internet-based technologies integrated in language curricula. *British Journal of Educational Technology*, *38*(5), 934–938. doi:10.1111/j.1467-8535.2007.00728.x

Liu, L., Feng, J., Pei, Q., Chen, C., Ming, Y., Shang, B., & Dong, M. (2020). Blockchain-enabled secure data sharing scheme in mobile-edge computing: An asynchronous advantage actor–critic learning approach. *IEEE Internet of Things Journal*, *8*(4), 2342–2353. doi:10.1109/JIOT.2020.3048345

Liu, X., Chen, S. C., Ma, J., & Yang, L. T. (2013). 3D video representation and design for ubiquitous environments. *Multimedia Tools and Applications*, *67*(1), 1–6. doi:10.100711042-013-1540-7

Lo, C. H., & Chalmers, A. (2003, April). Stereo vision for computer graphics: the effect that stereo vision has on human judgments of visual realism. In *Proceedings of the 19th spring conference on Computer graphics,* (pp. 109-117). 10.1145/984952.984971

Luo, F. L. (Ed.). (2020). *Machine learning for future wireless communications.*

Malekpoor, H., & Jam, S. (2013). Miniaturised asymmetric E-shaped microstrip patch antenna with folded-patch feed. *IET Microwaves, Antennas & Propagation*, *7*(2), 85–91.

McCormick, M. (1995). Integral 3D image for broadcast. In *Proc. 2nd International Display Workshop*, 1995.

Meisak, D., Macutkevic, J., Selskis, A., Kuzhir, P., & Banys, J. (2021). Dielectric relaxation spectroscopy and synergy effects in epoxy/MWCNT/Ni@ C composites. *Nanomaterials (Basel, Switzerland)*, *11*(2), 555. doi:10.3390/nano11020555 PMID:33672334

Mhatre, L., & Rai, N. (2017, February). Integration between wireless sensor and cloud. In *2017 International Conference on I-SMAC (IoT in Social, Mobile, Analytics and Cloud) (I-SMAC)* (pp. 779-782). IEEE.

Mills, J. (1996). Virtual classroom management and communicative writing pedagogy. In *Proceedings of European Writing Conferences*. Barcelona, Spain.

Mishra, R. K., & Patnaik, A. (2000, July). Neurospectral analysis of coaxial fed rectangular patch antenna. In IEEE Antennas and Propagation Society International Symposium. Transmitting Waves of Progress to the Next Millennium, 2, (pp. 1062-1065). IEEE

Mishra, R. K., & Patnaik, A. (1999a). Neurospectral computation for input impedance of rectangular microstrip antenna. *Electronics Letters*.

Mishra, R. K., & Patnaik, A. (1999b). Neurospectral computation for complex resonant frequency of microstrip resonators. *IEEE Microwave and Guided Wave Letters*, *9*(9), 351–353.

Murali, S., & Jamalipour, A. (2019). A lightweight intrusion detection for sybil attack under mobile RPL in the internet of things. *IEEE Internet of Things Journal*, *7*(1), 379–388. doi:10.1109/JIOT.2019.2948149

Nguyen, D. C., Cheng, P., Ding, M., Lopez-Perez, D., Pathirana, P. N., Li, J., Seneviratne, A., Li, Y., & Poor, H. V. (2020). Enabling AI in future wireless networks: A data life cycle perspective. *IEEE Communications Surveys and Tutorials*, *23*(1), 553–595. doi:10.1109/COMST.2020.3024783

Niemi, A., Joutsensalo, J., & Ristaniemi, T. (2000, September). Fuzzy channel estimation in multipath fading CDMA channel. In *11th IEEE International Symposium on Personal Indoor and Mobile Radio Communications, Proceedings*, 2, (pp. 1131-1135). IEEE. doi:10.1109/PIMRC.2000.881596

Nikhil, S., Singh, A. K., & Kumar, S. V. (2015). Design and performance of wearable ultra wide band textile antenna for medical application. *Microwave and Optical Technology Letters*, *57*(7).

O'Connor, M. C. (2010). Northern Arizona University to use existing RFID student cards for attendance tracking. *RFID journal, 24.*

Oliveros, M. A., García, A., & Valdez, B. (2015). Evaluation of a teaching sequence regarding science, technology and society values in higher education. *Creative Education*, *6*(16), 1768–1775. doi:10.4236/ce.2015.616179

Osman, M. A. R., Abd Rahim, M. K., Azfar Abdullah, M., Samsuri, N. A., Zubir, F., & Kamardin, K. (2011). Design, implementation and performance of ultra-wideband textile antenna. *Progress in Electromagnetics Research B. Pier B*, *27*, 307–325. doi:10.2528/PIERB10102005

Ouyang, Y., & Chappell, W. J. (2008). High frequency properties of electro-textiles for wearable antenna applications. *IEEE Transactions on Antennas and Propagation*, *56*(2), 381–389. doi:10.1109/TAP.2007.915435

Pang, B., Lee, L., & Vaithyanathan, S. (2002). *Thumbs up? Sentiment classification using machine learning techniques. arXiv preprint cs/0205070. Bishop, C. M., & Nasrabadi, N. M. (2006). Pattern recognition and machine learning, 4(4)*. Springer.

Parsi, K., & Laharika, M. (2013). A Comparative Study of Different Deployment Models in a Cloud. *International Journal of Advanced Research in Computer Science and Software Engineering*, *3*(5), 512–515.

Pillai, K. G. R., Radhakrishnan, K., Ramakrishnan, D., Yesudhas, H. R., Eanoch, G. J., Kumar, R., & Son, L. H. (2021). Compression based clustering technique for enhancing accuracy in web scale videos. *Multimedia Tools and Applications*, *80*(5), 7077–7101.

Pillai, V., Kumar, P., Hou, M. J., Ayyub, P., & Shah, D. O. (1995). Preparation of nanoparticles of silver halides, superconductors and magnetic materials using water-in-oil microemulsions as nano-reactors. *Advances in Colloid and Interface Science*, *55*, 241–269. doi:10.1016/0001-8686(94)00227-4

Piper, A. (1986). Conversation and the computer: A study of the conversational spin-off generated among learners of English as a foreign language working in groups. *System*, *14*(2), 187–198. doi:10.1016/0346-251X(86)90008-4

Polachan, K., Chatterjee, B., Weigand, S., & Sen, S. (2021). Human body–electrode interfaces for wide-frequency sensing and communication: A review. *Nanomaterials (Basel, Switzerland)*, *11*(8), 2152. doi:10.3390/nano11082152 PMID:34443980

Porozovs, J., Liepniece, L., & Voita, D. (2015). Evaluation of the teaching methods used in secondary school biology lessons. *Signum Temporis*, *7*(1), 60–66. doi:10.1515igtem-2016-0009

Potamianos, A., Fosler-Lussier, E., Ammicht, E., & Perakakis, M. (2007). Information Seeking Spoken Dialogue Systems Part II: Multimodal Dialogue. *IEEE Transactions on Multimedia*, *9*(3), 550–566. doi:10.1109/TMM.2006.887999

Putnik, G., Sluga, A., ElMaraghy, H., Teti, R., Koren, Y., Tolio, T., & Hon, B. (2013). Scalability in manufacturing systems design and operation: State-of-the-art and future developments roadmap. *CIRP Annals*, *62*(2), 751–774. doi:10.1016/j.cirp.2013.05.002

Quillian, M. R. (1969). The teachable language comprehender: A simulation program and theory of language. *Commun. Ass. Comput*, 459-476.

Radiant. (2022). *Texas Tech University Health Sciences Center in El Paso deploys campus-wide RFID asset tracking. Radiant.* https://radiantrfid.com/news/texas-tech -university-healt h-sciences-ce nter-in-e l-pas o-deploys-campus-wide-rfid -asset-tracking/

Rajan, A. P. (2013). Evolution of cloud storage as cloud computing infrastructure service. *arXiv preprint arXiv:1308.1303.*

Ramadan, A. H., Mervat, M., El-Hajj, A., Khoury, S., & Al-Husseini, M. (2009). A reconfigurable U-Koch microstrip antenna for wireless applications. *Progress in Electromagnetics Research, 93*, 355–367.

Ramakrishnan, D., & Radhakrishnan, K. (2022). Applying deep convolutional neural network (DCNN) algorithm in the cloud autonomous vehicles traffic model. *The International Arab Journal of Information Technology, 19*(2), 186–194.

Reisenwitz, T. H. (2016). Student evaluation of teaching: An investigation of nonresponse bias in an online context. *Journal of Marketing Education, 38*(1), 7–17. doi:10.1177/0273475315596778

Rockhart, J. F., Scott Morton, M. S., & Zannetos, Z. S. (1970). Associative learning project: phase I system.

Rogers, Y., Sharp, H., & Preece, J. (2002). *Interaction design: Beyond human-computer interaction.* Jon Wiley & Sons. Inc.

Rupani, S., & Doshi, N. (2019). A review of smart parking using internet of things (IoT). *Procedia Computer Science, 160*, 706–711. doi:10.1016/j.procs.2019.11.023

Salonen, P., & Rahmat-Samii, Y. (2006, November). Textile antennas: Effects of antenna bending on input matching and impedance bandwidth. In *2006 First European Conference on Antennas and Propagation* (pp. 1-5). IEEE.

Sangeetha, S. K. B., & Dhaya, R. (2022). Deep learning era for future 6G wireless communications—theory, applications, and challenges. *Artificial Intelligent Techniques for Wireless Communication and Networking*, 105-119.

Sangeetha, S. K. B., Dhaya, R., & Kanthavel, R. (2019). Improving performance of cooperative communication in heterogeneous manet environment. *Cluster Computing, 22*(5), 12389–12395. doi:10.100710586-017-1637-2

Sangeetha, S. K. B., Dhaya, R., Shah, D. T., Dharanidharan, R., & Reddy, K. P. S. (2021, February). An empirical analysis of machine learning frameworks for digital pathology in medical science. *Journal of Physics: Conference Series, 1767*(1), 012031.

Saravanan, P., Alam, S., & Mathur, G. N. (2003). Comparative study on the synthesis of γ-Fe2O3 and Fe3O4 nanocrystals using high-temperature solution-phase technique. *Journal of Materials Science Letters*, *22*(18), 1283–1285. doi:10.1023/A:1025470405000

Schulze, E. (1995, April). Synthesis of moving holographic stereograms with high-resolution spatial light modulators. In *Practical Holography IX* (Vol. 2406, pp. 124–131). SPIE.

Sebastiani, F. (2002). Machine learning in automated text categorization. [CSUR]. *ACM Computing Surveys*, *34*(1), 1–47. doi:10.1145/505282.505283

Seera, M., Lim, C. P., Kumar, A., Dhamotharan, L., & Tan, K. H. (2021). An intelligent payment card fraud detection system. *Annals of Operations Research*, 1–23.

Shaheen, S. (2005). Smart parking management field test: A bay area rapid transit (bart) district parking demonstration.

Shang, W. L., Chen, J., Bi, H., Sui, Y., Chen, Y., & Yu, H. (2021). Impacts of COVID-19 pandemic on user behaviors and environmental benefits of bike sharing: A big-data analysis. *Applied Energy*, *285*, 116429. doi:10.1016/j.apenergy.2020.116429 PMID:33519037

Sharma, A., Chaki, R., & Bhattacharya, U. (2011, April). Applications of wireless sensor network in Intelligent Traffic System: A review. In *3rd International Conference on Electronics Computer Technology, 5*, (pp. 53-57). IEEE.

Shoikova, E., Nikolov, R., & Kovatcheva, E. (2018, March). Smart digital education enhanced by AR and IoT data. In *Proceedings of the 12th International Technology, Education and Development Conference (INTED)*,(pp. 5-7). Valencia, Spain.

Silva, J. F., & Pinto, S. F. (2018). Linear and nonlinear control of switching power converters. In *Power Electronics Handbook* (pp. 1141–1220). Butterworth-Heinemann., doi:10.1016/B978-0-12-811407-0.00039-8

Simmons, R. F. (1971). Natural language for instructional communication. Artificial Intelligence and Heuristic Programming, Edinburgh Univ. Press, 191-198.

Simmons, R. S., & Silberman, H. F. (1967). A Plan for Research Toward Computer-Aided Instruction With Natural English. Technical Memorandum.

Simmons, R. F. (1970). Natural language question-answering systems: 1969. *Communications of the ACM*, *13*(1), 15–30.

Singh, A., & Sharma, S. (2008). *Skilled labour shortage threatens expansion in India.* Deccan Herald.

Singh, D. K., Kanaujia, B., Dwari, S., Pandey, G. P., & Kumar, S. (2015). Multiband circularly polarized stacked microstrip antenna. *Progress in Electromagnetics Research C*, *56*, 55–64. doi:10.2528/PIERC14121101

Son, J. B. (Ed.). (2004). Computer-assisted language learning: concepts, contexts and practices. iUniverse.

Stone, P., & Veloso, M. (2000). Multiagent systems: A survey from a machine learning perspective. *Autonomous Robots*, *8*(3), 345–383. doi:10.1023/A:1008942012299

Sun, X. B., Cao, M. Y., Hao, J. J., & Guo, Y. J. (2012). A rectangular slot antenna with improved bandwidth. *AEÜ. International Journal of Electronics and Communications*, *66*(6), 465–466.

Sun, Y., Peng, M., Zhou, Y., Huang, Y., & Mao, S. (2019). Application of machine learning in wireless networks: Key techniques and open issues. *IEEE Communications Surveys and Tutorials*, *21*(4), 3072–3108.

Swekis, P., Sukhanov, A. S., Chen, Y. C., Gloskovskii, A., Fecher, G. H., Panagiotopoulos, I., Sichelschmidt, J., Ukleev, V., Devishvili, A., Vorobiev, A., Inosov, D. S., Goennenwein, S. T. B., Felser, C., & Markou, A. (2021). Magnetic and Electronic Properties of Weyl Semimetal Co2MnGa Thin Films. *Nanomaterials (Basel, Switzerland)*, *11*(1), 251. doi:10.3390/nano11010251 PMID:33477868

Swets, J. A., & Feurzeig, W. (1965). Computer-Aided Instruction: Concepts and problem-solving techniques can be learned by conversing with a programmed-computer system. *Science*, *150*(3696), 572–576. doi:10.1126cience.150.3696.572 PMID:5837095

Tanaka, Y., Saiki, M., Katoh, M., & Endo, T. (2006). Development of image recognition for a parking assist system. *Proc. 13th World Congr. Intell. Transp. Syst. Services*, 1-7.

Taylor, E. F. (1967, January). Eliza Program Conversational Tutorial. [Ieee-Inst Electrical Electronics Engineers Inc.]. *IEEE Transactions on Education*, *10*(1), 64–64.

Thanner, C., & Eibelhuber, M. (2021). UV nanoimprint lithography: Geometrical impact on filling properties of nanoscale patterns. *Nanomaterials (Basel, Switzerland)*, *11*(3), 822. doi:10.3390/nano11030822 PMID:33806976

Thavamani, S., & Sinthuja, U. (2022, January). LSTM based Deep Learning Technique to Forecast Internet of Things Attacks in MQTT Protocol. In *2022 IEEE Fourth International Conference on Advances in Electronics, Computers and Communications (ICAECC)*, (pp. 1-4). IEEE.

Toda, T., Takahashi, S., & Iwata, F. (1995, April). Three-dimensional (3D) video system using grating image. In Practical Holography IX (2406), pp. 191-198). SPIE.

Tran, N. D. (2015). Reconceptualisation of approaches to teaching evaluation in higher education. *Issues in Educational Research*, *25*(1), 50–61.

Trayner, D. J., & Orr, E. (1996, April). Autostereoscopic display using holographic optical elements. In *Stereoscopic Displays and Virtual Reality Systems III* (Vol. 2653, pp. 65–74). SPIE.

Tsai, C. W., Lai, C. F., Chao, H. C., & Vasilakos, A. V. (2015). Big data analytics: A survey. *Journal of Big Data*, *2*(1), 1–32. doi:10.118640537-015-0030-3 PMID:26191487

Ullah, Z., Al-Turjman, F., Mostarda, L., & Gagliardi, R. (2020). Applications of artificial intelligence and machine learning in smart cities. *Computer Communications*, *154*, 313–323. doi:10.1016/j.comcom.2020.02.069

Underwood, J. H. (1984). *Linguistics, Computers, and the Language Teacher. A Communicative Approach*. Newbury House Publishers, Inc.

Uttal, W. R., Pasich, T., Rogers, M., & Hieronymus, R. (1969). Generative computer-assisted instruction. In Mental Health Res. Inst. 243. Mich., Commun.

Varela, F. J., & Bourgine, P. (Eds.). (1992). Toward a practice of autonomous systems: Proceedings of the First European Conference on Artificial Life. MIT press. Hydher, H., Tennakoon, P., & Jayakody, N. K. Recent Results of Machine Learning InspiredWireless Communications. ETIC.

VBCED. (2017). *Computer Assisted Instructions (CAI)*. Viswa Bharathi College of Education for Women, Veerachipalayam, Sankari West, Salem District. https://drarockiasamy.wordpress.com/computer-assisted-instructions-cai/

Vigorito, C. M., Ganesan, D., & Barto, A. G. (2007, June). Adaptive control of duty cycling in energy-harvesting wireless sensor networks. In *4th Annual IEEE communications society conference on sensor, mesh and ad hoc communications and networks,* (pp. 21-30). IEEE. 10.1109/SAHCN.2007.4292814

Viterbi, A. J. (1995). *CDMA: principles of spread spectrum communication*. Addison Wesley Longman Publishing Co., Inc.

Wang, C. X., Di Renzo, M., Stanczak, S., Wang, S., & Larsson, E. G. (2020). Artificial intelligence enabled wireless networking for 5G and beyond: Recent advances and future challenges. *IEEE Wireless Communications*, *27*(1), 16–23. doi:10.1109/MWC.001.1900292

Wang, F., & Wu, S. (2020, December). Research and Practice of Computer English Assisted Learning System. In *5th International Conference on Mechanical, Control and Computer Engineering (ICMCCE)* (pp. 1182-1185). IEEE.

Wang, H., Li, J., Zhang, H., & Zhou, Y. (2014, March). Benchmarking replication and consistency strategies in cloud serving databases: Hbase and cassandra. In *Workshop on big data benchmarks, performance optimization, and emerging hardware,* (pp. 71-82). Springer, Cham. 10.1007/978-3-319-13021-7_6

Wang, Q., Kuang, K., Gao, H., Chu, S., Yu, L., & Peng, W. (2021). Electromagnetically induced transparency-like effect by dark-dark mode coupling. *Nanomaterials (Basel, Switzerland)*, *11*(5), 1350. doi:10.3390/nano11051350 PMID:34065485

Warschauer, M. (1996). Computer-assisted language learning: An introduction. In S. Fotos (Ed.), *Multimedia language teaching*. Logos International.

Warschauer, M., & Healey, D. (1998). Computers and language learning: An overview. *Language Teaching*, *31*(2), 57–71. doi:10.1017/S0261444800012970

Weizenbaum, J. (1966). ELIZA—a computer program for the study of natural language communication between man and machine. *Communications of the ACM*, *9*(1), 36–45.

Wexler, J. D. (1970). A Generative Teaching System that Uses Information Nets and Skeleton Patterns. [Ph. D. dissertation]. University of Wisconsin, Madison.

Wikipedia. (2022, May 29). Computer-assisted language learning. In *Wikipedia, The Free Encyclopedia*. **Error! Hyperlink reference not valid.**

Willis, E. A., Szabo-Reed, A. N., Ptomey, L. T., Steger, F. L., Honas, J. J., Al-Hihi, E. M., Lee, R., Vansaghi, L., Washburn, R. A., & Donnelly, J. E. (2016). Distance learning strategies for weight management utilizing social media: A comparison of phone conference call versus social media platform. Rationale and design for a randomized study. *Contemporary Clinical Trials*, *47*, 282–288. doi:10.1016/j.cct.2016.02.005 PMID:26883282

Wu, P., Low, S., Liu, J. Y., Pienaar, J., & Xia, B. (2015). Critical success factors in distance learning construction programs at Central Queensland University: students' perspective. *Journal of Professional Issues in Engineering Education and Practice, 141*(1).

Wyatt, D. H. (1983). Three major approaches to developing computer-assisted language learning materials for microcomputers. *CALICO Journal*, *1*(2), 34–38. doi:10.1558/cj.v1i2.34-38

Xu, Y., Shieh, C. H., van Esch, P., & Ling, I. L. (2020). AI customer service: Task complexity, problem-solving ability, and usage intention. *Australasian Marketing Journal*, *28*(4), 189–199.

Yamazaki, S., Asakura, R., & Ohuchi, K. (2020). Throughput Analysis of Dynamic Multi-Hop Shortcut Communications for a Simple Model. IEICE TRANSACTIONS on Fundamentals of Electronics. *Communications and Computer Sciences*, *103*(7), 951–954.

Yang, T. C., Yang, S. J., & Hwang, G. J. (2014, July). Development of an interactive test system for students' improving learning outcomes in a computer programming course. In *IEEE 14th International Conference on Advanced Learning Technologies* (pp. 637-639). IEEE.

Yuen, A. H. (2006). Learning to program through interactive simulation. *Educational Media International*, *43*(3), 251–268. doi:10.1080/09523980600641452

Yuvaraju, M., & Monika, M. (2017). IoT based vehicle parking place detection using arduino. *International Journal of Engineering Sciences & Research Technology*, 536–542.

Zarinwall, A., Asadian-Birjand, M., Seleci, D. A., Maurer, V., Trautner, A., Garnweitner, G., & Fuchs, H. (2021). Magnetic Nanoparticle-Based Dianthin Targeting for Controlled Drug Release Using the Endosomal Escape Enhancer SO1861. *Nanomaterials (Basel, Switzerland)*, *11*(4), 1057. doi:10.3390/nano11041057 PMID:33924180

Zhang, C., Zhou, R., Lei, L., & Yang, X. (2021). Research on Automatic Parking System Strategy. *World Electric Vehicle Journal*, *12*(4), 200. doi:10.3390/wevj12040200

Zhao, Y. (2004). Problems in Researching Dialogue in E-learning in Higher Education. In *Economic and Social Research Council/Worldwide Universities Network research seminar series 'Researching Dialogue and Communities of Enquiry in E-learning in Higher Education.'*

Zhao, H. (2015). College physics teaching model design and evaluation research of students' seriousness. *The Open Cybernetics & Systemics Journal*, *9*(1), 2017–2020. doi:10.2174/1874110X01509012017

Zheng, Q., Luo, J., Luo, G., Ma, J., Xu, M., & Yao, H. (2010). Experimental study on adsorption of elemental mercury by liquid bromine-modified non-carbon-based adsorbent. [液溴改性非碳基吸附剂吸附元素汞的实验研究]. *Chinese Journal of Engineering Thermophysics*, (12), 2137–2140.

Zheng, Y., Jensen, A. D., Windelin, C., & Jensen, F. (2012). Review of technologies for mercury removal from flue gas from cement production processes. *Progress in Energy and Combustion Science*, *38*(5), 599–629. doi:10.1016/j.pecs.2012.05.001

Zhou, L., Li, H., & Sun, K. (2017). Teaching performance evaluation by means of a hierarchical multifactorial evaluation model based on type-2 fuzzy sets. *Applied Intelligence*, *46*(1), 34–44. doi:10.100710489-016-0816-9

Zhu, S., & Langley, R. (2007). Dual-band wearable antennas over EBG substrate. *Electronics Letters*, *43*(3), 1.

Related References

To continue our tradition of advancing academic research, we have compiled a list of recommended IGI Global readings. These references will provide additional information and guidance to further enrich your knowledge and assist you with your own research and future publications.

Aburezeq, I. M., & Dweikat, F. F. (2017). Cloud Applications in Language Teaching: Examining Pre-Service Teachers' Expertise, Perceptions and Integration. *International Journal of Distance Education Technologies*, *15*(4), 39–60. doi:10.4018/IJDET.2017100103

Acharjya, B., & Das, S. (2022). Adoption of E-Learning During the COVID-19 Pandemic: The Moderating Role of Age and Gender. *International Journal of Web-Based Learning and Teaching Technologies*, *17*(2), 1–14. https://doi.org/10.4018/IJWLTT.20220301.oa4

Adams, J. L., & Thomas, S. K. (2022). Non-Linear Curriculum Experiences for Student Learning and Work Design: What Is the Maximum Potential of a Chat Bot? In S. Ramlall, T. Cross, & M. Love (Eds.), *Handbook of Research on Future of Work and Education: Implications for Curriculum Delivery and Work Design* (pp. 299–306). IGI Global. https://doi.org/10.4018/978-1-7998-8275-6.ch018

Adera, B. (2017). Supporting Language and Literacy Development for English Language Learners. In J. Keengwe (Ed.), *Handbook of Research on Promoting Cross-Cultural Competence and Social Justice in Teacher Education* (pp. 339–354). Hershey, PA: IGI Global. doi:10.4018/978-1-5225-0897-7.ch018

Ahamer, G. (2017). Quality Assurance for a Developmental "Global Studies" (GS) Curriculum. In I. Management Association (Ed.), Educational Leadership and Administration: Concepts, Methodologies, Tools, and Applications (pp. 438-477). Hershey, PA: IGI Global. https://doi.org/ doi:10.4018/978-1-5225-1624-8.ch023

Ahamer, G. (2017). Quality Assurance for a Developmental "Global Studies" (GS) Curriculum. In I. Management Association (Ed.), Educational Leadership and Administration: Concepts, Methodologies, Tools, and Applications (pp. 438-477). Hershey, PA: IGI Global. https://doi.org/ doi:10.4018/978-1-5225-1624-8.ch023

Akayoğlu, S., & Seferoğlu, G. (2019). An Analysis of Negotiation of Meaning Functions of Advanced EFL Learners in Second Life: Negotiation of Meaning in Second Life. In M. Kruk (Ed.), *Assessing the Effectiveness of Virtual Technologies in Foreign and Second Language Instruction* (pp. 61–85). IGI Global. https://doi.org/10.4018/978-1-5225-7286-2.ch003

Akella, N. R. (2022). Unravelling the Web of Qualitative Dissertation Writing!: A Student Reflects. In A. Zimmerman (Ed.), *Methodological Innovations in Research and Academic Writing* (pp. 260–282). IGI Global. https://doi.org/10.4018/978-1-7998-8283-1.ch014

Alegre de la Rosa, O. M., & Angulo, L. M. (2017). Social Inclusion and Intercultural Values in a School of Education. In S. Mukerji & P. Tripathi (Eds.), *Handbook of Research on Administration, Policy, and Leadership in Higher Education* (pp. 518–531). Hershey, PA: IGI Global. doi:10.4018/978-1-5225-0672-0.ch020

Alexander, C. (2019). Using Gamification Strategies to Cultivate and Measure Professional Educator Dispositions. *International Journal of Game-Based Learning*, *9*(1), 15–29. https://doi.org/10.4018/IJGBL.2019010102

Anderson, K. M. (2017). Preparing Teachers in the Age of Equity and Inclusion. In I. Management Association (Ed.), Medical Education and Ethics: Concepts, Methodologies, Tools, and Applications (pp. 1532-1554). Hershey, PA: IGI Global. doi:10.4018/978-1-5225-0978-3.ch069

Awdziej, M. (2017). Case Study as a Teaching Method in Marketing. In D. Latusek (Ed.), *Case Studies as a Teaching Tool in Management Education* (pp. 244–263). Hershey, PA: IGI Global. doi:10.4018/978-1-5225-0770-3.ch013

Bakos, J. (2019). Sociolinguistic Factors Influencing English Language Learning. In N. Erdogan & M. Wei (Eds.), *Applied Linguistics for Teachers of Culturally and Linguistically Diverse Learners* (pp. 403–424). IGI Global. https://doi.org/10.4018/978-1-5225-8467-4.ch017

Banas, J. R., & York, C. S. (2017). Pre-Service Teachers' Motivation to Use Technology and the Impact of Authentic Learning Exercises. In L. Tomei (Ed.), *Exploring the New Era of Technology-Infused Education* (pp. 121–140). Hershey, PA: IGI Global. doi:10.4018/978-1-5225-1709-2.ch008

Barton, T. P. (2021). Empowering Educator Allyship by Exploring Racial Trauma and the Disengagement of Black Students. In C. Reneau & M. Villarreal (Eds.), *Handbook of Research on Leading Higher Education Transformation With Social Justice, Equity, and Inclusion* (pp. 186–197). IGI Global. https://doi.org/10.4018/978-1-7998-7152-1.ch013

Benhima, M. (2021). Moroccan English Department Student Attitudes Towards the Use of Distance Education During COVID-19: Moulay Ismail University as a Case Study. *International Journal of Information and Communication Technology Education*, *17*(3), 105–122. https://doi.org/10.4018/IJICTE.20210701.oa7

Beycioglu, K., & Wildy, H. (2017). Principal Preparation: The Case of Novice Principals in Turkey. In I. Management Association (Ed.), Educational Leadership and Administration: Concepts, Methodologies, Tools, and Applications (pp. 1152-1169). Hershey, PA: IGI Global. https://doi.org/doi:10.4018/978-1-5225-1624-8.ch054

Bharwani, S., & Musunuri, D. (2018). Reflection as a Process From Theory to Practice. In M. Khosrow-Pour, D.B.A. (Ed.), Encyclopedia of Information Science and Technology, Fourth Edition (pp. 1529-1539). Hershey, PA: IGI Global. doi:10.4018/978-1-5225-2255-3.ch132

Bhushan, A., Garza, K. B., Perumal, O., Das, S. K., Feola, D. J., Farrell, D., & Birnbaum, A. (2022). Lessons Learned From the COVID-19 Pandemic and the Implications for Pharmaceutical Graduate Education and Research. In C. Ford & K. Garza (Eds.), *Handbook of Research on Updating and Innovating Health Professions Education: Post-Pandemic Perspectives* (pp. 324–345). IGI Global. https://doi.org/10.4018/978-1-7998-7623-6.ch014

Bintz, W., Ciecierski, L. M., & Royan, E. (2021). Using Picture Books With Instructional Strategies to Address New Challenges and Teach Literacy Skills in a Digital World. In L. Haas & J. Tussey (Eds.), *Connecting Disciplinary Literacy and Digital Storytelling in K-12 Education* (pp. 38–58). IGI Global. https://doi.org/10.4018/978-1-7998-5770-9.ch003

Bohjanen, S. L., Cameron-Standerford, A., & Meidl, T. D. (2018). Capacity Building Pedagogy for Diverse Learners. In J. Keengwe (Ed.), *Handbook of Research on Pedagogical Models for Next-Generation Teaching and Learning* (pp. 195–212). Hershey, PA: IGI Global. doi:10.4018/978-1-5225-3873-8.ch011

Brewer, J. C. (2018). Measuring Text Readability Using Reading Level. In M. Khosrow-Pour, D.B.A. (Ed.), Encyclopedia of Information Science and Technology, Fourth Edition (pp. 1499-1507). Hershey, PA: IGI Global. doi:10.4018/978-1-5225-2255-3.ch129

Brookbanks, B. C. (2022). Student Perspectives on Business Education in the USA: Current Attitudes and Necessary Changes in an Age of Disruption. In A. Zhuplev & R. Koepp (Eds.), *Global Trends, Dynamics, and Imperatives for Strategic Development in Business Education in an Age of Disruption* (pp. 214–231). IGI Global. doi:10.4018/978-1-7998-7548-2.ch011

Brown, L. V., Dari, T., & Spencer, N. (2019). Addressing the Impact of Trauma in High Poverty Elementary Schools: An Ecological Model for School Counseling. In K. Daniels & K. Billingsley (Eds.), *Creating Caring and Supportive Educational Environments for Meaningful Learning* (pp. 135–153). IGI Global. https://doi.org/10.4018/978-1-5225-5748-7.ch008

Brown, S. L. (2017). A Case Study of Strategic Leadership and Research in Practice: Principal Preparation Programs that Work – An Educational Administration Perspective of Best Practices for Master's Degree Programs for Principal Preparation. In V. Wang (Ed.), *Encyclopedia of Strategic Leadership and Management* (pp. 1226–1244). Hershey, PA: IGI Global. doi:10.4018/978-1-5225-1049-9.ch086

Brzozowski, M., & Ferster, I. (2017). Educational Management Leadership: High School Principal's Management Style and Parental Involvement in School Management in Israel. In V. Potocan, M. Üngan, & Z. Nedelko (Eds.), *Handbook of Research on Managerial Solutions in Non-Profit Organizations* (pp. 55–74). Hershey, PA: IGI Global. doi:10.4018/978-1-5225-0731-4.ch003

Cahapay, M. B. (2020). Delphi Technique in the Development of Emerging Contents in High School Science Curriculum. *International Journal of Curriculum Development and Learning Measurement*, *1*(2), 1–9. https://doi.org/10.4018/IJCDLM.2020070101

Camacho, L. F., & Leon Guerrero, A. E. (2022). Indigenous Student Experience in Higher Education: Implementation of Culturally Sensitive Support. In P. Pangelinan & T. McVey (Eds.), *Learning and Reconciliation Through Indigenous Education in Oceania* (pp. 254–266). IGI Global. https://doi.org/10.4018/978-1-7998-7736-3.ch016

Cannaday, J. (2017). The Masking Effect: Hidden Gifts and Disabilities of 2e Students. In P. Dickenson, P. Keough, & J. Courduff (Eds.), *Preparing Pre-Service Teachers for the Inclusive Classroom* (pp. 220–231). Hershey, PA: IGI Global. doi:10.4018/978-1-5225-1753-5.ch011

Cederquist, S., Fishman, B., & Teasley, S. D. (2022). What's Missing From the College Transcript?: How Employers Make Sense of Student Skills. In Y. Huang (Ed.), *Handbook of Research on Credential Innovations for Inclusive Pathways to Professions* (pp. 234–253). IGI Global. https://doi.org/10.4018/978-1-7998-3820-3.ch012

Cockrell, P., & Gibson, T. (2019). The Untold Stories of Black and Brown Student Experiences in Historically White Fraternities and Sororities. In P. Hoffman-Miller, M. James, & D. Hermond (Eds.), *African American Suburbanization and the Consequential Loss of Identity* (pp. 153–171). IGI Global. https://doi.org/10.4018/978-1-5225-7835-2.ch009

Cohen, M. (2022). Leveraging Content Creation to Boost Student Engagement. In T. Driscoll III, (Ed.), *Designing Effective Distance and Blended Learning Environments in K-12* (pp. 223–239). IGI Global. https://doi.org/10.4018/978-1-7998-6829-3.ch013

Contreras, E. C., & Contreras, I. I. (2018). Development of Communication Skills through Auditory Training Software in Special Education. In M. Khosrow-Pour, D.B.A. (Ed.), Encyclopedia of Information Science and Technology, Fourth Edition (pp. 2431-2441). Hershey, PA: IGI Global. doi:10.4018/978-1-5225-2255-3.ch212

Cooke, L., Schugar, J., Schugar, H., Penny, C., & Bruning, H. (2020). Can Everyone Code?: Preparing Teachers to Teach Computer Languages as a Literacy. In J. Mitchell & E. Vaughn (Eds.), *Participatory Literacy Practices for P-12 Classrooms in the Digital Age* (pp. 163–183). IGI Global. https://doi.org/10.4018/978-1-7998-0000-2.ch009

Cooley, D., & Whitten, E. (2017). Special Education Leadership and the Implementation of Response to Intervention. In F. Topor (Ed.), *Handbook of Research on Individualism and Identity in the Globalized Digital Age* (pp. 265–286). Hershey, PA: IGI Global. doi:10.4018/978-1-5225-0522-8.ch012

Cosner, S., Tozer, S., & Zavitkovsky, P. (2017). Enacting a Cycle of Inquiry Capstone Research Project in Doctoral-Level Leadership Preparation. In I. Management Association (Ed.), Educational Leadership and Administration: Concepts, Methodologies, Tools, and Applications (pp. 1460-1481). Hershey, PA: IGI Global. doi:10.4018/978-1-5225-1624-8.ch067

Crawford, C. M. (2018). Instructional Real World Community Engagement. In M. Khosrow-Pour, D.B.A. (Ed.), Encyclopedia of Information Science and Technology, Fourth Edition (pp. 1474-1486). Hershey, PA: IGI Global. doi:10.4018/978-1-5225-2255-3.ch127

Crosby-Cooper, T., & Pacis, D. (2017). Implementing Effective Student Support Teams. In P. Dickenson, P. Keough, & J. Courduff (Eds.), *Preparing Pre-Service Teachers for the Inclusive Classroom* (pp. 248–262). Hershey, PA: IGI Global. doi:10.4018/978-1-5225-1753-5.ch013

Curran, C. M., & Hawbaker, B. W. (2017). Cultivating Communities of Inclusive Practice: Professional Development for Educators – Research and Practice. In C. Curran & A. Petersen (Eds.), *Handbook of Research on Classroom Diversity and Inclusive Education Practice* (pp. 120–153). Hershey, PA: IGI Global. doi:10.4018/978-1-5225-2520-2.ch006

Dass, S., & Dabbagh, N. (2018). Faculty Adoption of 3D Avatar-Based Virtual World Learning Environments: An Exploratory Case Study. In I. Management Association (Ed.), Technology Adoption and Social Issues: Concepts, Methodologies, Tools, and Applications (pp. 1000-1033). Hershey, PA: IGI Global. https://doi.org/ doi:10.4018/978-1-5225-5201-7.ch045

Davison, A. M., & Scholl, K. G. (2017). Inclusive Recreation as Part of the IEP Process. In C. Curran & A. Petersen (Eds.), *Handbook of Research on Classroom Diversity and Inclusive Education Practice* (pp. 311–330). Hershey, PA: IGI Global. doi:10.4018/978-1-5225-2520-2.ch013

DeCoito, I. (2018). Addressing Digital Competencies, Curriculum Development, and Instructional Design in Science Teacher Education. In M. Khosrow-Pour, D.B.A. (Ed.), Encyclopedia of Information Science and Technology, Fourth Edition (pp. 1420-1431). Hershey, PA: IGI Global. https://doi.org/ doi:10.4018/978-1-5225-2255-3.ch122

DeCoito, I., & Richardson, T. (2017). Beyond Angry Birds™: Using Web-Based Tools to Engage Learners and Promote Inquiry in STEM Learning. In I. Levin & D. Tsybulsky (Eds.), *Digital Tools and Solutions for Inquiry-Based STEM Learning* (pp. 166–196). Hershey, PA: IGI Global. doi:10.4018/978-1-5225-2525-7.ch007

Delmas, P. M. (2017). Research-Based Leadership for Next-Generation Leaders. In R. Styron Jr & J. Styron (Eds.), *Comprehensive Problem-Solving and Skill Development for Next-Generation Leaders* (pp. 1–39). Hershey, PA: IGI Global. doi:10.4018/978-1-5225-1968-3.ch001

Demiray, U., & Ekren, G. (2018). Administrative-Related Evaluation for Distance Education Institutions in Turkey. In K. Buyuk, S. Kocdar, & A. Bozkurt (Eds.), *Administrative Leadership in Open and Distance Learning Programs* (pp. 263–288). Hershey, PA: IGI Global. doi:10.4018/978-1-5225-2645-2.ch011

Dickenson, P. (2017). What do we Know and Where Can We Grow?: Teachers Preparation for the Inclusive Classroom. In P. Dickenson, P. Keough, & J. Courduff (Eds.), *Preparing Pre-Service Teachers for the Inclusive Classroom* (pp. 1–22). Hershey, PA: IGI Global. doi:10.4018/978-1-5225-1753-5.ch001

Ding, Q., & Zhu, H. (2021). Flipping the Classroom in STEM Education. In J. Keengwe (Ed.), *Handbook of Research on Innovations in Non-Traditional Educational Practices* (pp. 155–173). IGI Global. https://doi.org/10.4018/978-1-7998-4360-3.ch008

Dixon, T., & Christison, M. (2021). Teaching English Grammar in a Hybrid Academic ESL Course: A Mixed Methods Study. In K. Kelch, P. Byun, S. Safavi, & S. Cervantes (Eds.), *CALL Theory Applications for Online TESOL Education* (pp. 229–251). IGI Global. https://doi.org/10.4018/978-1-7998-6609-1.ch010

Donne, V., & Hansen, M. (2017). Teachers' Use of Assistive Technologies in Education. In L. Tomei (Ed.), *Exploring the New Era of Technology-Infused Education* (pp. 86–101). Hershey, PA: IGI Global. doi:10.4018/978-1-5225-1709-2.ch006

Donne, V., & Hansen, M. A. (2018). Business and Technology Educators: Practices for Inclusion. In I. Management Association (Ed.), Business Education and Ethics: Concepts, Methodologies, Tools, and Applications (pp. 471-484). Hershey, PA: IGI Global. https://doi.org/ doi:10.4018/978-1-5225-3153-1.ch026

Dos Santos, L. M. (2022). Completing Student-Teaching Internships Online: Instructional Changes During the COVID-19 Pandemic. In M. Alaali (Ed.), *Assessing University Governance and Policies in Relation to the COVID-19 Pandemic* (pp. 106–127). IGI Global. https://doi.org/10.4018/978-1-7998-8279-4.ch007

Dreon, O., Shettel, J., & Bower, K. M. (2017). Preparing Next Generation Elementary Teachers for the Tools of Tomorrow. In M. Grassetti & S. Brookby (Eds.), *Advancing Next-Generation Teacher Education through Digital Tools and Applications* (pp. 143–159). Hershey, PA: IGI Global. doi:10.4018/978-1-5225-0965-3.ch008

Durak, H. Y., & Güyer, T. (2018). Design and Development of an Instructional Program for Teaching Programming Processes to Gifted Students Using Scratch. In J. Cannaday (Ed.), *Curriculum Development for Gifted Education Programs* (pp. 61–99). Hershey, PA: IGI Global. doi:10.4018/978-1-5225-3041-1.ch004

Egorkina, E., Ivanov, M., & Valyavskiy, A. Y. (2018). Students' Research Competence Formation of the Quality of Open and Distance Learning. In V. Mkrttchian & L. Belyanina (Eds.), *Handbook of Research on Students' Research Competence in Modern Educational Contexts* (pp. 364–384). Hershey, PA: IGI Global. doi:10.4018/978-1-5225-3485-3.ch019

Ekren, G., Karataş, S., & Demiray, U. (2017). Understanding of Leadership in Distance Education Management. In I. Management Association (Ed.), Educational Leadership and Administration: Concepts, Methodologies, Tools, and Applications (pp. 34-50). Hershey, PA: IGI Global. https://doi.org/ doi:10.4018/978-1-5225-1624-8.ch003

Elmore, W. M., Young, J. K., Harris, S., & Mason, D. (2017). The Relationship between Individual Student Attributes and Online Course Completion. In K. Shelton & K. Pedersen (Eds.), *Handbook of Research on Building, Growing, and Sustaining Quality E-Learning Programs* (pp. 151–173). Hershey, PA: IGI Global. doi:10.4018/978-1-5225-0877-9.ch008

Ercegovac, I. R., Alfirević, N., & Koludrović, M. (2017). School Principals' Communication and Co-Operation Assessment: The Croatian Experience. In I. Management Association (Ed.), Educational Leadership and Administration: Concepts, Methodologies, Tools, and Applications (pp. 1568-1589). Hershey, PA: IGI Global. https://doi.org/ doi:10.4018/978-1-5225-1624-8.ch072

Everhart, D., & Seymour, D. M. (2017). Challenges and Opportunities in the Currency of Higher Education. In K. Rasmussen, P. Northrup, & R. Colson (Eds.), *Handbook of Research on Competency-Based Education in University Settings* (pp. 41–65). Hershey, PA: IGI Global. doi:10.4018/978-1-5225-0932-5.ch003

Farmer, L. S. (2017). Managing Portable Technologies for Special Education. In V. Wang (Ed.), *Encyclopedia of Strategic Leadership and Management* (pp. 977–987). Hershey, PA: IGI Global. doi:10.4018/978-1-5225-1049-9.ch068

Farmer, L. S. (2018). Optimizing OERs for Optimal ICT Literacy in Higher Education. In J. Keengwe (Ed.), *Handbook of Research on Mobile Technology, Constructivism, and Meaningful Learning* (pp. 366–390). Hershey, PA: IGI Global. doi:10.4018/978-1-5225-3949-0.ch020

Ferguson, B. T. (2019). Supporting Affective Development of Children With Disabilities Through Moral Dilemmas. In S. Ikuta (Ed.), *Handmade Teaching Materials for Students With Disabilities* (pp. 253–275). IGI Global. doi:10.4018/978-1-5225-6240-5.ch011

Fındık, L. Y. (2017). Self-Assessment of Principals Based on Leadership in Complexity. In I. Management Association (Ed.), Educational Leadership and Administration: Concepts, Methodologies, Tools, and Applications (pp. 978-991). Hershey, PA: IGI Global. https://doi.org/ doi:10.4018/978-1-5225-1624-8.ch047

Flor, A. G., & Gonzalez-Flor, B. (2018). Dysfunctional Digital Demeanors: Tales From (and Policy Implications of) eLearning's Dark Side. In I. Management Association (Ed.), The Dark Web: Breakthroughs in Research and Practice (pp. 37-50). Hershey, PA: IGI Global. https://doi.org/ doi:10.4018/978-1-5225-3163-0.ch003

Floyd, K. K., & Shambaugh, N. (2017). Instructional Design for Simulations in Special Education Virtual Learning Spaces. In T. Kidd & L. Morris Jr., (Eds.), *Handbook of Research on Instructional Systems and Educational Technology* (pp. 202–215). Hershey, PA: IGI Global. doi:10.4018/978-1-5225-2399-4.ch018

Freeland, S. F. (2020). Community Schools: Improving Academic Achievement Through Meaningful Engagement. In R. Kronick (Ed.), *Emerging Perspectives on Community Schools and the Engaged University* (pp. 132–144). IGI Global. https://doi.org/10.4018/978-1-7998-0280-8.ch008

Ghanbarzadeh, R., & Ghapanchi, A. H. (2019). Applied Areas of Three Dimensional Virtual Worlds in Learning and Teaching: A Review of Higher Education. In I. Management Association (Ed.), *Virtual Reality in Education: Breakthroughs in Research and Practice* (pp. 172-192). IGI Global. https://doi.org/10.4018/978-1-5225-8179-6.ch008

Giovannini, J. M. (2017). Technology Integration in Preservice Teacher Education Programs: Research-based Recommendations. In M. Grassetti & S. Brookby (Eds.), *Advancing Next-Generation Teacher Education through Digital Tools and Applications* (pp. 82–102). Hershey, PA: IGI Global. doi:10.4018/978-1-5225-0965-3.ch005

Good, S., & Clarke, V. B. (2017). An Integral Analysis of One Urban School System's Efforts to Support Student-Centered Teaching. In J. Keengwe & G. Onchwari (Eds.), *Handbook of Research on Learner-Centered Pedagogy in Teacher Education and Professional Development* (pp. 45–68). Hershey, PA: IGI Global. doi:10.4018/978-1-5225-0892-2.ch003

Guetzoian, E. (2022). Gamification Strategies for Higher Education Student Worker Training. In C. Lane (Ed.), *Handbook of Research on Acquiring 21st Century Literacy Skills Through Game-Based Learning* (pp. 164–179). IGI Global. https://doi.org/10.4018/978-1-7998-7271-9.ch009

Hamidi, F., Owuor, P. M., Hynie, M., Baljko, M., & McGrath, S. (2017). Potentials of Digital Assistive Technology and Special Education in Kenya. In C. Ayo & V. Mbarika (Eds.), *Sustainable ICT Adoption and Integration for Socio-Economic Development* (pp. 125–151). Hershey, PA: IGI Global. doi:10.4018/978-1-5225-2565-3.ch006

Hamim, T., Benabbou, F., & Sael, N. (2022). Student Profile Modeling Using Boosting Algorithms. *International Journal of Web-Based Learning and Teaching Technologies*, *17*(5), 1–13. https://doi.org/10.4018/IJWLTT.20220901.oa4

Henderson, L. K. (2017). Meltdown at Fukushima: Global Catastrophic Events, Visual Literacy, and Art Education. In R. Shin (Ed.), *Convergence of Contemporary Art, Visual Culture, and Global Civic Engagement* (pp. 80–99). Hershey, PA: IGI Global. doi:10.4018/978-1-5225-1665-1.ch005

Hudgins, T., & Holland, J. L. (2018). Digital Badges: Tracking Knowledge Acquisition Within an Innovation Framework. In I. Management Association (Ed.), Wearable Technologies: Concepts, Methodologies, Tools, and Applications (pp. 1118-1132). Hershey, PA: IGI Global. https://doi.org/doi:10.4018/978-1-5225-5484-4.ch051

Hwang, R., Lin, H., Sun, J. C., & Wu, J. (2019). Improving Learning Achievement in Science Education for Elementary School Students via Blended Learning. *International Journal of Online Pedagogy and Course Design*, *9*(2), 44–62. https://doi.org/10.4018/IJOPCD.2019040104

Jančec, L., & Vodopivec, J. L. (2019). The Implicit Pedagogy and the Hidden Curriculum in Postmodern Education. In J. Vodopivec, L. Jančec, & T. Štemberger (Eds.), *Implicit Pedagogy for Optimized Learning in Contemporary Education* (pp. 41–59). IGI Global. https://doi.org/10.4018/978-1-5225-5799-9.ch003

Janus, M., & Siddiqua, A. (2018). Challenges for Children With Special Health Needs at the Time of Transition to School. In I. Management Association (Ed.), Autism Spectrum Disorders: Breakthroughs in Research and Practice (pp. 339-371). Hershey, PA: IGI Global. doi:10.4018/978-1-5225-3827-1.ch018

Jesus, R. A. (2018). Screencasts and Learning Styles. In M. Khosrow-Pour, D.B.A. (Ed.), Encyclopedia of Information Science and Technology, Fourth Edition (pp. 1548-1558). Hershey, PA: IGI Global. doi:10.4018/978-1-5225-2255-3.ch134

John, G., Francis, N., & Santhakumar, A. B. (2022). Student Engagement: Past, Present, and Future. In S. Ramlall, T. Cross, & M. Love (Eds.), *Handbook of Research on Future of Work and Education: Implications for Curriculum Delivery and Work Design* (pp. 329–341). IGI Global. https://doi.org/10.4018/978-1-7998-8275-6.ch020

Karpinski, A. C., D'Agostino, J. V., Williams, A. K., Highland, S. A., & Mellott, J. A. (2018). The Relationship Between Online Formative Assessment and State Test Scores Using Multilevel Modeling. In M. Khosrow-Pour, D.B.A. (Ed.), Encyclopedia of Information Science and Technology, Fourth Edition (pp. 5183-5192). Hershey, PA: IGI Global. doi:10.4018/978-1-5225-2255-3.ch450

Kats, Y. (2017). Educational Leadership and Integrated Support for Students with Autism Spectrum Disorders. In I. Management Association (Ed.), Educational Leadership and Administration: Concepts, Methodologies, Tools, and Applications (pp. 101-114). Hershey, PA: IGI Global. https://doi.org/ doi:10.4018/978-1-5225-1624-8.ch007

Kaya, G., & Altun, A. (2018). Educational Ontology Development. In M. Khosrow-Pour, D.B.A. (Ed.), Encyclopedia of Information Science and Technology, Fourth Edition (pp. 1441-1450). Hershey, PA: IGI Global. doi:10.4018/978-1-5225-2255-3.ch124

Keough, P. D., & Pacis, D. (2017). Best Practices Implementing Special Education Curriculum and Common Core State Standards using UDL. In P. Dickenson, P. Keough, & J. Courduff (Eds.), *Preparing Pre-Service Teachers for the Inclusive Classroom* (pp. 107–123). Hershey, PA: IGI Global. doi:10.4018/978-1-5225-1753-5.ch006

Kilburn, M., Henckell, M., & Starrett, D. (2018). Factors Contributing to the Effectiveness of Online Students and Instructors. In M. Khosrow-Pour, D.B.A. (Ed.), Encyclopedia of Information Science and Technology, Fourth Edition (pp. 1451-1462). Hershey, PA: IGI Global. doi:10.4018/978-1-5225-2255-3.ch125

Koban Koç, D. (2021). Gender and Language: A Sociolinguistic Analysis of Second Language Writing. In E. Hancı-Azizoglu & N. Kavaklı (Eds.), *Futuristic and Linguistic Perspectives on Teaching Writing to Second Language Students* (pp. 161–177). IGI Global. https://doi.org/10.4018/978-1-7998-6508-7.ch010

Konecny, L. T. (2017). Hybrid, Online, and Flipped Classrooms in Health Science: Enhanced Learning Environments. In I. Management Association (Ed.), Flipped Instruction: Breakthroughs in Research and Practice (pp. 355-370). Hershey, PA: IGI Global. https://doi.org/ doi:10.4018/978-1-5225-1803-7.ch020

Kupietz, K. D. (2021). Gaming and Simulation in Public Education: Teaching Others to Help Themselves and Their Neighbors. In N. Drumhiller, T. Wilkin, & K. Srba (Eds.), *Simulation and Game-Based Learning in Emergency and Disaster Management* (pp. 41–62). IGI Global. https://doi.org/10.4018/978-1-7998-4087-9.ch003

Kwee, C. T. (2022). Assessing the International Student Enrolment Strategies in Australian Universities: A Case Study During the COVID-19 Pandemic. In M. Alaali (Ed.), *Assessing University Governance and Policies in Relation to the COVID-19 Pandemic* (pp. 162–188). IGI Global. https://doi.org/10.4018/978-1-7998-8279-4.ch010

Lauricella, S., & McArthur, F. A. (2022). Taking a Student-Centred Approach to Alternative Digital Credentials: Multiple Pathways Toward the Acquisition of Microcredentials. In D. Piedra (Ed.), *Innovations in the Design and Application of Alternative Digital Credentials* (pp. 57–69). IGI Global. https://doi.org/10.4018/978-1-7998-7697-7.ch003

Llamas, M. F. (2019). Intercultural Awareness in Teaching English for Early Childhood: A Film-Based Approach. In E. Domínguez Romero, J. Bobkina, & S. Stefanova (Eds.), *Teaching Literature and Language Through Multimodal Texts* (pp. 54–68). IGI Global. https://doi.org/10.4018/978-1-5225-5796-8.ch004

Lokhtina, I., & Kkese, E. T. (2022). Reflecting and Adapting to an Academic Workplace Before and After the Lockdown in Greek-Speaking Cyprus: Opportunities and Challenges. In A. Zhuplev & R. Koepp (Eds.), *Global Trends, Dynamics, and Imperatives for Strategic Development in Business Education in an Age of Disruption* (pp. 126–148). IGI Global. https://doi.org/10.4018/978-1-7998-7548-2.ch007

Lovell, K. L. (2017). Development and Evaluation of Neuroscience Computer-Based Modules for Medical Students: Instructional Design Principles and Effectiveness. In J. Stefaniak (Ed.), *Advancing Medical Education Through Strategic Instructional Design* (pp. 262–276). Hershey, PA: IGI Global. doi:10.4018/978-1-5225-2098-6.ch013

Maher, D. (2019). The Use of Course Management Systems in Pre-Service Teacher Education. In J. Keengwe (Ed.), *Handbook of Research on Blended Learning Pedagogies and Professional Development in Higher Education* (pp. 196–213). IGI Global. https://doi.org/10.4018/978-1-5225-5557-5.ch011

Makewa, L. N. (2019). Teacher Technology Competence Base. In L. Makewa, B. Ngussa, & J. Kuboja (Eds.), *Technology-Supported Teaching and Research Methods for Educators* (pp. 247–267). IGI Global. https://doi.org/10.4018/978-1-5225-5915-3.ch014

Mallett, C. A. (2022). School Resource (Police) Officers in Schools: Impact on Campus Safety, Student Discipline, and Learning. In G. Crews (Ed.), *Impact of School Shootings on Classroom Culture, Curriculum, and Learning* (pp. 53–70). IGI Global. https://doi.org/10.4018/978-1-7998-5200-1.ch004

Marinho, J. E., Freitas, I. R., Leão, I. B., Pacheco, L. O., Gonçalves, M. P., Castro, M. J., Silva, P. D., & Moreira, R. J. (2022). Project-Based Learning Application in Higher Education: Student Experiences and Perspectives. In A. Alves & N. van Hattum-Janssen (Eds.), *Training Engineering Students for Modern Technological Advancement* (pp. 146–164). IGI Global. https://doi.org/10.4018/978-1-7998-8816-1.ch007

McCleskey, J. A., & Melton, R. M. (2022). Rolling With the Flow: Online Faculty and Student Presence in a Post-COVID-19 World. In S. Ramlall, T. Cross, & M. Love (Eds.), *Handbook of Research on Future of Work and Education: Implications for Curriculum Delivery and Work Design* (pp. 307–328). IGI Global. https://doi.org/10.4018/978-1-7998-8275-6.ch019

McCormack, V. F., Stauffer, M., Fishley, K., Hohenbrink, J., Mascazine, J. R., & Zigler, T. (2018). Designing a Dual Licensure Path for Middle Childhood and Special Education Teacher Candidates. In D. Polly, M. Putman, T. Petty, & A. Good (Eds.), *Innovative Practices in Teacher Preparation and Graduate-Level Teacher Education Programs* (pp. 21–36). Hershey, PA: IGI Global. doi:10.4018/978-1-5225-3068-8.ch002

McDaniel, R. (2017). Strategic Leadership in Instructional Design: Applying the Principles of Instructional Design through the Lens of Strategic Leadership to Distance Education. In V. Wang (Ed.), *Encyclopedia of Strategic Leadership and Management* (pp. 1570–1584). Hershey, PA: IGI Global. doi:10.4018/978-1-5225-1049-9.ch109

McKinney, R. E., Halli-Tierney, A. D., Gold, A. E., Allen, R. S., & Carroll, D. G. (2022). Interprofessional Education: Using Standardized Cases in Face-to-Face and Remote Learning Settings. In C. Ford & K. Garza (Eds.), *Handbook of Research on Updating and Innovating Health Professions Education: Post-Pandemic Perspectives* (pp. 24–42). IGI Global. https://doi.org/10.4018/978-1-7998-7623-6.ch002

Meintjes, H. H. (2021). Learner Views of a Facebook Page as a Supportive Digital Pedagogical Tool at a Public South African School in a Grade 12 Business Studies Class. *International Journal of Smart Education and Urban Society*, *12*(2), 32–45. https://doi.org/10.4018/IJSEUS.2021040104

Melero-García, F. (2022). Training Bilingual Interpreters in Healthcare Settings: Student Perceptions of Online Learning. In J. LeLoup & P. Swanson (Eds.), *Handbook of Research on Effective Online Language Teaching in a Disruptive Environment* (pp. 288–310). IGI Global. https://doi.org/10.4018/978-1-7998-7720-2.ch015

Meletiadou, E. (2022). The Use of Peer Assessment as an Inclusive Learning Strategy in Higher Education Institutions: Enhancing Student Writing Skills and Motivation. In E. Meletiadou (Ed.), *Handbook of Research on Policies and Practices for Assessing Inclusive Teaching and Learning* (pp. 1–26). IGI Global. https://doi.org/10.4018/978-1-7998-8579-5.ch001

Memon, R. N., Ahmad, R., & Salim, S. S. (2018). Critical Issues in Requirements Engineering Education. In I. Management Association (Ed.), Computer Systems and Software Engineering: Concepts, Methodologies, Tools, and Applications (pp. 1953-1976). Hershey, PA: IGI Global. doi:10.4018/978-1-5225-3923-0.ch081

Mendenhall, R. (2017). Western Governors University: CBE Innovator and National Model. In K. Rasmussen, P. Northrup, & R. Colson (Eds.), *Handbook of Research on Competency-Based Education in University Settings* (pp. 379–400). Hershey, PA: IGI Global. doi:10.4018/978-1-5225-0932-5.ch019

Mense, E. G., Griggs, D. M., & Shanks, J. N. (2018). School Leaders in a Time of Accountability and Data Use: Preparing Our Future School Leaders in Leadership Preparation Programs. In E. Mense & M. Crain-Dorough (Eds.), *Data Leadership for K-12 Schools in a Time of Accountability* (pp. 235–259). Hershey, PA: IGI Global. doi:10.4018/978-1-5225-3188-3.ch012

Mense, E. G., Griggs, D. M., & Shanks, J. N. (2018). School Leaders in a Time of Accountability and Data Use: Preparing Our Future School Leaders in Leadership Preparation Programs. In E. Mense & M. Crain-Dorough (Eds.), *Data Leadership for K-12 Schools in a Time of Accountability* (pp. 235–259). Hershey, PA: IGI Global. doi:10.4018/978-1-5225-3188-3.ch012

Mestry, R., & Naicker, S. R. (2017). Exploring Distributive Leadership in South African Public Primary Schools in the Soweto Region. In I. Management Association (Ed.), Educational Leadership and Administration: Concepts, Methodologies, Tools, and Applications (pp. 1041-1064). Hershey, PA: IGI Global. doi:10.4018/978-1-5225-1624-8.ch050

Monaghan, C. H., & Boboc, M. (2017). (Re) Defining Leadership in Higher Education in the U.S. In V. Wang (Ed.), *Encyclopedia of Strategic Leadership and Management* (pp. 567–579). Hershey, PA: IGI Global. doi:10.4018/978-1-5225-1049-9.ch040

Morall, M. B. (2021). Reimagining Mobile Phones: Multiple Literacies and Digital Media Compositions. In C. Moran (Eds.), *Affordances and Constraints of Mobile Phone Use in English Language Arts Classrooms* (pp. 41-53). IGI Global. https://doi.org/10.4018/978-1-7998-5805-8.ch003

Mthethwa, V. (2022). Student Governance and the Academic Minefield During COVID-19 Lockdown in South Africa. In M. Alaali (Ed.), *Assessing University Governance and Policies in Relation to the COVID-19 Pandemic* (pp. 255–276). IGI Global. https://doi.org/10.4018/978-1-7998-8279-4.ch015

Muthee, J. M., & Murungi, C. G. (2018). Relationship Among Intelligence, Achievement Motivation, Type of School, and Academic Performance of Kenyan Urban Primary School Pupils. In M. Khosrow-Pour, D.B.A. (Ed.), Encyclopedia of Information Science and Technology, Fourth Edition (pp. 1540-1547). Hershey, PA: IGI Global. https://doi.org/ doi:10.4018/978-1-5225-2255-3.ch133

Naranjo, J. (2018). Meeting the Need for Inclusive Educators Online: Teacher Education in Inclusive Special Education and Dual-Certification. In D. Polly, M. Putman, T. Petty, & A. Good (Eds.), *Innovative Practices in Teacher Preparation and Graduate-Level Teacher Education Programs* (pp. 106–122). Hershey, PA: IGI Global. doi:10.4018/978-1-5225-3068-8.ch007

Nkabinde, Z. P. (2017). Multiculturalism in Special Education: Perspectives of Minority Children in Urban Schools. In J. Keengwe (Ed.), *Handbook of Research on Promoting Cross-Cultural Competence and Social Justice in Teacher Education* (pp. 382–397). Hershey, PA: IGI Global. doi:10.4018/978-1-5225-0897-7.ch020

Nkabinde, Z. P. (2018). Online Instruction: Is the Quality the Same as Face-to-Face Instruction? In J. Keengwe (Ed.), *Handbook of Research on Digital Content, Mobile Learning, and Technology Integration Models in Teacher Education* (pp. 300–314). Hershey, PA: IGI Global. doi:10.4018/978-1-5225-2953-8.ch016

Nugroho, A., & Albusaidi, S. S. (2022). Internationalization of Higher Education: The Methodological Critiques on the Research Related to Study Overseas and International Experience. In H. Magd & S. Kunjumuhammed (Eds.), *Global Perspectives on Quality Assurance and Accreditation in Higher Education Institutions* (pp. 75–89). IGI Global. https://doi.org/10.4018/978-1-7998-8085-1.ch005

Nulty, Z., & West, S. G. (2022). Student Engagement and Supporting Students With Accommodations. In P. Bull & G. Patterson (Eds.), *Redefining Teacher Education and Teacher Preparation Programs in the Post-COVID-19 Era* (pp. 99–116). IGI Global. https://doi.org/10.4018/978-1-7998-8298-5.ch006

O'Connor, J. R. Jr, & Jackson, K. N. (2017). The Use of iPad® Devices and "Apps" for ASD Students in Special Education and Speech Therapy. In Y. Kats (Ed.), *Supporting the Education of Children with Autism Spectrum Disorders* (pp. 267–283). Hershey, PA: IGI Global. doi:10.4018/978-1-5225-0816-8.ch014

Okolie, U. C., & Yasin, A. M. (2017). TVET in Developing Nations and Human Development. In U. Okolie & A. Yasin (Eds.), *Technical Education and Vocational Training in Developing Nations* (pp. 1–25). Hershey, PA: IGI Global. doi:10.4018/978-1-5225-1811-2.ch001

Pack, A., & Barrett, A. (2021). A Review of Virtual Reality and English for Academic Purposes: Understanding Where to Start. *International Journal of Computer-Assisted Language Learning and Teaching*, *11*(1), 72–80. https://doi.org/10.4018/IJCALLT.2021010105

Pashollari, E. (2019). Building Sustainability Through Environmental Education: Education for Sustainable Development. In L. Wilson, & C. Stevenson (Eds.), *Building Sustainability Through Environmental Education* (pp. 72-88). IGI Global. https://doi.org/10.4018/978-1-5225-7727-0.ch004

Paulson, E. N. (2017). Adapting and Advocating for an Online EdD Program in Changing Times and "Sacred" Cultures. In I. Management Association (Ed.), Educational Leadership and Administration: Concepts, Methodologies, Tools, and Applications (pp. 1849-1876). Hershey, PA: IGI Global. https://doi.org/ doi:10.4018/978-1-5225-1624-8.ch085

Petersen, A. J., Elser, C. F., Al Nassir, M. N., Stakey, J., & Everson, K. (2017). The Year of Teaching Inclusively: Building an Elementary Classroom for All Students. In C. Curran & A. Petersen (Eds.), *Handbook of Research on Classroom Diversity and Inclusive Education Practice* (pp. 332–348). Hershey, PA: IGI Global. doi:10.4018/978-1-5225-2520-2.ch014

Pfannenstiel, K. H., & Sanders, J. (2017). Characteristics and Instructional Strategies for Students With Mathematical Difficulties: In the Inclusive Classroom. In C. Curran & A. Petersen (Eds.), *Handbook of Research on Classroom Diversity and Inclusive Education Practice* (pp. 250–281). Hershey, PA: IGI Global. doi:10.4018/978-1-5225-2520-2.ch011

Phan, A. N. (2022). Quality Assurance of Higher Education From the Glonacal Agency Heuristic: An Example From Vietnam. In H. Magd & S. Kunjumuhammed (Eds.), *Global Perspectives on Quality Assurance and Accreditation in Higher Education Institutions* (pp. 136–155). IGI Global. https://doi.org/10.4018/978-1-7998-8085-1.ch008

Preast, J. L., Bowman, N., & Rose, C. A. (2017). Creating Inclusive Classroom Communities Through Social and Emotional Learning to Reduce Social Marginalization Among Students. In C. Curran & A. Petersen (Eds.), *Handbook of Research on Classroom Diversity and Inclusive Education Practice* (pp. 183–200). Hershey, PA: IGI Global. doi:10.4018/978-1-5225-2520-2.ch008

Randolph, K. M., & Brady, M. P. (2018). Evolution of Covert Coaching as an Evidence-Based Practice in Professional Development and Preparation of Teachers. In V. Bryan, A. Musgrove, & J. Powers (Eds.), *Handbook of Research on Human Development in the Digital Age* (pp. 281–299). Hershey, PA: IGI Global. doi:10.4018/978-1-5225-2838-8.ch013

Rell, A. B., Puig, R. A., Roll, F., Valles, V., Espinoza, M., & Duque, A. L. (2017). Addressing Cultural Diversity and Global Competence: The Dual Language Framework. In L. Leavitt, S. Wisdom, & K. Leavitt (Eds.), *Cultural Awareness and Competency Development in Higher Education* (pp. 111–131). Hershey, PA: IGI Global. doi:10.4018/978-1-5225-2145-7.ch007

Richards, M., & Guzman, I. R. (2020). Academic Assessment of Critical Thinking in Distance Education Information Technology Programs. In I. Management Association (Ed.), *Learning and Performance Assessment: Concepts, Methodologies, Tools, and Applications* (pp. 1-19). IGI Global. https://doi.org/10.4018/978-1-7998-0420-8.ch001

Riel, J., Lawless, K. A., & Brown, S. W. (2017). Defining and Designing Responsive Online Professional Development (ROPD): A Framework to Support Curriculum Implementation. In T. Kidd & L. Morris Jr., (Eds.), *Handbook of Research on Instructional Systems and Educational Technology* (pp. 104–115). Hershey, PA: IGI Global. doi:10.4018/978-1-5225-2399-4.ch010

Roberts, C. (2017). Advancing Women Leaders in Academe: Creating a Culture of Inclusion. In S. Mukerji & P. Tripathi (Eds.), *Handbook of Research on Administration, Policy, and Leadership in Higher Education* (pp. 256–273). Hershey, PA: IGI Global. doi:10.4018/978-1-5225-0672-0.ch012

Rodgers, W. J., Kennedy, M. J., Alves, K. D., & Romig, J. E. (2017). A Multimedia Tool for Teacher Education and Professional Development. In C. Martin & D. Polly (Eds.), *Handbook of Research on Teacher Education and Professional Development* (pp. 285–296). Hershey, PA: IGI Global. doi:10.4018/978-1-5225-1067-3.ch015

Romanowski, M. H. (2017). Qatar's Educational Reform: Critical Issues Facing Principals. In I. Management Association (Ed.), Educational Leadership and Administration: Concepts, Methodologies, Tools, and Applications (pp. 1758-1773). Hershey, PA: IGI Global. https://doi.org/ doi:10.4018/978-1-5225-1624-8.ch080

Ruffin, T. R., Hawkins, D. P., & Lee, D. I. (2018). Increasing Student Engagement and Participation Through Course Methodology. In M. Khosrow-Pour, D.B.A. (Ed.), Encyclopedia of Information Science and Technology, Fourth Edition (pp. 1463-1473). Hershey, PA: IGI Global. doi:10.4018/978-1-5225-2255-3.ch126

Sabina, L. L., Curry, K. A., Harris, E. L., Krumm, B. L., & Vencill, V. (2017). Assessing the Performance of a Cohort-Based Model Using Domestic and International Practices. In I. Management Association (Ed.), Educational Leadership and Administration: Concepts, Methodologies, Tools, and Applications(pp. 913-929). Hershey, PA: IGI Global. https://doi.org/ doi:10.4018/978-1-5225-1624-8.ch044

Samkian, A., Pascarella, J., & Slayton, J. (2022). Towards an Anti-Racist, Culturally Responsive, and LGBTQ+ Inclusive Education: Developing Critically-Conscious Educational Leaders. In E. Cain-Sanschagrin, R. Filback, & J. Crawford (Eds.), *Cases on Academic Program Redesign for Greater Racial and Social Justice* (pp. 150–175). IGI Global. https://doi.org/10.4018/978-1-7998-8463-7.ch007

Santamaría, A. P., Webber, M., & Santamaría, L. J. (2017). Effective School Leadership for Māori Achievement: Building Capacity through Indigenous, National, and International Cross-Cultural Collaboration. In I. Management Association (Ed.), Educational Leadership and Administration: Concepts, Methodologies, Tools, and Applications (pp. 1547-1567). Hershey, PA: IGI Global. https://doi.org/ doi:10.4018/978-1-5225-1624-8.ch071

Santamaría, L. J. (2017). Culturally Responsive Educational Leadership in Cross-Cultural International Contexts. In I. Management Association (Ed.), Educational Leadership and Administration: Concepts, Methodologies, Tools, and Applications (pp. 1380-1400). Hershey, PA: IGI Global. https://doi.org/ doi:10.4018/978-1-5225-1624-8.ch064

Segredo, M. R., Cistone, P. J., & Reio, T. G. (2017). Relationships Between Emotional Intelligence, Leadership Style, and School Culture. *International Journal of Adult Vocational Education and Technology*, *8*(3), 25–43. doi:10.4018/IJAVET.2017070103

Shalev, N. (2017). Empathy and Leadership From the Organizational Perspective. In Z. Nedelko & M. Brzozowski (Eds.), *Exploring the Influence of Personal Values and Cultures in the Workplace* (pp. 348–363). Hershey, PA: IGI Global. doi:10.4018/978-1-5225-2480-9.ch018

Siamak, M., Fathi, S., & Isfandyari-Moghaddam, A. (2018). Assessment and Measurement of Education Programs of Information Literacy. In R. Bhardwaj (Ed.), *Digitizing the Modern Library and the Transition From Print to Electronic* (pp. 164–192). Hershey, PA: IGI Global. doi:10.4018/978-1-5225-2119-8.ch007

Siu, K. W., & García, G. J. (2017). Disruptive Technologies and Education: Is There Any Disruption After All? In I. Management Association (Ed.), Educational Leadership and Administration: Concepts, Methodologies, Tools, and Applications (pp. 757-778). Hershey, PA: IGI Global. https://doi.org/ doi:10.4018/978-1-5225-1624-8.ch037

Slagter van Tryon, P. J. (2017). The Nurse Educator's Role in Designing Instruction and Instructional Strategies for Academic and Clinical Settings. In J. Stefaniak (Ed.), *Advancing Medical Education Through Strategic Instructional Design* (pp. 133–149). Hershey, PA: IGI Global. doi:10.4018/978-1-5225-2098-6.ch006

Slattery, C. A. (2018). Literacy Intervention and the Differentiated Plan of Instruction. In *Developing Effective Literacy Intervention Strategies: Emerging Research and Opportunities* (pp. 41–62). Hershey, PA: IGI Global. doi:10.4018/978-1-5225-5007-5.ch003

Smith, A. R. (2017). Ensuring Quality: The Faculty Role in Online Higher Education. In K. Shelton & K. Pedersen (Eds.), *Handbook of Research on Building, Growing, and Sustaining Quality E-Learning Programs* (pp. 210–231). Hershey, PA: IGI Global. doi:10.4018/978-1-5225-0877-9.ch011

Souders, T. M. (2017). Understanding Your Learner: Conducting a Learner Analysis. In J. Stefaniak (Ed.), *Advancing Medical Education Through Strategic Instructional Design* (pp. 1–29). Hershey, PA: IGI Global. doi:10.4018/978-1-5225-2098-6.ch001

Spring, K. J., Graham, C. R., & Ikahihifo, T. B. (2018). Learner Engagement in Blended Learning. In M. Khosrow-Pour, D.B.A. (Ed.), Encyclopedia of Information Science and Technology, Fourth Edition (pp. 1487-1498). Hershey, PA: IGI Global. doi:10.4018/978-1-5225-2255-3.ch128

Storey, V. A., Anthony, A. K., & Wahid, P. (2017). Gender-Based Leadership Barriers: Advancement of Female Faculty to Leadership Positions in Higher Education. In V. Wang (Ed.), *Encyclopedia of Strategic Leadership and Management* (pp. 244–258). Hershey, PA: IGI Global. doi:10.4018/978-1-5225-1049-9.ch018

Stottlemyer, D. (2018). Develop a Teaching Model Plan for a Differentiated Learning Approach. In *Differentiated Instructional Design for Multicultural Environments: Emerging Research and Opportunities* (pp. 106–130). Hershey, PA: IGI Global. doi:10.4018/978-1-5225-5106-5.ch005

Stottlemyer, D. (2018). Developing a Multicultural Environment. In *Differentiated Instructional Design for Multicultural Environments: Emerging Research and Opportunities* (pp. 1–27). Hershey, PA: IGI Global. doi:10.4018/978-1-5225-5106-5.ch001

Swagerty, T. (2022). Digital Access to Culturally Relevant Curricula: The Impact on the Native and Indigenous Student. In E. Reeves & C. McIntyre (Eds.), *Multidisciplinary Perspectives on Diversity and Equity in a Virtual World* (pp. 99–113). IGI Global. https://doi.org/10.4018/978-1-7998-8028-8.ch006

Swami, B. N., Gobona, T., & Tsimako, J. J. (2017). Academic Leadership: A Case Study of the University of Botswana. In N. Baporikar (Ed.), *Innovation and Shifting Perspectives in Management Education* (pp. 1–32). Hershey, PA: IGI Global. doi:10.4018/978-1-5225-1019-2.ch001

Swanson, K. W., & Collins, G. (2018). Designing Engaging Instruction for the Adult Learners. In M. Khosrow-Pour, D.B.A. (Ed.), Encyclopedia of Information Science and Technology, Fourth Edition (pp. 1432-1440). Hershey, PA: IGI Global. doi:10.4018/978-1-5225-2255-3.ch123

Swartz, B. A., Lynch, J. M., & Lynch, S. D. (2018). Embedding Elementary Teacher Education Coursework in Local Classrooms: Examples in Mathematics and Special Education. In D. Polly, M. Putman, T. Petty, & A. Good (Eds.), *Innovative Practices in Teacher Preparation and Graduate-Level Teacher Education Programs* (pp. 262–292). Hershey, PA: IGI Global. doi:10.4018/978-1-5225-3068-8.ch015

Taliadorou, N., & Pashiardis, P. (2017). Emotional Intelligence and Political Skill Really Matter in Educational Leadership. In I. Management Association (Ed.), Educational Leadership and Administration: Concepts, Methodologies, Tools, and Applications (pp. 1274-1303). Hershey, PA: IGI Global. https://doi.org/ doi:10.4018/978-1-5225-1624-8.ch060

Tandoh, K. A., & Ebe-Arthur, J. E. (2018). Effective Educational Leadership in the Digital Age: An Examination of Professional Qualities and Best Practices. In J. Keengwe (Ed.), *Handbook of Research on Digital Content, Mobile Learning, and Technology Integration Models in Teacher Education* (pp. 244–265). Hershey, PA: IGI Global. doi:10.4018/978-1-5225-2953-8.ch013

Tobin, M. T. (2018). Multimodal Literacy. In M. Khosrow-Pour, D.B.A. (Ed.), Encyclopedia of Information Science and Technology, Fourth Edition (pp. 1508-1516). Hershey, PA: IGI Global. doi:10.4018/978-1-5225-2255-3.ch130

Torres, K. M., Arrastia-Chisholm, M. C., & Tackett, S. (2019). A Phenomenological Study of Pre-Service Teachers' Perceptions of Completing ESOL Field Placements. *International Journal of Teacher Education and Professional Development*, *2*(2), 85–101. https://doi.org/10.4018/IJTEPD.2019070106

Torres, M. C., Salamanca, Y. N., Cely, J. P., & Aguilar, J. L. (2020). All We Need is a Boost! Using Multimodal Tools and the Translanguaging Strategy: Strengthening Speaking in the EFL Classroom. *International Journal of Computer-Assisted Language Learning and Teaching*, *10*(3), 28–47. doi:10.4018/IJCALLT.2020070103

Torres, M. L., & Ramos, V. J. (2018). Music Therapy: A Pedagogical Alternative for ASD and ID Students in Regular Classrooms. In P. Epler (Ed.), *Instructional Strategies in General Education and Putting the Individuals With Disabilities Act (IDEA) Into Practice* (pp. 222–244). Hershey, PA: IGI Global. doi:10.4018/978-1-5225-3111-1.ch008

Toulassi, B. (2017). Educational Administration and Leadership in Francophone Africa: 5 Dynamics to Change Education. In S. Mukerji & P. Tripathi (Eds.), *Handbook of Research on Administration, Policy, and Leadership in Higher Education* (pp. 20–45). Hershey, PA: IGI Global. doi:10.4018/978-1-5225-0672-0.ch002

Umair, S., & Sharif, M. M. (2018). Predicting Students Grades Using Artificial Neural Networks and Support Vector Machine. In M. Khosrow-Pour, D.B.A. (Ed.), Encyclopedia of Information Science and Technology, Fourth Edition (pp. 5169-5182). Hershey, PA: IGI Global. doi:10.4018/978-1-5225-2255-3.ch449

Vettraino, L., Castello, V., Guspini, M., & Guglielman, E. (2018). Self-Awareness and Motivation Contrasting ESL and NEET Using the SAVE System. In M. Khosrow-Pour, D.B.A. (Ed.), Encyclopedia of Information Science and Technology, Fourth Edition (pp. 1559-1568). Hershey, PA: IGI Global. doi:10.4018/978-1-5225-2255-3.ch135

Wiemelt, J. (2017). Critical Bilingual Leadership for Emergent Bilingual Students. In I. Management Association (Ed.), Educational Leadership and Administration: Concepts, Methodologies, Tools, and Applications (pp. 1606-1631). Hershey, PA: IGI Global. doi:10.4018/978-1-5225-1624-8.ch074

Wolf, F., Seyfarth, F. C., & Pflaum, E. (2018). Scalable Capacity-Building for Geographically Dispersed Learners: Designing the MOOC "Sustainable Energy in Small Island Developing States (SIDS)". In U. Pandey & V. Indrakanti (Eds.), *Open and Distance Learning Initiatives for Sustainable Development* (pp. 58–83). Hershey, PA: IGI Global. doi:10.4018/978-1-5225-2621-6.ch003

Woodley, X. M., Mucundanyi, G., & Lockard, M. (2017). Designing Counter-Narratives: Constructing Culturally Responsive Curriculum Online. *International Journal of Online Pedagogy and Course Design*, *7*(1), 43–56. doi:10.4018/IJOPCD.2017010104

Yell, M. L., & Christle, C. A. (2017). The Foundation of Inclusion in Federal Legislation and Litigation. In C. Curran & A. Petersen (Eds.), *Handbook of Research on Classroom Diversity and Inclusive Education Practice* (pp. 27–52). Hershey, PA: IGI Global. doi:10.4018/978-1-5225-2520-2.ch002

Zinner, L. (2019). Fostering Academic Citizenship With a Shared Leadership Approach. In C. Zhu & M. Zayim-Kurtay (Eds.), *University Governance and Academic Leadership in the EU and China* (pp. 99–117). IGI Global. https://doi.org/10.4018/978-1-5225-7441-5.ch007

About the Contributors

R. Dhaya has 16 years experience in teaching and research in the field of Computer Science and Engineering. She published more than 80 research papers in peer reviewed international Journals. She was the recipient of IEI Young women Engineer award. Her areas of interests are wireless sensor networks, embedded systems, Machine Learning, Communication Systems.

R. Kanthavel has 22 years' experience in teaching and research in the field of information and Communication Engineering. He has the credit of more than 100 research articles in peer reviewed international Journals. His areas of interests are computer networking, Machine Learning and AI, Co-operative communication, computing and mobile networks.

***

S. Kannadhasan is working as an Assistant Professor in the department of Electronics and Communication Engineering in Cheran College of Engineering, Kaur, Tamilnadu, India. He is currently doing research in the field of Smart Antenna for Anna University. He is ten years of teaching and research experience. He obtained his B.E in ECE from Sethu Institute of Technology, Kariapatti in 2009 and M.E in Communication Systems from Velammal College of Engineering and Technology, Madurai in 2013. He obtained his M.B.A in Human Resources Management from Tamilnadu Open University, Chennai. He obtained his PGVLSI in Post Graduate diploma in VLSI design from Annamalai University, Chidambaram in 2011 and PGDCA in Post Graduate diploma in Computer Applications from Tamil University in 2014. He obtained his PGDRD in Post Graduate diploma in Rural Development from Indira Gandhi National Open University in 2016. He has published around 18 papers in the reputed indexed international journals and more than 125 papers presented/published in national, international journal and conferences. Besides he has contributed a book chapter also. He also serves as a board member, reviewer, speaker, session chair, advisory and technical committee of various colleges and conferences. He is also to attend the various workshop, seminar, conferences, faculty development programme, STTP and Online courses. His areas of interest are Smart Antennas, Digital Signal Processing, Wireless Communication, Wireless Networks, Embedded System, Network Security, Optical Communication, Microwave Antennas, Electromagnetic Compatability and Interference, Wireless Sensor Networks, Digital Image Processing, Satellite Communication, Cognitive Radio Design and Soft Computing techniques. He is Member of IEEE, ISTE, IEI, IETE, CSI, IAENG, SEEE, IEAE, INSC, IARDO, ISRPM, IACSIT, ICSES, SPG, SDIWC, IJSPR and EAI Community

R. Nagarajan received his B.E. in Electrical and Electronics Engineering from Madurai Kamarajar University, Madurai, India, in 1997. He received his M.E. in Power Electronics and Drives from Anna University, Chennai, India, in 2008. He received his Ph.D in Electrical Engineering from Anna University, Chennai, India, in 2014. He has worked in the industry as an Electrical Engineer. He is currently working as Professor of Electrical and Electronics Engineering at Gnanamani College of Technology, Namakkal, Tamilnadu, India. He has published more than 70 papers in International Journals and Conferences. His research interest includes Power Electronics, Power System, Communication Engineering, Network Security, Soft Computing Techniques, Cloud Computing, Big Data Analysis and Renewable Energy Sources

H. Shaheen is presently working as Associate Professor in the Department of Computer Science and Engineering ,MVJ College of Engineering, Bangalore Affiliated to VTU, Karnataka. She received the B. Tech and ME degree from Anna University, Chennai. She completed her PhD at Karpagam Academy of Higher Education, Coimbatore. Her Research interests include Artificial Intelligence, Mobile and Pervasive Computing, Blockchain, Network Security and Web Services. She Published more than 23 papers in refereed international journals and 7 papers in National and International conferences as tutorial Presenter. She is an active member of ISTE,IAENG and also Editorial Board member in IJRAST and Reviewer in ASTESJ. Also published more than 15 books and 6 Patent journals. Received IASTE Best Women Faculty – 2018 by International Association for Science and Technical Education.

Kanagaraj Venusamy obtained his MBA degree in Production Management from Manonmanium Sundaranar University, Tamilnadu, India in 2011 and B.E (Electronics and Communication Engineering) in 2005 from Anna University, M.E in Mechatronics Engineering, India in 2019 from Anna university affiliated college. Presently pursuing Doctorate in Management studies at Bharathidasan university, Tamilnadu, India. His main interests of research are control systems, industrial automation, artificial intelligence, robotics, drone, IoT, entrepreneurship and human resource management. He had 12 years of teaching experience in reputed institution in India and Oman and two year of industrial experience at Saudi Arabia. He has technically assisted various short term course for students, faculty development program and International Robotics Competition. He has acted as co principle investigator in sultanate of Oman government funded research projects. Currently working as a Control Systems Instructor in University of Technology and Applied Sciences - Al Mussanah.

Index

S

V

W

Recommended Reference Books

IGI Global's reference books can now be purchased from three unique pricing formats:
Print Only, E-Book Only, or Print + E-Book.
Shipping fees may apply.

www.igi-global.com

Participatory Pedagogy: Emerging Research and Opportunities
ISBN: 9781522589648
EISBN: 9781522589655
© 2021; 156 pp.
List Price: US$ 155

Transformative Pedagogical Perspectives on Home Language Use in Classrooms
ISBN: 9781799840756
EISBN: 9781799840763
© 2021; 282 pp.
List Price: US$ 185

Advancing Online Course Design and Pedagogy for the 21st Century Learning Environment
ISBN: 9781799855989
EISBN: 9781799856009
© 2021; 382 pp.
List Price: US$ 195

Deep Fakes, Fake News, and Misinformation in Online Teaching and Learning Technologies
ISBN: 9781799864745
EISBN: 9781799864752
© 2021; 271 pp.
List Price: US$ 195

Enhancing Higher Education Accessibility Through Open Education and Prior Learning
ISBN: 9781799875710
EISBN: 9781799875734
© 2021; 252 pp.
List Price: US$ 195

Connecting Disciplinary Literacy and Digital Storytelling in K-12 Education
ISBN: 9781799857709
EISBN: 9781799857716
© 2021; 378 pp.
List Price: US$ 195

Do you want to stay current on the latest research trends, product announcements, news, and special offers?
Join IGI Global's mailing list to receive customized recommendations, exclusive discounts, and more.
Sign up at: www.igi-global.com/newsletters.

Publisher of Timely, Peer-Reviewed Inclusive Research Since 1988

IGI Global
PUBLISHER of TIMELY KNOWLEDGE

www.igi-global.com | Sign up at www.igi-global.com/newsletters | facebook.com/igiglobal | twitter.com/igiglobal

CPSIA information can be obtained
at www.ICGtesting.com
Printed in the USA
BVHW012024201022
649532BV00003B/38

9 781668 450581